W9-AEU-252

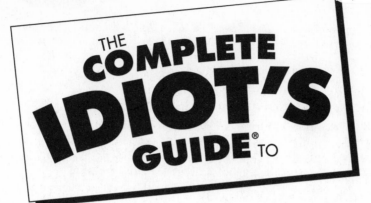

THE COMPLETE IDIOT'S GUIDE® TO

Comfort Food

by Leslie Bilderback, CMB

ALPHA

A member of Penguin Group (USA) Inc.

This book is dedicated to my grandmother, Mildred Reed. Even though she hates cooking, her meals were always the most comforting to me as a child. No one whips up a batch of instant pudding like Grandma Reed.

ALPHA BOOKS

Published by the Penguin Group

Penguin Group (USA) Inc., 375 Hudson Street, New York, New York 10014, USA.

Penguin Group (Canada), 90 Eglinton Avenue East, Suite 700, Toronto, Ontario M4P 2Y3, Canada (a division of Pearson Penguin Canada Inc.)

Penguin Books Ltd., 80 Strand, London WC2R 0RL, England

Penguin Ireland, 25 St. Stephen's Green, Dublin 2, Ireland (a division of Penguin Books Ltd.)

Penguin Group (Australia), 250 Camberwell Road, Camberwell, Victoria 3124, Australia (a division of Pearson Australia Group Pty. Ltd.)

Penguin Books India Pvt. Ltd., 11 Community Centre, Panchsheel Park, New Delhi—110 017, India

Penguin Group (NZ), 67 Apollo Drive, Rosedale, North Shore, Auckland 1311, New Zealand (a division of Pearson New Zealand Ltd.)

Penguin Books (South Africa) (Pty.) Ltd., 24 Sturdee Avenue, Rosebank, Johannesburg 2196, South Africa

Penguin Books Ltd., Registered Offices: 80 Strand, London WC2R 0RL, England

Copyright © 2007 by Leslie Bilderback, CMB

All rights reserved. No part of this book shall be reproduced, stored in a retrieval system, or transmitted by any means, electronic, mechanical, photocopying, recording, or otherwise, without written permission from the publisher. No patent liability is assumed with respect to the use of the information contained herein. Although every precaution has been taken in the preparation of this book, the publisher and author assume no responsibility for errors or omissions. Neither is any liability assumed for damages resulting from the use of information contained herein. For information, address Alpha Books, 800 East 96th Street, Indianapolis, IN 46240.

THE COMPLETE IDIOT'S GUIDE TO and Design are registered trademarks of Penguin Group (USA) Inc.

International Standard Book Number: 978-1-59257-633-3
Library of Congress Catalog Card Number: 2007924615

09 08 07   8 7 6 5 4 3 2 1

Interpretation of the printing code: The rightmost number of the first series of numbers is the year of the book's printing; the rightmost number of the second series of numbers is the number of the book's printing. For example, a printing code of 07-1 shows that the first printing occurred in 2007.

Printed in the United States of America

Note: This publication contains the opinions and ideas of its author. It is intended to provide helpful and informative material on the subject matter covered. It is sold with the understanding that the author and publisher are not engaged in rendering professional services in the book. If the reader requires personal assistance or advice, a competent professional should be consulted.

The author and publisher specifically disclaim any responsibility for any liability, loss, or risk, personal or otherwise, which is incurred as a consequence, directly or indirectly, of the use and application of any of the contents of this book.

Most Alpha books are available at special quantity discounts for bulk purchases for sales promotions, premiums, fundraising, or educational use. Special books, or book excerpts, can also be created to fit specific needs.

For details, write: Special Markets, Alpha Books, 375 Hudson Street, New York, NY 10014.

Publisher: *Marie Butler-Knight*
Editorial Director: *Mike Sanders*
Managing Editor: *Billy Fields*
Acquisitions Editor: *Michele Wells*
Development Editor: *Lynn Northrup*
Senior Production Editor: *Janette Lynn*
Copy Editor: *Amy Borrelli*

Cartoonist: *Shannon Wheeler*
Cover Designer: *Kurt Owens*
Book Designer: *Trina Wurst*
Indexer: *Johnna Vanhoose Dinse*
Layout: *Ayanna Lacey*
Proofreader: *Aaron Black*

Contents at a Glance

Contents

Appendixes

Introduction

When I was just starting out as a professional chef, I worked in quite a nice place that was often patronized by people celebrating special evenings. I would commonly get requests for my recipes, and I happily obliged. Every now and then I would receive messages back saying that the recipe I sent was not what they had enjoyed in the restaurant. Because most of my repertoire was boosted from other chefs anyway, I was not at all tightfisted with my recipes. I never held anything back. The recipes I sent really were the ones I used. But there was a crucial difference between the meals my customers made at home, and the ones they ate in the restaurant: the experience was missing. The to-die-for chocolate cake at the restaurant was likely accompanied by the handsome husband, a shower of affection, and the promise of more to come at the end of the evening. The recipe just doesn't play the same when you make it for the Cub Scout bake sale.

Sensory Memory

This phenomenon makes special food out of the ordinary. When I traveled through Europe after college with my future husband, we had very little money, and sustained ourselves on bread, cheese, and salami. It is still my favorite lunch, although it never tastes quite as good, because I am not sitting on the banks of the Seine. My husband talks about the greatest beverage he ever had in his life, a bottle of Lemon Crush. It was served from a cooler of ice and salt, so it tasted a little salty-sweet. Of course, he had it while visiting the Mayan ruins of Tikal. It really doesn't have the same effect when he chugs one after soccer practice. But every time he does, he remembers Tikal.

This is called sensory memory. These are memories evoked by our senses. It's why you are whisked back to your college days when you hear an old favorite song. It's why you are reminded of your grandmother when you smell her perfume. And it's why you get a warm feeling of contentment when you eat certain foods. For me, the best sensory memories come from food. They take me to a time and place so specific, so detailed, so identifiable, that it takes the eating experience to a new level of enjoyment.

Food that evokes a positive sensory memory has come to be known as *comfort food*. Comfort food means different things to different people, but most agree that it refers to foods we equate with the warm fuzzy feelings of childhood, happiness, and love. They are the foods we remember fondly, and the ones we turn to in times of stress. They are not necessarily culinary masterworks; in fact, they are usually simple, familiar dishes. They are not necessarily foods that even required much cooking. But they are foods that bring us relief and joy.

Why do these foods help us? Researchers have pinpointed a biochemical system in laboratory rats related to comfort foods. When rats get stressed (cats moving in next door, higher cheese prices, that annoying Mickey), hormones are released that stimulate a craving for high-fat, high-sugar foods. The rats eat, and not surprisingly, they get fat. But they're happy, so it's all good.

Of course, as you might expect, most comfort foods are seriously bad for us. They usually contain a high amount of fat and carbohydrates, two nutrients that Americans get too much of as it is. But hey, we're talking comfort here. I am not encouraging you to totally abandon sensible nutrition, and I am not suggesting that eating these foods will cure your woes. But they are good, and they'll make you smile, which is sometimes all you need to get through the day. So once in awhile, a little comfort cooking is definitely in order.

The Recipes

I have compiled what is quite possibly the most complete list of comfort foods known to man. (Well, I think it's pretty thorough.) The recipes are organized by meal and food group. Because there is always more than one way to make everything, many recipes include abbreviated variations to the classic preparations. As a bonus, I have included additional *Dress It Up* recipes for those whose culinary taste and curiosity lean toward more gourmet fare. These are updated, fancier versions of the familiar favorites, suitable for even the most upscale affairs.

Tools and Techniques

Comfort food is home cooking, and home cooking utilizes basic home-cooking methods and utensils. Because these recipes originated decades (in some cases, centuries) ago, there is very little specialized equipment necessary. In most cases, I have given both the classic tools, and some modern options.

Pans

Sauté pans, skillets, and frying pans are all basically the same thing; a round, flat, shallow pan. The word *sauté* means to jump, and the sauté pan has a slanted lip designed to keep the food moving. With a flick of the wrist a trained chef can keep the food jumping all day. If your wrist muscles are not fully developed, you can stir with a spoon to obtain the same results. Whenever you see the term *sauté*, it is an indication that the food is meant to be stirred around in the pan throughout the cooking process. The large surface area of this pan promotes quick, even browning.

A skillet usually refers to a heavier pan, often cast iron. The side of the pan is straight, designed to hold fat for frying. Skillets are typically used for prolonged pan-frying or deep-fat-frying.

Saucepans are round pans with tall sides and, typically, one long handle. They are designed for simmering or boiling large amounts of liquids, and are called for in recipes for sauces, soups, stocks, boiling vegetables, and grains. They are usually identified by quart capacity, but in general, a well-equipped kitchen should have a small, medium, and large saucepan. A larger pan, with a capacity of 1 gallon or more, is generally called a stockpot. The long handle has been replaced with two short handles for easy lifting. A pasta pot is a small stockpot, usually with a colander insert, which makes draining the pasta a snap.

When necessary I have indicated if a pan should be nonstick, cast iron, or simply heavy. Nonstick is preferable for most egg cookery and for delicate frying that would be ruined by the food sticking. Cast iron is suggested for most deep-frying because it holds the heat well, distributes it evenly, and is so heavy that it is difficult to accidentally tip it over. A heavy pan should be aluminum or have an aluminum core. Aluminum heats slowly and evenly, and does not allow scorching. Occasionally I will suggest stainless steel, but not often. I find it heats too quickly, and burns easily.

Utensils

Blenders, countertop or handheld electric mixers, food processors, and immersion blenders are all pretty modern, and while they make cooking easier, they are not mandatory. In most cases, I provide the tried-and-true old-fashioned methods, like hand whisking, in addition to the modern, time-saving techniques. I have provided detailed descriptions of specialized techniques, such as deep-frying, at the head of the chapter, and sidebars where required.

Handheld tools are generally a matter of preference. I have indicated the industry-standard choices, but I know you will do whatever you want. For instance, many recipes require a whisk, but I often grab a fork instead. For many applications a fork works just as well, and it's much easier to clean.

One of the most confusing tools is the spatula. There are simply too many tools that go by that name. I have tried to specify the type of spatula called for in each recipe. Rubber spatulas are used for scraping and folding, while flipping spatulas are for turning over hot foods. There are plastic heat-resistant versions of these, which are ideal when working on sensitive nonstick surfaces.

Time

There was a time when one family member (usually mom) spent the entire day cooking. Consequently, some of these dishes require more time than you are perhaps accustomed to spending in the kitchen. In many cases, I have included quick variations. But I also want to encourage you to set aside some time if you can. In many cases, cooking the food is as comforting as eating it. If you have never done much cooking, I would like to introduce you to the pleasures of the kitchen. If you cook, but can't be bothered with lengthy steps, I want to encourage you to stop and smell the rosemary. As long as you allot the time for it, cooking a slow meal can be very rewarding—in some cases, even therapeutic.

The Ingredients

Classic home cooking often calls for ingredients local to the area of the recipes origin. For instance, chili con carne, a Texas original, calls for chiles and chili powder. You may run into difficulty finding these ingredients in some parts of our country. Those of you living in these regions may need to do a little Internet shopping. I have provided sources for you, as well as easier-to-find substitutions.

Similarly, you may come across an ingredient that you're unfamiliar with. Even great home cooks I know were stumped by some of the things these recipes call for. In such cases, I have provided explanations and sources. We have become a nation of premixed, precooked, ready-to-eat ingredients, and the real thing is often mysterious. Rest assured that nothing within these pages is unattainable, and most of it is readily available.

If you come across something you don't recognize, and there is no explanation, take a peek at the glossary in this book. It is an extensive, encyclopedic reference of culinary terms, techniques, and ingredients.

A Word About Substitutions

It seems that everyone is concerned about some part of their diet. If you're not watching your fat intake, you're watching the sugar or the salt. It is perfectly fine to substitute low-fat, fat-free, low-cholesterol, sugar-free, low-salt, soy-based, or dairy-free products into these recipes. Sugar substitutes work fine in the baking recipes, too, as does whole-grain flour.

Several recipes call for wine or other alcohol, and despite what you may have been told, the alcohol does not completely cook out in recipes, even when flambéed. Any liquid in an equal amount can be substituted, such as water, broth, or even non-alcoholic wine. Just bear in mind its flavor. Wine is acidic, which plays a part in the balance of flavor. When substituting for wine, I usually add a small percentage of lemon or vinegar to compensate.

Whenever you make substitutions, it's a good idea to try the recipe once before you make it for company. After all, these are comfort food recipes, and while a whole-grain, soy-protein meatloaf with turkey bacon may be healthy, it may not comfort your guests quite as much as the real thing.

How This Book Is Organized

This book is divided into four parts:

Part 1, "Rise and Shine," features all of your favorite breakfast foods, from waffles to eggs Benedict to blueberry muffins.

Part 2, "Lunch Break," gives you sandwiches, soups, and salads for your lunch box or lunch parties.

Part 3, "Supper Time," features dinner ideas for every time of year, from summer backyard barbecues to holiday roasts, and everything to go with them.

Part 4, "Sweet Stuff and Snacks," shares everyone's favorite desserts, whether it's cakes, pies, cookies, custards, or candies. And there's recipes here for the snackers, too, including after-school treats and party favorites.

You'll also find three handy appendixes: a glossary, lists of common ingredient substitutions and equivalents, and conversion tables.

Extras

I am passionate about food and cooking, and my brain is crammed full of interesting (sometimes useless, but usually entertaining) information that I cannot help but pass on to you. You'll find these throughout the book in the form of four sidebars:

Kitchen Tips

Check these boxes for time-saving suggestions and practical advice. Some of these come from professional kitchens, and some from ingenious grandmas. Whatever works!

Tidbits

Here you'll find miscellaneous bits of information, such as anecdotes or interesting background on the origin of a recipe.

> **Listen to Mom!**
>
> Think of these cautions as gentle nagging in print. Of course, I want to keep you safe, and prevent you from messing up. But mostly, I want your recipes to be successful so that you'll continue cooking comforting food for yourself, your family, and your friends.

> **Chefspeak**
>
> Obscure and unfamiliar terms and techniques are explained in these boxes. The culinary language is quite specific. Even something as basic as *boiling* has a very specific culinary definition and use.

Acknowledgments

Thanks to Mom for opening up her recipe files and sharing her comfort foods with me. Thanks to the best proofreader ever, my husband Bill. Thanks to Emma and Claire for helping me test recipes, especially the cookies and cakes. Thanks to all my testers, especially Chef Michael Harants.

Special Thanks to the Technical Reviewer

The Complete Idiot's Guide to Comfort Food was reviewed by an expert who double-checked the accuracy of what you'll learn here, to help us ensure that this book gives you everything you need to know about cooking up comfort foods. Special thanks are extended to Lisa Vislocky.

Lisa Vislocky is a fourth-year doctoral student in the Department of Nutritional Sciences at the University of Connecticut, where she studies sports nutrition and exercise science while fulfilling her didactic requirements to become a Registered Dietician. Lisa was also the technical editor for *The Complete Idiot's Guide to Fondues and Hot Dips*.

Trademarks

All terms mentioned in this book that are known to be or are suspected of being trademarks or service marks have been appropriately capitalized. Alpha Books and Penguin Group (USA) Inc. cannot attest to the accuracy of this information. Use of a term in this book should not be regarded as affecting the validity of any trademark or service mark.

Part 1

Rise and Shine

Breakfast is a meal often missed or rushed through by busy Americans. We swig a cup of coffee on the way out the door, or maybe cram a piece of toast in our mouth during carpool. I'll bet many of you skip the meal altogether. Haven't you heard that a good breakfast is the foundation of a healthy day? Well, it is. But I know. You're busy. Perhaps this is why a well-made breakfast is the most comforting meal there is.

Think about all the lovely breakfasts you've had. Where were you? Who was it making them for you? Who were you eating with? What did it mean to have such a luxurious waste of time?

These recipes run the gamut from basic everyday breakfast to Mother's-Day-brunch-worthy fare, all of them tried and true. So put down the paper and get in the kitchen.

Chapter 1

All-American Breakfasts

In This Chapter

- The amazing egg and its sidekicks
- Home-style cereals
- Hot off the griddle
- Wonderful waffles

I used to dread breakfast when I was a child. Maybe it was because nothing was ever very good. The eggs were always brown and rubbery, the cereal was too sweet, and the instant oatmeal, sweetened with artificial maple, was thick and gummy. My parents tried everything to get me to eat breakfast, to no avail. Eventually I progressed to simply skipping it altogether.

When I learned how to cook professionally, I discovered a big wide world of breakfasts. Foods that were reserved in my family for sleepover parties and Mother's Day brunch were suddenly available to me 24/7. In fact, I began eating breakfast for lunch, and even dinner. I still do that. I can't seem to get enough of pancakes, waffles, scrambled egg concoctions, fancy poached eggs, and real, delicious, nutty cereals.

If you are a traditional breakfast scoffer, these recipes will turn you around. And if you're a breakfast lover like me, you'll find some interesting ideas in this chapter. So hop out of bed, jump into your bunny slippers, and fire up the stove.

Eggs

Eggs are truly a miracle food. They're loaded with protein, they can be whipped into completely different forms, and they come individually packaged, naturally. They're cheap, too. So it's easy to see why they became a breakfast staple.

I was never a fan of eggs as a kid, however. It wasn't until I learned how to cook eggs the French way that I fell in love with them. French eggs are never brown and rubbery. They are creamy and moist (of course, all the added cream and butter don't hurt).

Egg cookery is not as easy as it sounds. Eggs cook fast, and it's easy to take them too far. The eggs with runny yolks, like over easy and sunny-side up, are by far the hardest. But with a little practice, you'll be a pro in no time.

Kitchen Tips

Whatever style of eggs you cook, invest in a nonstick pan. It doesn't have to be fancy, but the nonstick coating will make cooking and cleanup a whole lot easier. When cooking in your nonstick pan, *never* use metal utensils; they will scrape off the nonstick coating. Instead, use a wooden spoon, or get yourself a heatproof rubber spatula. Similarly, when cleaning, use a brush or sponge, never use a scouring pad. Your pans will last longer, and so will your patience. If you don't have a nonstick pan, melt plenty of butter in the pan, and trick a friend into doing the dishes.

I prefer cooking eggs in butter, because nothing tastes better. I use unsalted butter because it browns less, and it gives me and my guests control over the amount of salt we eat. But I understand that not everyone can justify the added cholesterol butter brings to the table. If that's you, try using a polyunsaturated oil, such as safflower oil or corn oil, instead. When you're watching your cholesterol, every little bit helps. Of course, you may want to lay off the eggs too, or use only the whites, as the whites are fat-free.

When cooking for company, I usually make two eggs per guest, unless it's my dad, who takes four. Once the eggs are done, I put them in a covered casserole dish and keep them warm in an oven set on low until the rest of the breakfast is ready. Fried eggs, which include over easy, over medium, over hard, and sunny-side up, must be made to order. They cool and break if you try to hold them for any length of time. So get everything else you're serving ready before you begin.

Cereal

Cereal is the most popular breakfast food in America. It's fast, convenient, relatively inexpensive, and comes in so many varieties that it takes up an entire aisle at the grocery store. For my kids, a trip down the cereal aisle is the main attraction of any trip to the grocery store. It's a fun excursion, despite my strict rules about what they can and cannot choose. One of our family birthday traditions includes the breakfast of your choice, with no restrictions. You can bet they head right for the sugariest, most chocolaty, fruity, marshmallowy, cookie-flavored cereal that they can find. (And inevitably, they only get through about half the box before they're tired of it.)

What you may not know is that, if chosen right, cereal is the healthiest breakfast choice there is. It provides an ample supply of the one food group our society is severely lacking: whole grains. This lack of whole grains in the American diet was the impetus for the creation of cereal in the first place.

In the 1820s, a Presbyterian minister named Sylvester Graham was preaching a vegetarian diet filled with whole grains, and a lifestyle of cleanliness and exercise. He had a following, but was largely considered to be a nutcase. However, his crackers, made with his "Graham whole grain flour," became a hit.

Another proponent of a vegetarian diet, James Jackson, created the first cereal out of Graham's flour and bran nuggets. It was called granula, and is the great grandfather of today's granola. (You'll find a recipe for granola later in this chapter.)

In the 1890s the Kellogg brothers were experimenting with whole-wheat dough at their sanitarium in Battle Creek, Michigan. Their creation of the wheat flaked cereal is said to have been accidental.

After a stay at Kellogg's Battle Creek Sanitarium, C. W. Post set up shop in Battle Creek and began experimenting with whole grains. There he created Grape-Nuts and Post-Toasties, two cereals still popular today.

The cereal recipes in this chapter are hearty, healthy (for the most part), and delicious. They're a good choice for everyday eating, and can be dressed up for company, too.

The Griddle

Food cooked on a griddle has a long history in culinary arts. These foods are descended from the mush our ancestors slapped on a hot rock over an open fire. There is evidence of bread and baking in ancient Egypt, and it is thought that grain and baking technologies spread from there to Greece, Rome, and then throughout the Roman Empire. This is why you can find flat bread in every culture. There is Middle Eastern *pita*, eastern Mediterranean *lavosh*, French *crepes*, Norwegian *lefse*, Russian *blini*, Ethiopian *injera*, Mexican *tortillas*, Indian *naan* and *chapati*, Sri Lankan *papadum*, Italian *foccacia*, Jewish *matzo*, Chinese green-onion pancakes, and Thai *khanom buang*, to name but a few. They are all made out of indigenous grains, served or filled with native meats, fruits, and vegetables, and are often used as a utensil.

The best griddles are made from cast iron. Cast iron cooks slowly and more evenly than anything else. If you buy a new cast-iron griddle it must first be *seasoned*. To season your pan, coat it evenly with a thin layer of shortening, coconut oil, or lard. Bake it at 300°F for 30 minutes. Pour off any excess liquid fat, and continue baking for 2 hours. Cool the pan upside-down on a stack of newspaper. The first few times you use the pan, use a lot of fat to continue the seasoning process. You can also repeat the seasoning steps a couple more times for a really good seal. Seasoned pans should never be scrubbed, as this would remove the oiled coating and expose new crevices for food to stick to. A light wipe with warm water is sufficient cleaning. This gentle cleaning will also prolong the life of the pan.

> **Chefspeak**
>
> **Seasoning** a cast-iron pan keeps the food from sticking by filling in and smoothing out the roughness that we can't see with the naked eye.

Pancakes

A well-made pancake may be the best comfort food of them all. Do they conjure up memories of terrific sleepovers at your best friend's house in fourth grade? Or perhaps they recall the morning after a particularly raucous Friday night in college? I find them most comforting when they are served spur of the moment for dinner, with good syrup, softened sweet butter, and a dollop of homemade strawberry jam.

For a superior pancake, let the batter rest for about 10 minutes before cooking. This extra time allows the dry ingredients to fully absorb the wet ones, and it gives the baking powder some extra time to work. The batter fills with carbon dioxide bubbles that expand on the griddle, creating lighter pancakes.

Waffles

Bronze-age irons with grid marks have been excavated from Celtic bogs. Blacksmiths at some point began adding decorative elements to the irons, including cultural symbols and family crests. Two flat sheets of iron were hinged and stuck on a long handle. They were probably filled with gruel and held over an open flame. The breads that came out were often used as utensils, like most flat breads.

Today there are dozens of waffle irons available to the consumer. A Belgian waffle iron typically has deeper holes, but can be used for any type of batter. There are waffle cone irons; pizzelle and krumkake irons for making crisp waffle cookies; waffle stick or dipper irons; flip-over waffle irons; single, double, and quadruple waffle irons; square, round, heart-shaped, and Hello-Kitty waffle irons. In fact, if you're married, I bet you got a waffle iron as a wedding gift. It's probably in your cupboard right now, back behind the Jack LaLanne Power Juicer and the Black & Decker Fry-Mate.

If your waffle iron is coated with a nonstick surface, keep any sort of metal away from it. You'll scratch off the surface, and then the waffles will stick for sure. If you need help removing the cooked waffles from the iron, use a wooden pick or chopstick.

Scrambled Eggs

The cream in this recipe makes the eggs extra light and luscious. Half-and-half works, too, as does milk, and even water, although the latter produces a somewhat less luscious dish.

Serves 4
Prep time: 5 minutes
Cook time: 5 minutes

8 large eggs

¼ cup heavy cream

Salt and pepper

4 TB. (½ stick) butter

1. Preheat the oven to 200°F. Crack eggs into a bowl, add cream, and add salt and pepper to taste. Whisk to combine.

2. Warm the frying pan over medium heat, add the butter and let it melt until it sizzles. Tilt the pan to coat it evenly. Add the eggs all at once, and begin stirring. Reduce heat and stir gently until the eggs coagulate. The eggs are done when they are firm, but still yellow and moist. Transfer to the casserole dish, cover, and keep warm in the oven until you're ready to serve.

Hangtown Fry

Placerville, California, is a gold-country town formerly known as Hangtown. There, a lucky miner entered the El Dorado Hotel and told the chef to make him the most expensive thing he could think of. This is what he got.

Serves 4
Prep time: 10 minutes
Cook time: 20 minutes

4 slices of bacon, diced

1 cup all-purpose flour

1 tsp. each salt and pepper

1 (8-oz.) jar or can of oysters, drained, or 12 fresh shucked oysters

8 large eggs

¼ cup milk

½ tsp. salt

1 tsp. pepper

1. Fry diced bacon until crisp. Mix together flour and 1 teaspoon each of salt and pepper. Add the oysters, toss to coat, and shake off excess flour. Add floured oysters to the bacon pan and fry until golden.

2. Mix together eggs, milk, ½ teaspoon salt, and 1 teaspoon pepper, and whisk to combine. Add all at once to bacon and oysters, and reduce the heat. Stir eggs gently until they begin to set. The eggs are done when they are firm, but still moist. Serve immediately with sourdough toast.

Fried Eggs

The trick to making good fried eggs is cracking them into a small bowl or ramekin before they go in the pan to keep the yolks whole. It also helps to have a very hot pan with plenty of butter.

1 TB. butter   **2 large eggs**

Serves 1	
Prep time: 5 minutes	
Cook time: 5 minutes	

1. Warm the frying pan over medium heat, add the butter, and let it melt until it sizzles. Tilt the pan to coat it evenly.

2. Crack the eggs into the small bowl or ramekin. Pour the eggs into the hot butter all at once, then reduce the heat. Cook for 1 to 2 minutes, until the white is cooked. Jiggle the pan to help loosen the eggs, and flip it over gently and continue cooking to desired doneness.

What's your preference? Over easy are flipped and cooked until the white is hard, but the yolk is still runny. Over-medium eggs have a half-set yolk, and an over-hard yolk is firm. Sunny-side-up eggs are not flipped, but cooked until the white is set and the yolk is still runny.

Fried Egg Sandwich: Try your favorite fried egg between two slices of buttered toast. Or go all out and add bacon, sausage, or ham. Eat your heart out, McMuffin!

Tidbits

I once worked on a Navy ship where the eggs were fried on a big flat-top griddle. It was quite a skill, keeping them from sliding across the griddle as the ship rocked back and forth. In fact, it was a skill I didn't possess, which is why I was banned from egg duty.

Poached Eggs

If you make these delicate eggs ahead of time, float them in cool water to keep them from overcooking and breaking.

Serves 4
Prep time: 5 minutes
Cook time: 15–20 minutes

1 tsp. salt	**8 eggs**
2 tsp. vinegar	

1. Bring about 1 quart of water, salt, and vinegar to a boil. At the boil, reduce the heat and keep it at a bare simmer.

2. Break one egg into a small dish or ramekin, then slide the egg from the dish down the side of the pan into the simmering water. Simmer 3 to 5 minutes until the white is firm, but the yolk is still soft. Carefully remove the egg with a slotted spoon and transfer to a bowl of cold water. Repeat with remaining eggs.

3. Hold the poached eggs in a bowl of cold water until you're ready to serve them. To reheat, bring the water back to a simmer, and drop the eggs in briefly just before serving.

Eggs Florentine: So named because the main ingredient is spinach, which was brought into popularity supposedly by Catherine de Medici, Florentine wife of France's King Henry II, the dish consists of a poached egg perched on top of creamed or sautéed spinach, and covered with Mornay sauce, which is a white béchamel sauce enriched with Swiss cheese.

Poached Eggs and Corned Beef Hash: Pile the hash in the center of the plate, and nestle a poached egg on top. You can warm up a can of hash, or make it from scratch. Fry up some onions in melted butter, then add leftover cooked potatoes and meat (corned beef or anything else, including barbecue, steak, chicken, even seafood). This has got to be one of my very favorite breakfasts.

Eggs Benedict

This recipe came form New York City in the 1890s, but both Delmonico's and the Waldorf-Astoria claim it as their own. Whoever invented it should be crowned King of the Sunday Brunch.

1¼ lbs. (5 sticks) butter, melted

6 egg yolks

2 TB. lemon juice

2 TB. cold water

Salt and white pepper

4 English muffins, split and toasted

4 TB. (½ stick) butter

8 slices Canadian bacon or ham, warmed

8 poached eggs (see recipe earlier in this chapter)

Serves 4
Prep time: 45 minutes
Cook time: 20 minutes

1. To make the hollandaise sauce: Melt 5 sticks butter and set it aside until it is cool enough to hold your finger in, but still liquid. Fill the lower portion of the double boiler with water and bring it to a simmer.

2. In the upper portion of the double boiler combine the egg yolks, lemon juice, and cold water. Whisk vigorously for 1 to 2 minutes, until the color begins to lighten. Put the double boiler together, and continue to whisk until the eggs become thick and creamy.

3. Remove the thickened yolks from the double boiler, and while whisking, start drizzling the melted butter into the yolks *very slowly*. It should take about 3 minutes to incorporate all the butter. When all the butter is in, season the sauce with salt and white pepper.

4. Butter each toasted English muffin, and place two halves on each serving plate. Place a slice of Canadian bacon or ham on top of the muffin. Reheat the poached eggs and place one on top of each bacon slice. Ladle about ¼ cup of sauce on top of each egg. Serve immediately.

Listen to Mom!

When making an egg-based sauce like hollandaise, never ever stop whisking while it's sitting over hot water. The eggs will immediately congeal and turn your creamy sauce into scrambled eggs.

Dress It Up: Eggs Sardou

This dish is similar to Eggs Benedict, but the additional elements make it extraordinary.

Serves 4
Prep time: 45 minutes
Cook time: 20 minutes

8 artichoke bottoms, fresh, canned and drained, or frozen and thawed (not artichoke hearts)

1 (2-oz.) can anchovy filets, chopped

1 recipe Creamed Spinach, warmed (see Chapter 9)

8 poached eggs

1 recipe hollandaise sauce (see earlier eggs Benedict recipe)

½ cup chopped ham

1. Preheat oven to 400°F. Line a cookie sheet with the artichoke bottoms. Sprinkle the chopped anchovies evenly on each artichoke bottom. Bake for 10 minutes to warm thoroughly.

2. Place two artichoke bottoms on each serving plate. Spoon 2 tablespoons of creamed spinach on the top of each. Place a warm poached egg on top of the spinach, and ladle ¼ cup of hollandaise sauce over the egg. Sprinkle the top of each egg with a pinch of chopped ham. Serve immediately.

Tidbits

This New Orleans favorite is said to have been created at Antoine's restaurant for the French playwright Victorien Sardou.

Strata

This delicious and super-easy breakfast bread pudding was all the rage in the 1930s and is still enjoyed today.

1 medium onion, diced

2 TB. butter

2 TB. chopped fresh parsley (or 1 tsp. dried)

15 slices day-old bread, crusts removed

2 cups sharp cheddar cheese, grated

2 cups diced ham (or other breakfast meat)

6 eggs

3 cups milk

1 tsp. dry mustard

½ tsp. grated nutmeg

1 tsp. salt

½ tsp. pepper

1 cup heavy cream

Serves 6
Prep time: 30 minutes (plus 1–12 hours of refrigeration)   **Cook time:** 45 minutes

1. Sauté onions in butter over medium heat until they are light golden brown. Add chopped parsley and set aside to cool.

2. Coat a casserole dish with pan spray or butter. Dice the bread into 1-inch cubes, and layer half on the bottom of the greased casserole dish. Top with cheese, ham, sautéed onions, and the remaining bread.

3. Break eggs into a large bowl and whisk to combine. Add milk, mustard, nutmeg, salt, and pepper, and mix well. Pour this mixture over the casserole, then refrigerate for 1 hour, or overnight.

4. Preheat oven to 350°F. Just before baking, top the strata with the cream. Bake 45 minutes, until firm and golden brown. Rest 5 minutes before serving.

Three-Cheese Strata: Omit the meat, and double the amount of cheese to 4 cups. I like the combination of jack, Swiss, and havarti.

Roasted Winter Squash Strata: Layer your bread with cheese and roasted butternut and acorn squash. To roast the squash, slice them in half or quarters, remove the seeds, rub with olive oil, and bake at 450°F until tender and brown, about 45 minutes. Then scoop out the squash and roughly chop.

Frittata

This easy egg dish actually tastes better the next day.

Serves 6
Prep time: 20 minutes
Cook time: 30 minutes

1 medium yellow onion, diced

2 TB. olive oil

2 cloves garlic, minced

8 oz. sliced mushrooms

4 oz. bulk sausage

¼ cup chopped fresh basil (or 2 TB. dried)

8 eggs

1 cup grated cheddar cheese

1 tsp. grated nutmeg

Salt and pepper

1. Preheat oven to 350°F. Coat a casserole dish with pan spray or butter.

2. Sauté onions in olive oil until golden brown. Add garlic, mushrooms, and sausage and continue cooking until the meat is browned. Turn off the heat and stir in basil, eggs, cheese, and nutmeg, and season with salt and pepper. Transfer the mixture to the casserole dish. Bake for 30 minutes until firm and golden brown. Frittata can be served hot, room temperature, or cold. It will keep in the refrigerator for up to 2 days, and can freeze for up to 1 week.

Spinach Frittata: Omit the sausage and add 2 cups of frozen spinach (thawed and well drained), or fresh spinach sautéed in butter and garlic.

Southwestern Frittata: Omit the sausage and add up to 3 cups of the following Southwestern-inspired ingredients: corn; green chilies; roasted red, green, or yellow bell peppers; chili peppers; tomatoes; tomatillos; olives; or black beans. Omit the basil and season with cumin, cilantro, salt, and pepper.

California Crab Frittata: Omit the sausage and add 1 cup of fresh, frozen, canned, or imitation crabmeat, two chopped scallions, two minced cloves of garlic, one large diced tomato, one diced avocado, and one (14-oz.) can of artichoke hearts, drained and chopped. Omit the basil and season with ¼ cup fresh chopped, (or 1 tablespoon dried) thyme.

Joe's Special

If you are watching your carbohydrates, this is a perfect meal for you—it's quick to prepare, has loads of protein and iron, and is oh-so-satisfying.

1 medium yellow onion, chopped

2 TB. olive oil

2 cloves garlic, minced

½ lb. ground beef

8 oz. sliced mushrooms

1 tsp. nutmeg

1 tsp. oregano

4 cups fresh spinach, or 1 (10-oz.) package frozen spinach, thawed and drained

6 eggs, whisked together

1½ tsp. salt

½ tsp. pepper

Serves 4–6	
Prep time: 10 minutes	
Cook time: 20 minutes	

1. Sauté onions in olive oil over medium heat until they begin to brown. Add garlic, ground beef, mushrooms, nutmeg, and oregano, and cook, stirring occasionally, until the meat is browned. Pour off excess fat.

2. Add the spinach, eggs, salt, and pepper. Reduce the heat and stir gently until the spinach wilts and the eggs begin to set. When finished, the eggs will be firm, but still moist. Serve immediately.

Tidbits

Every restaurant in San Francisco ever owned, operated, or frequented by anyone named Joe claims this dish as their own. I always thought it came from Little Joes in North Beach, where "rain or shine, there's always a line."

Hash Browns

Serve your hash browns up faster by boiling your potatoes the night before.

Serves 4
Prep time: 40 minutes
Cook time: 20 minutes

2 large baking or russet potatoes, peeled

Salt and pepper

½ cup canola oil

2 TB. butter

1. Boil potatoes until tender. Drain and cool.

2. Grate the cooked potatoes into a large bowl. (Potatoes can also be diced.) Season with salt and pepper. Divide the grated potatoes into four equal portions.

3. Coat the bottom of the sauté pan with ¼ inch of oil and butter, and place over high heat. When the butter begins to sizzle, add one portion of grated potato. Press down to form a patty, and fry until golden brown, about 5 minutes per side. Transfer finished hash browns to a serving platter and hold in a 200°F oven until ready to serve.

Biscuits and Sausage Gravy

You can also make this down-home treat with your favorite breakfast meat, or use leftover gravy from the night before.

1 lb. uncooked breakfast sausage, diced

2 TB. butter

2 TB. all-purpose flour

4–5 cups milk

Salt and pepper

4 biscuits, halved

Serves 4	
Prep time: 30 minutes	
Cook time: 30 minutes	

1. In a large sauté pan, cook sausage over medium heat until browned. Drain off excess fat. Add butter and let it melt. Add flour, stirring until the butter is absorbed.

2. Whisk in the milk ½ cup at a time. Wait for it to be absorbed before adding the next ½ cup. Add milk until desired consistency is reached. Season with salt and pepper. Pour hot gravy over biscuits and serve.

Kitchen Tips

This basic gravy is an easy variation of the French sauce béchamel. It is thickened with a roux, consisting of equal parts melted fat (in this case butter) and flour. Traditionalists will tell you that the fat for this gravy should come from the sausage alone. That is, in fact, the way traditional gravy is made. The resulting gravy is much richer and, dare I say greasier, than what we are accustomed to today. If you're a purist, omit the butter, pour off all but 2 tablespoons of the sausage fat, and take heart. Sausage fat is no worse for you than butter.

Granola

Don't restrict this cereal to breakfast duty—granola also makes a great snack, and guilt-free dessert.

Serves 8
Prep time: 10 minutes
Cook time: 60 minutes

1 cup canola oil

½ cup honey

1 tsp. vanilla extract

4 cups rolled oats (not quick cooking)

½ cup whole-wheat flour

½ cup oat bran

½ cup wheat germ

½ cup hulled sunflower seeds

1 cup raisins

1 cup dates

1 cup chopped almonds

1. Preheat oven to 325°F. In a small saucepan, combine the oil, honey, and vanilla. Warm it over medium heat until it begins to simmer.

2. Meanwhile, in a large bowl combine the oats, flour, oat bran, wheat germ, and sunflower seeds. Pour the warm oil mixture over the oat mixture and toss it together to thoroughly moisten everything. Spread the granola onto an ungreased cookie sheet in an even, thin layer. Lower the oven temperature and toast at 250°F for 1 hour, stirring every 10 minutes to promote even browning.

3. Cool, then mix in raisins, dates, and almonds. Serve with milk, yogurt, or eat it as is for a great snack. Store in an airtight container for up to 1 week at room temperature, or in the refrigerator for up to 1 month.

Aloha Granola: Replace the sunflower seeds, raisins, and almonds with up to 3 cups of your favorite tropical fruits and nuts. I like to use shredded coconut, macadamia nuts, Brazil nuts, banana chips, dried pineapple, dried mango, and dried papaya. Try serving this granola with coconut milk instead of regular milk.

Apple-Spice Granola: Replace ¼ cup of the honey with ¼ cup of brown sugar. Before adding the oil mixture to the oats, mix in 1 teaspoon each of cinnamon, nutmeg, ginger, and cardamom, and ¼ teaspoon of clove. Replace the dates with 1 cup of chopped dried apples. Serve with milk and a dollop of applesauce or grated fresh apples.

Dress It Up: Breakfast Parfait

This is a beautiful way to serve a healthy breakfast. Don't you dare save it for company! You deserve breakfast this good every day.

4 cups sliced fresh fruit, such as berries, peaches, pears, or citrus

2 cups nonfat plain or vanilla yogurt

2 cups granola (see previous recipe)

¼ cup honey

Serves 4
Prep time: 10 minutes

1. Put ½ cup of fruit in the bottom of each parfait glass. Layer ¼ cup of yogurt over the fruit, then ¼ cup granola. Repeat the layering, finishing with the granola on top.

2. Before serving, drizzle 1 tablespoon of honey on top of each glass, and garnish with a whole fresh berry or wedge of fruit.

Kitchen Tips

Berries are the usual choice of fruit in this recipe, but they are really only good in the spring and summer. I prefer using whatever is fresh, ripe, and in season. In the summer I like peaches and apricots. In the fall, try ripe, juicy pears and pomegranate seeds. Winter is citrus season, so look for fancy tangerines, mandarins, and blood oranges.

Grits

If you're from the South, you've probably been taught that grits is an acronym for *grains in the South*, but it's actually a reference to its raw texture.

<table>
<tr><td>

Serves 4

Prep time: 5 minutes

Cook time: 30 minutes
</td></tr>
</table>

4½ cups water   **1 cup grits**

1 tsp. salt   **4 TB. (½ stick) butter**

1. In a large saucepan, bring water and salt to a boil. Stir in grits slowly, and reduce heat to a simmer.

2. Cook for 30 minutes, stirring occasionally, until the grits are thick and tender. Remove from heat, stir in butter, and serve.

Cheesy Grits: Add 1 cup of grated cheddar cheese with the butter. (I prefer sharp white cheddar.) Serve with a dollop of sour cream.

Baked Grits: Cook grits on the stovetop for only 5 minutes. Remove from heat and allow to cool slightly. Add two beaten eggs, ½ cup of milk, 4 tablespoons of butter, 1 cup of your favorite cheese, and up to 1 cup of cooked crumbled bacon, diced ham, or cooked sausage. Pour into a greased casserole dish and bake at 350°F for 30 minutes, until set and golden brown.

Fried Grits: Let cooked grits cool for 10 minutes, then stir in one egg. Pour onto a brownie pan, cover, and chill until firm. Slice solidified grits into serving-sized pieces and fry in melted butter until golden brown on each side.

Tidbits

Corn porridge has been eaten for centuries all over the world, beginning with the ancient cultures of Mesoamerica. When you order grits, what you usually get is hominy grits, made from dried, ground hominy. Hominy is corn that has been treated in an alkali solution (traditionally lye) to soften the husk, remove the germ, and improve the flavor. The same product is ground finer to produce *masa harina*, the flour used to make corn tortillas and tamales. You can find grits from untreated corn, but it's not the norm.

Pancakes

Both the batter and the finished pancakes freeze well. Plan ahead and cook a bunch to last the week.

1½ cups all-purpose flour

3 TB. sugar

2½ tsp. baking powder

½ tsp. salt

1½ cups milk

2 TB. melted butter or vegetable oil

2 eggs

Serves 4
Prep time: 15 minutes
Cook time: 20 minutes

1. Heat griddle over high heat. In a medium-sized bowl sift together flour, sugar, baking powder, and salt. In a separate bowl, combine milk, butter, and eggs. Whisk together thoroughly. Pour the egg mixture into the sifted dry ingredients and stir to combine and just moisten the dry. Be careful not to overmix. Lumps are okay.

2. Test the griddle by sprinkling on a little water. If it sizzles and evaporates, it's ready. If your griddle is not seasoned, oil it lightly with some vegetable oil or pan spray. Lower the heat to medium and ladle out the pancake batter. Cook for 1 to 2 minutes, until bubbles appear. Flip the pancake and cook the other side, about 1 to 2 minutes. Adjust the heat of your griddle as necessary. Repeat with remaining batter. Serve immediately, or keep warm in a 200°F oven, covered with foil or a clean dishtowel.

Kitchen Tips

Adjust the heat on your griddle accordingly. Cast iron holds heat well, but even over a low flame it will continue to heat up during prolonged cooking. If the pancakes are browning too fast, turn down the heat, wait about 5 minutes, then resume cooking.

Buttermilk Pancakes: Replace the milk with an equal amount of buttermilk for a tangy, old-fashioned buttermilk pancake.

Fruity Pancakes: Just before cooking, gently fold in 1 cup of your favorite fruit. Try blueberries, bananas, pears, or whatever's ripe.

Whole-Wheat Pancakes: Replace the all-purpose flour with whole-wheat flour (preferably stone ground) for a healthier, yet still-delicious pancake option.

Dress It Up: Blini and Caviar

These Russian pancakes, though considered today to be quite elegant and refined, are nothing more than humble peasant cakes. French chefs working in Russia's Imperial Court brought blini back home to France in the 1800s, topped them with sour cream, smoked fish, or caviar, and made history.

Serves 8	
Prep time: 3 hours	
Cook time: 20 minutes	

1 (2-oz.) package yeast	2 TB. butter, melted
2 cups warm milk	1 tsp. salt
1½ cups all-purpose flour, divided	1 cup sour cream
½ cup buckwheat flour	4 oz. caviar (beluga or sevruga if available)
3 eggs, separated	

Chefspeak

Buckwheat is not wheat at all. It's not even really a grain. It is the seed from an herb related to rhubarb. It is most often ground into flour, but when toasted and cooked like rice, it goes by the name Kasha. Find Kasha and buckwheat flour wherever healthy foods are sold.

1. In a large bowl, combine yeast and warm milk, and stir to combine. Add 1 cup all-purpose flour and the *buckwheat* flour, and beat in well. Cover the bowl tightly with plastic wrap and set aside in a warm place to double in volume, about 1 hour.

2. When the batter has doubled, add to it three egg yolks, melted butter, remaining ½ cup of flour, and salt. Beat until well combined. Cover the bowl again, and let the batter double in volume again, about 1 hour.

3. When the batter has doubled, preheat griddle over high heat. Whip egg whites until stiff, and fold them into the batter. Test the griddle by sprinkling on a little water. If it sizzles and evaporates, it's ready. If your griddle is not seasoned, oil it lightly with some vegetable oil or pan spray. Lower the heat to medium and ladle out ¼ cup of blini batter. Cook for 1 to 2 minutes, until bubbles appear. Flip the blini and cook the other side, about 1 to 2 minutes. Adjust the heat of your griddle as necessary. Repeat with remaining batter.

4. Serve each blini topped with a dollop of sour cream and a smidgeon of caviar.

Waffles

Don't forget National Waffle Day, August 24, which celebrates the U.S. patent of the waffle iron in 1869.

1½ cups cake flour	**3 eggs, separated**
2½ tsp. baking powder	**4 TB. (½ stick) butter, melted**
1 TB. sugar	**1½ cups milk**
½ tsp. salt	

Serves 4
Prep time: 15 minutes
Cook time: 30 minutes

1. *Triple sift* together flour, baking powder, sugar, and salt. Set aside.

2. In a separate bowl combine the egg yolks, melted butter, and milk. Whisk together thoroughly.

3. In another bowl, whip the egg whites until they are stiff. (To see if they are stiff enough, scoop out some of the whipped whites and turn the spoon over so the dripping peak faces up. Stiff egg whites hold the peak erect.)

4. Pour the egg yolk mixture into the flour and stir together briefly. Lumps are okay. Add the stiff egg whites to this mixture and fold together gently until they are just combined. Cook batter in a waffle iron, following the manufacturer's instructions.

Chefspeak

Triple sifting is a technique that helps ensure a light batter. Each time the flour goes through the sifter it picks up more air. The more you sift, the lighter the recipe will turn out. You could conceivably sift all day, but I usually get bored after three passes.

Buttermilk or Sour Cream Waffles: Replace the milk with buttermilk or sour cream for a tangy breakfast treat. The sour cream version will be a little bit thicker, so you can increase the amount to 2 cups.

Sourdough Waffles: Replace 1 cup of milk with 1 cup of sourdough starter for a San Francisco treat.

Dress It Up: Old-Fashioned Yeasted Belgian Waffles

Belgian waffles are simply regular waffles made in an iron with deeper holes. You can make them using a regular waffle recipe, but I prefer this old-fashioned yeasted one.

Serves 4
Prep time: 90 minutes
Cook time: 30 minutes

1 (¼-oz.) package active dry yeast

3 cups warm milk

4 cups all-purpose flour

½ cup sugar

1 tsp. salt

3 eggs, separated

1 cup sour cream

6 oz. (1½ sticks) butter, melted

1 TB. vanilla extract

1. In a small bowl dissolve yeast in the warm milk. Set it aside until it begins to bubble, about 15 minutes.

2. Triple sift together the flour, sugar, and salt. Set aside.

3. In another bowl, combine the egg yolks, sour cream, melted butter, vanilla, and yeasted milk. Mix thoroughly to combine. Pour this milk mixture over the sifted dry ingredients, and stir together gently until just combined. Lumps are okay.

4. In another bowl, whip the egg whites until they are stiff. Add them to the batter and fold together gently until just combined. Cover the batter with plastic wrap and set aside to rise until it is doubled in volume, about 1 hour.

5. Cook batter in a waffle iron, following the manufacturer's instructions. Serve with syrup and butter.

Tidbits

Belgian waffles didn't really become popular until the 1960 World's Fair in Brussels, Belgium, where a restaurateur served waffles with fruit and cream. Four years later they appeared at the Bel-Gem waffle stand, the most popular attraction in the Belgium Village of the 1964 New York World's Fair.

French Toast

Try making this recipe with day-old sweet rolls, croissants, or challah. The richer and thicker the bread, the more luscious the French toast will be.

2 eggs	**1 tsp. grated nutmeg**
1 cup half-and-half or milk	**Grated zest of 1 lemon**
2 tsp. sugar	**4 TB. butter**
½ tsp. salt	**4 slices day-old bread**
1 tsp. vanilla extract	

Serves 2	
Prep time: 10 minutes	
Cook time: 15 minutes	

1. In a large bowl, combine the eggs and half-and-half or milk, and whisk together thoroughly. Add the sugar, salt, vanilla, nutmeg, and lemon zest, and stir to combine.

2. Melt 1 to 2 tablespoons of butter in a sauté pan. Dip the bread, one slice at a time, into the egg mixture. Place the slice in the pan, and fry it in the butter until it is golden brown, about 2 minutes per side. Repeat with remaining bread, adding butter to the pan as needed. Serve immediately with butter and syrup.

Tidbits

Why is it called French toast? Because it is modeled after the French *pain perdu*, which means "lost bread." The lost bread is the bread that is too stale to eat. But stale bread is the best bread to use for this recipe. It has lost its moisture, and therefore has more room to soak up the moisture of the egg custard.

Cinnamon French Toast: Add a teaspoon of mixed spices, such as a pinch each of ground cinnamon, ginger, and allspice to the egg mixture, and serve with apples or bananas sautéed in butter. Sprinkle the top with toasted nuts.

French Toast Sandwiches: For big breakfast eaters, layer a fried egg and bacon, ham, or sausage between two slices of French toast.

Breakfast Baking

In This Chapter

- ◆ Myriad muffins
- ◆ Streusel, scones, and crumpets
- ◆ Coffee cake and bread
- ◆ Sweet buns and popovers

I love baking, but I rarely get the opportunity to bake at home. Everyone I know is watching carbs, or counting calories, or they just know better. When I do bake, I am chastised for presenting temptation. And it's hard for me to justify baking a cake for myself. Consequently, baking is saved for special occasions, like birthdays and holidays.

There is one exception, and that's breakfast. It seems that where the pancake goes, so, too, shall go the muffin. Few people would eat an actual cake for breakfast (at least not in public). But everyone eats muffins, which are really nothing more than cute little baby cakes. Now what could be more comforting than that? I think that in our collective conscience we have all agreed that as long as there is fruit of some kind anywhere on the table, a sweet roll can be a part of this balanced breakfast.

Muffins

The best part of muffins, by far, is the top, or as we professionals call it, the crown. The tops are so popular that stores and catalogs sell shallow muffin pans designed to maximize the top and minimize everything else. To maximize the tops in a regular muffin pan, fill the batter to the top, and bake the muffins at a high temperature. Most batters can take a 425°F oven. The leavening will react faster, creating more gas before the crust has a chance to solidify. Rotate the pan halfway through baking for even browning, and check the center muffins for doneness by pressing the top. Your finger should bounce back immediately to the touch. Inserting a pick only works if there are no goopy ingredients floating in your batter. If you skewer a blueberry or chocolate chip, it will give you a false reading.

The batters used for muffins can also be baked in loaf pans. These breads make excellent gifts, not to mention excellent toast. Bake them in pans lined with a strip of parchment paper or foil to make getting them out of the pan easy. Remember to bake them at a much lower temperature than the muffins, about 325°F. If they bake too hot, the crust will burn while the center remains raw. Be patient. Baking at such a low temperature can take well over an hour.

The Cut-In Technique

Streusel, scones, and in later chapters biscuits and pie dough are all made using the cut-in technique. This is a method of incorporating fat and flour together, not by beating or creaming, but by crumbling. The butter and flour do not actually combine, but remain separate, the butter in small chunks floating within the flour. It should never look like a paste. This peaceful coexistence of fat and flour is the key to tender, flaky baked goods. In the oven, the moisture contained within the fat evaporates into steam, pushing up the dough, and leaving little pockets of air that our mouth reads as flakiness.

I like to keep the butter in what I call pea-size pieces. While they do not have to be round, they should be approximately that small. To get your butter small, but keep it from melting and joining with the flour into a paste, keep your ingredients cold. I like to freeze the diced butter before adding it, and if the temperature in my kitchen is particularly warm I'll even freeze the flour for 10 or 15 minutes.

I like to use my fingers to break down the butter because I can better monitor the butter size. Many bakers like to keep their hands out of it entirely, preferring to use a *pastry blender*, a couple of knives or forks, or even a food processor (a technique that requires mastery). When I use my hands, I am careful to pinch the chunks with only my fingertips.

Chefspeak

The **pastry blender** is a groovy little tool used to break fat into flour. It's been used for decades, and I bet if you don't have one, your grandma does. It consists of a bow of a few wires connected to a handle.

Adding Alternately

Many batter recipes call for the dry and wet ingredients to be added alternately into creamy butter and eggs. The term *alternately* means that the dry and wet ingredients are divided into three or four batches, and added into the batter one at a time, first the dry, then the wet, then the dry, and so on. This method ensures that the ingredients are well incorporated. It is also a smart way to avoid making a mess on your counter-top, which usually happens when large amounts of anything are added into a recipe.

Preparing Pans

Most baked goods need to be baked in something, usually a pan of some sort. Batters and doughs that are poured into dry pans will certainly stick to them, and are impossible to remove in one piece. This drastically reduces the pleasure factor of baking. To avoid this nasty scenario, pans should be greased or coated with a lining of paper or foil.

Parchment paper is the lining of choice for professional bakers. It is available in rolls at most supermarkets, or in sheets through specialty baking suppliers. (Try shop. bakerscatalogue.com.) It is easy to cut to fit into any pan, and is easy to clean up. (Just throw it away!) Lining a pan with paper also prolongs the life of your pans because the dirty pans require less scrubbing.

Corn Muffins

These muffins are so closely related to cornbread they can easily jump from morning to afternoon or evening. Serve them with butter, honey, and jam, or use them to soak up extra barbecue sauce on rib night.

Makes 12 muffins	
Prep time: 20 minutes	
Cook time: 30 minutes	

2 cups all-purpose flour	8 oz. (2 sticks) butter
1 TB. baking powder	1 cup brown sugar
1 tsp. salt	2 eggs
2 cups cornmeal	2 cups buttermilk

1. Preheat oven to 375°F. Coat muffin pan with pan spray and line with muffin cups. Sift together the flour, baking powder, and salt. Stir in the cornmeal and set aside.

2. Combine butter and sugar, and beat together until creamy. Add eggs one at a time. Add the dry ingredients alternately with the buttermilk.

3. Fill muffin cups to the rim with muffin batter. Bake until risen and golden brown, about 20 minutes. A pick inserted into the middle muffin should come out clean.

4. Cool muffin pan for 15 minutes before removing muffins. Store muffins in an airtight container at room temperature for 2 days, or freeze for up to 2 weeks. Refresh in a 200°F oven for 15 minutes before serving.

Cheesy Green-Chili Corn Muffins: Reduce the amount of sugar in the recipe to ½ cup, and fold into the finished batter a 4-oz. can of diced green chilies and 1 cup of grated cheddar or jack cheese.

Cilantro Corn Muffins: Reduce the amount of sugar in the recipe to ½ cup, and fold into the finished batter 2 cups of defrosted and drained frozen corn and ¼ cup chopped fresh cilantro.

Bran Muffins

If you've shied away from bran muffins because you think they are health food, I have good news for you. They have oil and sugar, which makes them deliciously unhealthy. They are still healthier than having a Twinkie for breakfast, though, so enjoy in good health!

2 eggs	1 cup wheat germ
3 TB. canola oil	2¾ cups wheat bran
⅓ cup honey	⅔ cup oat bran
⅓ cup brown sugar	2 tsp. baking powder
⅓ cup molasses	2 tsp. baking soda
1 TB. vanilla extract	1 tsp. ground ginger
1½ cups buttermilk	1 tsp. ground cinnamon
½ cup whole-wheat flour	1 tsp. ground nutmeg
½ cup all-purpose flour	

> *Makes 12 muffins*
>
> **Prep time:** 20 minutes
> **Cook time:** 30 minutes

1. Preheat oven to 375°F. Coat muffin pan with pan spray and line with muffin cups. Combine eggs, oil, honey, sugar, molasses, vanilla, and buttermilk and beat together thoroughly. Set aside.

2. In a separate bowl, combine the flours, wheat germ, brans, baking powder, baking soda, and spices and mix well. Pour the egg mixture into the flour mixture and stir together until just incorporated.

3. Fill muffin cups to the rim with muffin batter. Bake until risen and golden brown, about 20 minutes. A pick inserted into the middle muffin should come out clean.

4. Cool muffin pan for 15 minutes before removing muffins. Store muffins in an airtight container at room temperature for 2 days, or freeze for up to 2 weeks. Refresh in a 200°F oven for 15 minutes before serving.

Raisin Bran Muffins: Fold into the finished batter 1 cup of raisins or other dried fruits.

Granola Muffins: Fold into the finished batter 2 cups of your favorite crunchy granola cereal (see Chapter 1 for a recipe).

Oatmeal Muffins: Omit the wheat bran and replace it with 2½ cups rolled oats.

 Tidbits

Bran is the outer husk of a grain. It contains no oils, proteins, or vitamins, but it is still excellent food because it is 100 percent fiber, which Americans typically don't get enough of. Consuming at least 25 grams of fiber a day can help prevent all sorts of health problems, including diabetes, heart disease, and certain types of cancer.

Blueberry Muffins

Use frozen blueberries instead of fresh to prevent smashing the berries as you stir them into the batter. Even if I have the finest fresh blueberries at the height of their season, I freeze them solid before incorporating them into a batter or dough.

Makes 12 muffins	
Prep time: 20 minutes	
Cook time: 30 minutes	

3½ cups cake flour	8 oz. (2 sticks) butter
1 tsp. baking powder	1 cup sugar
1 tsp. salt	2 eggs
1 cup buttermilk	1½ cups frozen blueberries
2 tsp. vanilla	1 recipe streusel (optional; see following recipe)

1. Preheat oven to 375°F. Coat muffin pan with pan spray and line with muffin cups. Sift together cake flour, baking powder, and salt; set aside. Combine buttermilk and vanilla in another bowl, and set aside.

2. Combine butter and sugar, and beat together until creamy. Add eggs one at a time. Add the sifted dry ingredients alternately with the buttermilk. Carefully fold in blueberries by hand.

3. Fill muffin cups to the rim with muffin batter. Top with streusel, if desired, or a sprinkling of granulated sugar. Bake until risen and golden brown, about 20 minutes. A pick inserted into the middle muffin should come out clean.

4. Cool muffin pan for 15 minutes before removing muffins. Store muffins in an airtight container at room temperature for 2 days, or freeze for up to 2 weeks. Refresh in a 200°F oven for 15 minutes before serving.

Cranberry-Orange Muffins: When creaming butter and sugar, add the grated zest of two oranges. Replace the blueberries with an equal amount of dried cranberries or chopped fresh cranberries.

Lemon-Poppy Seed Muffins: When creaming butter and sugar, add the grated zest of four lemons. Mix ⅓ cup poppy seeds with the flour. When the muffins come out of the oven, drizzle on a lemon glaze made by mixing 1 cup sifted powdered sugar with ¼ cup lemon juice.

Chocolate Chip Muffins: Replace the blueberries with an equal amount of chocolate chips and up to 1 cup of chopped nuts, if desired.

Monkey-Chunk Muffins: Go all out and add ½ cup chocolate chips, ½ cup chopped nuts, and 1 chopped ripe banana.

Kitchen Tips

The zest is the outermost, colored portion of a citrus peel. It is the zest that carries the colorful, flavorful oils coveted by so many bakers. The best way to remove it is with a small hand grater. The smallest holes of a standing box cheese grater work great (no pun intended), as does a microplane, a rasp developed with grating zest in mind. Forget that little tool known as the zester. It produces tiny strings of zest that must be minced by hand before being added into a recipe.

Streusel

This topping is also known as crisp, crumb, and crumble. Most of the recipes in this chapter can only be improved by adding streusel, so whip up a big batch and have it on hand in your freezer to top muffins, coffee cakes, and pies.

2 cups all-purpose flour

1 cup sugar (brown sugar, white sugar, or a combination)

1 cup butter, chilled and diced

Makes 4 cups
Prep time: 10 minutes

1. In a large bowl, combine flour and sugar. Mix well, then cut in butter, using fingertips or a pastry blender, until chunks are pea-sized. The streusel is ready if it holds together when squeezed, but easily crumbles apart. Be careful not to over mix, or the streusel will become gummy.

2. Generously crumble the streusel on top of the item to be baked, and proceed as directed. Store leftover streusel in the freezer for up to 1 month.

Nutty Streusel: Add up to 1 cup of finely chopped nuts of your choice, 1 cup of rolled oats, and 1 to 2 tablespoons of your favorite spices.

English Muffins

It is thought that the English muffin is America's attempt to replicate the crumpet, a staple tea offering in Britain. I like mine smeared with Nutella, a spread available in grocery stores.

Makes 6 muffins	
Prep time: 90 minutes	
Cook time: 15 minutes	

1½ cups warm milk	1 tsp. salt
1 package active dry yeast	1 TB. butter
1 TB. sugar	2 cups all-purpose flour

1. In a large bowl, combine warm milk, yeast, and sugar, mixing well. Add salt, butter, and flour, beating together for 8 to 10 minutes, until a smooth dough forms. Cover with plastic wrap and set aside to rise in a warm spot until doubled in volume, about 1 hour.

2. Heat griddle over high heat. Test the griddle by sprinkling on a little water. If it sizzles and evaporates, it's ready. If your griddle is not seasoned, oil it lightly with some vegetable oil or pan spray. Lower the heat to medium. Place 6 muffin rings on the griddle and fill them halfway with muffin batter. Cover the rings loosely with foil and cook until browned on the bottom, about 5 minutes. Using a spatula or tongs, flip the muffin and ring over. Cover and cook this side another 5 minutes. Cool completely before splitting and serving.

Kitchen Tips

English muffin rings are available in specialty cookware stores, and online (try shop.bakerscatalogue.com). When I was a kid, my mom and I saved tuna fish cans, washed them thoroughly, and trimmed the tops and bottoms off to make our own ring molds.

Dress It Up: Crumpets

English muffins and crumpets are very similar in shape and in preparation. But crumpets are not at all sweet, and are meant to be toasted whole, never split like an English muffin.

1½ cups warm milk

1 package active dry yeast

1 egg

1 TB. butter

½ tsp. salt

1 cup all-purpose flour

2–4 TB. butter

Makes 12 crumpets	
Prep time: 90 minutes
Cook time: 20 minutes

1. In a large bowl, combine warm milk, yeast, and egg, mixing well. Add 1 TB. butter, salt, and flour, beating together for about 5 minutes, until a smooth dough forms. Cover with plastic wrap and set aside to rise in a warm spot until doubled in volume, about 1 hour.

2. Heat griddle over high heat. Test the griddle by sprinkling on a little water. If it sizzles and evaporates, it's ready. Lower the heat to medium. Melt a little butter on the griddle. Place the muffin rings on the griddle and fill them half–way with batter. Cover the rings loosely with foil and cook until browned on the bottom, about 5 minutes. Using a spatula or tongs, flip the crumpet and ring over. Cover and cook this side another 5 minutes. Cool completely before serving with butter and jam.

Listen to Mom!

When baking with yeast, the milk should be warmed just enough so that you can hold your finger in it. The temperature should be about 100°F, which is just above body temperature. If it is too hot, it will kill the yeast, and your dough will never rise. If the milk is cold, the recipe will still work, but the dough will take longer to rise. This is thought by many bakers (myself included) to be preferable, since the longer a dough rises, the more flavor it develops.

Currant Scones

This sweet, flaky Scottish biscuit was traditionally made with oats, patted into circles, and cut into triangular wedges like a pie. Today they come in many shapes, and are often served with lemon curd and clotted cream.

Makes 6 scones
Prep time: 15 minutes
Cook time: 20 minutes

1 egg

1 tsp. vanilla

½ cup milk

3 cups all-purpose flour

1 tsp. salt

1 TB. plus 1 tsp. baking powder

1 cup sugar

8 oz. (2 sticks) butter, chilled and diced

1 cup dried currants

1 egg yolk

½ cup cream

1 cup sugar

1. Preheat oven to 375°F. Line a cookie sheet with parchment paper. In a small bowl, whisk together the egg, vanilla, and milk and set aside. In a separate large bowl, sift together flour, salt, baking powder, and sugar.

2. Cut the chilled butter into the dry ingredients, breaking it into small, pea-size pieces with your fingertips or a pastry blender. Stir in the currants.

3. Make a well in the center of the flour-butter mixture, and pour in the milk mixture. Stir gently until just moistened. Turn the dough out onto a lightly floured work surface and fold it seven or eight times, until it holds together. Flatten the dough out into a disc 1-inch thick. Cut the disc into six to eight wedges, and place each wedge on the cookie sheet, evenly spaced.

4. Whisk together the egg yolk and cream. Brush it generously on the top of each scone, and sprinkle the tops generously with sugar. Bake until golden brown, about 15 minutes. Store cooled scones at room temperature in an airtight container for 2 days, or freeze for up to 2 weeks. Refresh in a 200°F oven for 15 minutes before serving.

Blueberry Scones: After the butter is cut into the dry ingredients, add 1 cup of frozen blueberries. Stir in the milk carefully, and fold the dough gently so as not to crush the berries.

Lemon Scones: Add the grated zest of four lemons to the dry ingredients. You can do the same with oranges, tangerines, or limes.

Coffee Cake

For years my kids would never eat coffee cake because they thought it would taste like coffee. Now, a little older, and lot more Starbucks savvy, they're fans.

3 cups cake flour	1½ cups brown sugar
1½ tsp. baking soda	3 eggs
1 tsp. salt	1 TB. vanilla
2 tsp. cinnamon	1 cup sour cream
12 oz. (1½ sticks) butter	1 recipe streusel (see earlier recipe)

Serves 6
Prep time: 15 minutes
Cook time: 45 minutes

1. Preheat oven to 350°F. Coat the baking pan with melted butter or pan spray. Sift together the flour, baking soda, salt, and cinnamon and set aside.

2. In a large bowl, beat together the butter and brown sugar until creamy. Add the eggs one at a time, mixing until smooth, and add the vanilla. Add the sifted dry ingredients alternately with the sour cream, and mix until well blended.

3. Pour half of the batter into the pan and sprinkle half the streusel evenly on top. Cover with remaining batter, and top with rest of streusel. Bake for 45 minutes, until golden brown, and a pick inserted into the center of the cake comes out clean.

4. Cool the cake for 15 minutes before removing from pan and cutting. Store coffee cake for 2 days at room temperature wrapped air-tight, or freeze for up to 2 weeks. Refresh in a 200°F oven for 15 minutes before serving.

Nut Cake: Try adding 1 cup of chopped Brazil nuts, cashews, or hazelnuts to your streusel topping.

Fresh-Fruit Crumb Cake: Before the final topping of streusel, add a layer of ripe fresh fruit. Chop large fruits like peaches into small chunks or thin slices. Stay away from watery fruits like melons, and for best results, sauté apples and pears in butter until tender.

Tropical Coffee Cake: Transport yourself to Polynesia by adding 1 teaspoon of allspice to the cake batter with the flour, and replacing the sour cream with 1 cup of canned coconut milk. Fill the pan with batter, then top it with thin slices of mango, pineapple, and kiwi fruit before sprinkling on streusel made with an added ½ cup of shredded coconut and ½ cup of chopped macadamia nuts.

Cinnamon Swirl Bread

This bread makes the world's greatest toast, and not a half-bad French toast. The dough itself is a basic, versatile sweet dough, as you will see in the variations.

Serves 6–8

Prep time: 2 hours
Cook time: 90 minutes

1½ cups warm water

2 (¼-oz.) packages active dry yeast

½ cup brown sugar

2 eggs

4 oz. (1 stick) butter, softened

1 tsp. salt

4–5 cups bread flour

⅓ cup cinnamon

⅔ cup sugar

4 oz. (1 stick) butter, melted

1 egg

½ tsp. salt

1 TB. water

1. In a medium bowl, combine the warm water, yeast, and sugar, mixing well to combine. Add the eggs, 1 stick softened butter, and salt, mixing thoroughly.

2. Add 2 cups flour, and stir to combine. Continue adding flour to create a firm dough. Turn the dough out onto a floured surface and knead, adding flour only when necessary, until the dough becomes smooth and elastic, about 8 to 10 minutes. Return to the bowl, cover with plastic wrap, and set in a warm place to rise until doubled in volume, about 1 hour.

3. Combine the cinnamon and sugar, and set aside. Turn dough out onto a floured surface and with a rolling pin, roll into an 18×24 rectangle. Brush the entire surface with melted butter, then sprinkle generously with cinnamon and sugar. Starting on a long edge, roll the dough up into a log.

4. Cut the log into two 9-inch loaves. Place each loaf in a loaf pan, cover with plastic wrap, and set aside to rise again for 30 minutes. Preheat oven to 350°F.

5. In a small bowl, make an egg wash by combining the egg, salt, and water. Brush it on top of the loaves, and bake them until golden brown and firm, about 1 hour. Test for doneness with an instant-read thermometer. The internal temperature should be above 200°F. Cool for 15 minutes before removing the bread from the pan. Cool completely before slicing. Store bread for 2 days at room temperature, wrapped airtight, or

freeze for up to 2 weeks. Refresh in a 200°F oven for 15 minutes before serving.

Kitchen Tips

There are many variables that determine the amount of flour a bread recipe needs. Temperature, humidity, measurement accuracy, and type and manufacturer of flour all contribute. There is only one sure way to know how much is enough, and that is by looking and feeling. The dough should be smooth and soft, but not sticky, and not so tough that it's hard to knead. Reserve the last cup or two called for in any bread recipe and add it slowly, a little at a time. Let each addition work in completely before you decide if more is needed. Sometimes, the recipe will need more than called for, sometimes less. That's what makes baking so exciting!

Sweet Rolls: Slice log into 1-inch wheels. Place wheels on a cookie sheet lined with parchment paper. Brush with egg wash and bake at 350°F until golden brown, about 20 minutes. Dust the warm rolls with powdered sugar before serving.

Harvest Loaf: Spice up the cinnamon and sugar with an additional 1 teaspoon nutmeg, 1 teaspoon ginger, 1 teaspoon cardamom, and ¼ teaspoon clove. After sprinkling on the sugar mixture, sprinkle 2 cups of your favorite dried fruits and toasted nuts. Try mixing chopped apricots, dried cranberries, golden raisins, chopped dates, walnuts, pecans, hazelnuts, and cashews.

Monkey Bread: After the dough has risen, divide it into pieces and roll each piece into a tight ball the size of a golf ball. Dip each ball into melted butter, and roll it in cinnamon and sugar. Pack the balls tightly into a greased angel food pan. Bake in a 325°F oven for 1 hour. Turn the bread out onto a serving platter and let the monkeys rip it apart.

Dress It Up: Sticky Buns

These buns can be baked in pans, as written, or you can use a large muffin pan for perfectly round, individual buns.

Makes 10 buns
Prep time: 2 hours
Cook time: 30 minutes

1 cup brown sugar

2 TB. honey

8 oz. (2 sticks) butter, softened

¼ cup milk

1 TB. cinnamon

2 TB. bread flour

2 cups chopped pecans

1 recipe Cinnamon Swirl Bread, rolled into a log (see previous recipe)

1. Preheat oven to 350°F. Generously coat cake pans with pan spray, and line with a circle of parchment paper or foil. Coat paper with spray as well.

2. Mix together the brown sugar, honey, butter, milk, cinnamon, and flour into a smooth paste. Divide the paste between the two pans, and spread evenly. Sprinkle 1 cup of nuts into each pan.

3. Slice the log of cinnamon swirl dough into 10 buns, and place five buns in each pan, on top of the nuts, cut-side up. Bake until golden brown and bubbly, about 20 minutes. Let the pan cool for 15 minutes before inverting it onto a serving plate.

Listen to Mom! _____

Be careful of hot sugar burns! Use oven mitts and caution when inverting the sticky buns. That topping is like molten lava. Let it cool before you eat it, too.

Popovers

A well-made popover is like a buttery cream puff, but lighter. My grandpa was the King of Popovers (when Grandma would let him into the kitchen). I still use his heavy cast-iron pan.

4 eggs, room temperature

2 cups milk, room temperature

2 cups all-purpose flour

1 tsp. salt

Makes 12 popovers
Prep time: 30 minutes
Cook time: 35 minutes

1. Preheat oven to 400°F. Place the popover pan into the oven to heat it up. Combine all ingredients in a blender, and blend until well combined.

2. Pour the batter into the pan, filling each cup to the rim. Bake for 15 minutes, then turn the heat down to 375°F and bake another 20 minutes, until golden brown. Serve immediately!

Listen to Mom!

Lots of poofing in the oven is the key to a good popover, and temperature is the key to a good poofing. If the ingredients or the oven are too cold, there will not be enough energy to push the batter up into a beautiful, poofy crown. So be sure the ingredients have lost the chill from the fridge, be sure to preheat your pan, and don't open the oven door during the first 30 minutes of baking. If you do, the temperature will drop dramatically, and the popovers will fall.

Whole-Wheat Popovers: Replace the all-purpose flour with an equal amount of whole-wheat flour.

Blueberry Popovers: After filling the pan with batter, drop a few blueberries into each cup, and bake as directed. Try it with other fruits, too, such as sautéed apples or pears, bananas, or peaches.

Cinnamon Popovers: Add 1 teaspoon of ground cinnamon to the batter before blending. Try it with nutmeg or allspice, too.

Part 2

Lunch Break

Where do you have lunch? At your desk? In the cafeteria? Are you lucky
enough to have it with friends, or do you grab whatever you can at the
drive-through? If I had my way, all business would stop from noon to
one o'clock so that we could all enjoy a well-made sandwich and a warm
cup of soup. Unfortunately, life just ain't that way.

You can simulate my utopian vision by packing yourself and your family a
lunch made with love and care. It's infinitely more exciting to open a lunch
bag than it is to watch them slop the mystery meat onto your tray.

The recipes in this section can be made for lunch on the go, or presented
with flair at your next bridge party. (Does anyone play bridge anymore?)
Some are hearty meals on their own, and some can double as a first course
or side dish for more elaborate entertaining. You'll be sure to find the
perfect recipe to fill your Partridge Family lunch box, or grace your white
linen table.

Chapter 3

Sandwiches from Coast to Coast

In This Chapter

◆ What makes a great sandwich

◆ Classic favorites

◆ Hearty grilled sandwiches

◆ Salad sandwiches

◆ Sandwiches stacked high

You may have had a sandwich for lunch almost every day for your entire life. But were you aware that there is a proper method of sandwich assembly? Well, don't worry. If you're not following the rules, the sandwich cops are not going to storm in and bust you. But if you were to attend a large culinary school, you would likely be faced with Sandwich Making 101. Proper sandwich assembly requires careful consideration of the ingredients, their moisture content, their proximity to the bread, and the probability of moisture penetration. Any moist fillings, like watery tomatoes, must be separated from the bread by a moisture barrier, such as a leaf of lettuce, a slice of meat, or cheese. A thin layer of butter or mayonnaise serves the same purpose. The fat prevents moisture from penetrating the bread and making it soggy.

Sandwich Meat

Salty cured meats lend themselves particularly well to sandwich making. They are satisfying, inexpensive, readily available, and so easy to prepare that anyone can do it. I find them particularly satisfying when made of last night's leftovers.

All of these meats share a history of preservation. Before refrigeration, meat had to be saved in some way, unless one was prepared to eat an entire animal in one sitting. Ham is the thigh and butt of an animal (usually pork, but not always) that has been cured. Curing is a traditional form of meat preservation, which can be done dry or wet. Dry curing involves heavily salting, drying, and aging the meat. Wet curing uses brine, which is heavily salted water flavored with herbs and spices. The meat is soaked in the brine for several days, until the salt penetrates the meat, killing off any bacteria in the process. Corned beef is cured beef. Pastrami is cured beef that has been smoked.

It is possible to make your own ham, corned beef, and pastrami. A cool dark place, like a cellar or wine room, is required for dry curing. Recipes for wet brines vary, but usually involve coriander, allspice, sugar, vinegar, pepper, and plenty of salt. Luckily, you can find ham, pastrami, and corned beef at every deli in America. Be sure you get them sliced extra thin.

Between Two Slices

What's a sandwich without great bread? These days there are seemingly endless varieties to suit every taste and recipe: from rich dark pumpernickel to nutty whole-grain breads to tangy sourdough to simple white bread. To make a great sandwich, the bread must be the proper density. Too many holes means the filling will ooze through onto your hands. If the bread is too thick there is a chance the flavors of the filling will be lost; too thin and you risk it falling apart.

The recipes that follow give suggestions for bread, but use your imagination. Don't forget about rolls, flat bread, pita bread, bagels, and croissants. Even lettuce leaves can stand in for bread for the carb-conscious!

BLT

I once worked at a critically acclaimed restaurant in San Francisco. But every day for lunch we'd walk up the street to a tiny soul-food café and order a BLT on white toast. That, my friend, is good food.

4 slices sandwich bread or your choice

2 TB. mayonnaise

2 large crisp lettuce leaves, washed and dried

1 large ripe tomato, sliced into four ¼-inch slices

4 slices crisp cooked bacon

Serves 2	
Prep time: 10 minutes	
Cook time: 5 minutes	

1. Toast the bread and spread mayonnaise evenly on each piece.

2. For each sandwich, layer on top of one slice of bread one leaf of lettuce, one slice of tomato, and two crisscrossed slices of bacon. Top with a second slice of bread, press down and cut on the diagonal.

3. For company, stick a toothpick in the center of each half to hold it all together.

Kitchen Tips

There are certainly dozens of things you could do to this sandwich to dress it up, such as using artisan bread, homemade mayonnaise, heirloom tomatoes, extra-thick smoked bacon, or gourmet baby lettuce. All of that would be good, but none of it is necessary. The beauty of the BLT is in its simplicity. All the elements combine in sublime synchronicity; acid balancing salt, crumbly against crunchy, hot versus cold. It's nothing but a little bite of heaven.

California ABLT: Add sliced avocado to the BLT. If you want to get really West Coast about it, use alfalfa sprouts instead of lettuce.

The Submarine

This sandwich probably originated in Connecticut, where sailors from a submarine base enjoyed it while on liberty. Many places claim to have originated the sub, but wouldn't dream of calling it that. It's a hero in New York, a grinder in parts of New England, a hoagie in Philadelphia (from the Hog Island shipyard), and an Italian in Maine.

Serves 2
Prep time: 10 minutes

1 (12-inch) French or Italian roll

2 TB. mayonnaise

2 TB. mustard

¼ lb. sliced deli meats of your choice (choose at least 2 meats)

2 oz. sliced cheese of your choice

½ cup shredded lettuce

1 red onion, thinly sliced

Optional condiments, including pepperoncinis, pimentos, jalapenos, pickles, or olives

¼ cup Italian dressing, or an equal amount of olive oil and red-wine vinegar

Salt and pepper

1. Slice roll in half lengthwise, leaving one side intact, like a hinge. Open up the roll and spread one side with mayonnaise, the other with mustard.

2. Arrange the deli meats evenly across the open roll, then layer the cheese on top, lining the entire open surface of the roll. Place the lettuce, onions, and condiments evenly down the center of the open roll. Drizzle Italian dressing over the sandwich ingredients, and sprinkle with salt and pepper to taste.

3. Close the roll back up, and slice into two 6-inch sandwiches. The sub can also be cut into 1-inch pieces for party snacking.

The Dagwood: Made popular by Chick Young's immortal comic strip *Blondie,* this was the only thing Dagwood Bumstead knew how to make. It stands out from the sub for its use of sliced bread, with the ingredients stacked up high. The idea here is to make this sandwich ludicrously large.

The Po'boy: Here is the Southern version, available all across the Gulf Coast, but mostly known as a New Orleans specialty. Make it as you would the sub, but replace the deli meats with fried oysters, shrimp, soft-shell crabs, and crayfish.

Dress It Up: Muffaletta

New Orleans is home to a well-established Italian community that perpetuates some time-honored Italian traditions. Among them is this sandwich, based on a Sicilian recipe.

1 cup large pimento-stuffed green olives, sliced

1 cup kalamata olives, pitted and sliced

½ cup pickled cauliflower, sliced

½ cup pepperoncini, chopped

½ cup cocktail onions, chopped

¼ cup capers, drained

3 cloves garlic, minced

1 stalk celery, thinly sliced

1 carrot, grated

1 TB. celery seed

1 TB. dried oregano

Salt and pepper

2 cups olive oil

1 large round loaf of Italian bread

¼ lb. sliced mortadella

¼ lb. sliced ham

¼ lb. sliced Italian salami

¼ lb. sliced mozzarella cheese

¼ lb. sliced provolone cheese

Serves 6
Prep time: 24 hours (includes time for refrigeration)

1. In a large bowl, combine the olives, cauliflower, pepperoncini, onions, capers, garlic, celery, carrot, spices, and olive oil. Stir together and refrigerate overnight.

2. Slice the Italian loaf in half horizontally, and on each open half spread a generous amount of olive salad mixture. On the bottom half pile on the meats and cheeses, then replace the top of the bread.

3. Wrap the sandwich tightly in plastic wrap, and place it on a large pie plate. Invert another pie pan on top, and weight it down with some canned foods. Refrigerate for 1 hour. To serve, unwrap the sandwich and slice it into wedges.

Tidbits

The muffaletta is the one thing I cannot leave New Orleans without. In fact, whenever someone I know travels to The Big Easy, I put in my order, and wait patiently for hand delivery. (I actually think they taste better after 8 hours of travel.) If you can stand the lines, get yours in the French Quarter at its alleged spot of origin, Central Grocery, on Decatur Street. Once you've experienced it there, feel free to try the others.

The Reuben

The origin of this sandwich is hotly debated. New Yorkers credit Arnold Reuben of Reuben's Restaurant on 59th Street. Nebraskans say it came from poker player Reuben Kay of Omaha. Regardless, it gained popularity after it took first place in a national sandwich competition in 1956.

Serves 2
Prep time: 10 minutes
Cook time: 15 minutes

4 TB. butter, softened

4 slices light rye bread

½ cup Thousand Island dressing

¼ lb. corned beef

½ cup sauerkraut

4 slices Swiss cheese

1. Butter one side of each slice of bread. For each sandwich, lay one slice in a nonstick skillet, buttered side down. Spread Thousand Island dressing evenly on each slice, then layer the bread with half the corned beef, sauerkraut, and Swiss cheese. Spread the second slice of bread with Thousand Island dressing and place it on top. Butter the top of the sandwich.

2. Over medium heat, cook the sandwiches until the bottom is golden brown, about 5 minutes. Carefully flip them over, and brown the other side. Cut the sandwich on the diagonal and serve.

Kitchen Tips

In a pinch, it's easy to make Thousand Island dressing by combining ½ cup ketchup to 1 cup mayonnaise. If you want to take a little more time, add 1 teaspoon pickle relish, 1¼ cup chopped onion, and one chopped hard-boiled egg. Some people also like a little heat, and add chili sauce or prepared horseradish. This dressing is named for the Thousand Island region of upstate New York, along the St. Lawrence River and Lake Ontario, where it was first served to vacationers.

Tuna Salad Sandwich

You can boost the health-food status of this recipe by replacing the mayonnaise with yogurt, light sour cream, or fat-free mayonnaise.

1 (6-oz.) can water-packed tuna

¼ cup mayonnaise

1 TB. Dijon mustard

1 stalk celery, diced

Optional: 2 TB. diced onion, 1 TB. capers, 1 TB. pickle relish

Salt and pepper

4 slices sandwich bread of your choice

Serves 2
Prep time: 10 minutes

1. In a large bowl, combine tuna, mayonnaise, mustard, celery, and any additional ingredients. Season to taste with salt and pepper, and mix until well combined.

2. Divide tuna salad between two slices of bread, and spread evenly. Top each with a second slice of bread, cut on the diagonal, and serve.

Tidbits

What's the difference between tunas? First, there are different types of fish. White-meat tuna must be albacore. Everything else is called light meat and includes yellowfin, blue-fin, and skipjack tunas. You can buy tuna packed in various forms, including solid pack (the most expensive), chunk, flake, and grated (the cheapest). Tuna packed in oil has twice the calories of water-packed tuna, and only about half the amount of beneficial omega 3 fatty acids.

Tuna Melt: Anything can be a melt simply by adding cheese and grilling it. I like Swiss cheese with tuna, but your favorite cheese will work. Add two thin slices of cheese to the sandwich before putting on the top slice of bread. Butter the top of the sandwich, and place it in a nonstick skillet over low heat, butter side down. While the bottom slice is toasting, butter the top of the sandwich. When the bottom is toasted to a golden brown, flip it and toast the other side. Melts are best cooked slowly so that the filling can warm and the cheese can thoroughly melt.

Dress It Up: Crab Salad Sandwich

Rather than turn it into a sandwich, this salad can rest on a bed of baby greens, fill a hollowed-out tomato, or perch delicately atop cucumber slices for a stunning hors d'oeuvre.

Serves 4
Prep time: 40 minutes

4 TB. softened butter

2 TB. Dijon mustard

1 (2-oz.) can chopped pimentos, drained

8 slices sourdough bread

1 (4-oz.) package cream cheese, softened

¼ cup mayonnaise

1 TB. lime juice

2 tsp. Old Bay seasoning

4 scallions, chopped

2 stalks celery, chopped

1 cup fresh, canned, frozen (defrosted), or imitation crab meat

2 bunches watercress or baby greens, washed and dried

1. In a medium bowl blend together the butter, mustard, and pimentos. Spread this mixture thinly onto each slice of bread.

2. In another bowl, combine the cream cheese, mayonnaise, lime juice, and Old Bay. Blend together until creamy, then stir in the chopped scallions, celery, and crab meat.

3. For each sandwich, place ½ cup of crab salad onto one slice of bread. Top the salad with a generous handful of watercress, then place another slice of bread on top. Press the sandwich gently and cut on the diagonal.

Kitchen Tips

The key to this recipe is the Old Bay seasoning. This perfect combination of celery seeds, ginger, bay leaf, mustard, and chili peppers whisks me off to the ocean whenever I taste it. This sandwich is a great choice for warm summer seaside entertaining … or when you just want to feel like you're at the seaside.

Shrimp Salad Sandwich: Replace the crab meat with 1 cup of cooked bay shrimp.

Egg Salad Sandwich

This recipe is great when there are few ingredients at hand. Sometimes I keep it simple with only mayo, mustard, salt, and pepper. But when company comes I add a little spice and crunch.

4 eggs

¼ cup mayonnaise

1 TB. Dijon mustard

1 stalk celery, chopped

2 radishes, minced

1 scallion, chopped

1 TB. capers

Salt and pepper

4 slices sandwich bread of your choice

Serves 2
Prep time: 45 minutes
Cook time: 20 minutes

1. Place eggs in small saucepan and cover with water. Bring to a boil over high heat for 5 minutes. Turn off heat and let eggs sit in the hot water for 20 minutes. Transfer to a bowl of ice water and chill for 10 minutes.

2. Peel the cooled eggs, chop them, and place them in a large bowl. Add the mayonnaise, mustard, celery, radishes, scallion, and capers. Stir well to combine, then season with salt and pepper.

3. Divide egg salad evenly between two slices of bread. Top each with a second slice of bread, cut on the diagonal, and serve.

Kitchen Tips

An egg slicer is a nifty device that slices hard boiled eggs into perfect, thin slices. The egg sits in a little tray and a dozen or so wires come down on it like a tiny paper cutter. To chop an egg, slice it once into wheels, then turn it 90 degrees and slice it again. It's much quicker, easier, and neater than using a knife.

Dress It Up: Deviled Eggs

Okay, so technically this is not a sandwich, but I had to include it in this chapter. My favorite time of year to make this recipe is right after Easter, when hard-boiled eggs are tinted with the beautiful colors of residual Easter-egg dye.

Serves 8
Prep time: 45 minutes
Cook time: 20 minutes

8 eggs

¼ cup mayonnaise

1 TB. Dijon mustard

½ tsp. onion powder

Salt and pepper

Paprika for dusting

1. Place eggs in small saucepan and cover with water. Bring to a boil over high heat for 5 minutes. Turn off heat and let eggs sit in the hot water for 20 minutes. Transfer to a bowl of ice water and chill for 10 minutes.

2. Peel the cooled eggs, and slice them in half, lengthwise. Carefully remove the yolks from the whites, set the whites on a plate, and place the yolks in a large bowl. To the yolks, add the mayonnaise, mustard, and onion powder, stirring well to combine. Season with salt and pepper.

3. Spoon the yolk mixture into a piping bag and pipe it decoratively into the empty whites. Lightly dust the top with paprika, and serve. Store deviled eggs in the refrigerator for up to 24 hours.

Kitchen Tips

Piping bags are easy to find, and easy to use. Most large supermarkets carry them, as do craft supply stores. The choice of tip is a matter of preference, but I like to use a star tip for deviled eggs. Be sure the egg yolk mixture is smooth, or it won't flow through the tip. If you have no piping bag, a plastic bag works in a pinch. Just fill the bag with the deviled egg mix, seal the top, cut off one small corner, and squeeze the yolk through the hole. Since the plastic bag has no decorative tip, try adding a small leaf of chervil or flat-leaf parsley on top of each egg to make it pretty.

The Club Sandwich

There are several theories as to the origin of this double-decker sandwich. The Saratoga Club House, in Saratoga Springs, New York, claims to have created it, while others believe it was popularized at the 1904 St. Louis World's Fair. Then there are those who think it was born from train travel and the double-decker club cars.

6 slices white sandwich bread, toasted

¼ cup mayonnaise

4 leaves of crisp lettuce, washed and dried

4 slices of ripe tomato

4 slices crisp cooked bacon

¼ lb. sliced chicken or turkey

Serves 2
Prep time: 30 minutes
Cook time: 5 minutes

1. Spread each slice of toast with a thin even layer of mayonnaise. For each sandwich start with one slice of toast, and stack two leaves of lettuce, two slices of tomato, and two slices of bacon, crisscrossed. Place a second slice of toast on the bacon, and pile on the sliced chicken or turkey. Place the last slice of toast over the poultry, mayo side down.

2. Press the sandwich gently, and place four frilly toothpicks through the sandwich from top to bottom, ¼-inch from each of the four edges of the sandwich. Using a sharp serrated knife, slice the sandwich from corner to corner into four triangles. Serve the sandwich slices on their side so the colorful interior layers are exposed.

Dress It Up: The Monte Cristo

This crazy sandwich blurs the line between breakfast, lunch, and dessert. Batter-dipped and grilled or deep fried, it is properly dusted with powdered sugar and served with strawberry or raspberry jam, current jelly, or maple syrup.

Serves 2	
Prep time: 10 minutes	
Cook time: 20 minutes	

1 egg

⅓ cup milk

⅔ cup All-purpose flour

½ tsp. salt

1½ tsp. baking powder

2 cups vegetable oil

2 TB. butter, softened

4 slices white sandwich bread

¼ lb. sliced turkey

¼ lb. sliced Swiss cheese

¼ lb. sliced ham

¼ cup powdered sugar

½ cup red current jelly, strawberry or raspberry jam, or maple syrup

1. In a medium bowl, whisk together the egg and milk. Sift together the flour, salt, and baking powder, and add it to the egg mixture. Stir to combine, then set aside for 10 minutes.

2. Fill the frying pan 2 inches deep with vegetable oil, and place over high heat. Spread the softened butter evenly on one side of each slice of bread. For each sandwich, layer the turkey, cheese, and ham between two slices of buttered bread.

3. When the oil reaches 375°F, dip the sandwich into the batter, coating it well, and place it carefully into the hot oil. Fry until golden brown, about 5 minutes per side.

4. Remove fried sandwich from oil and drain on paper towels. Serve with a dusting of powdered sugar and a side of red current jelly, jam, or maple syrup.

Tidbits

Thought to be a 1950s American rendition of the French Croque Monsieur, the Monte Cristo first gained popularity as a standard menu item in several Disneyland restaurants. It is most associated with the Blue Bayou restaurant, which is adjacent to, and a part of, the Pirates of the Caribbean ride. Shiver me timbers! As with many recipes, the origin of the Monte Cristo is often disputed, and its creation is simultaneously claimed by the scurvy scallywags of the Brown Derby restaurant of Hollywood, and the Hotel del Coronado of San Diego.

Chapter 4

Salads for Every Occasion

In This Chapter

- ◆ Getting your greens
- ◆ Salad as a main course
- ◆ Salads on the side
- ◆ Layered salads
- ◆ Chopped and composed salads

My grandmother doesn't cook much anymore, but when I was a kid, she was the queen of entertaining. Now, don't misunderstand me. She hated cooking. But she loved entertaining, and set the most beautiful tables in town. They were the height of 1960s chic, with table linens and matching dishware for every occasion imaginable. Everything was impeccably arranged, with the proper silverware for each course on the menu, a bread plate, matching glassware, candlesticks, and centerpieces.

She was also quite a bridge player, and consequently had dozens of little salad-sized plates that fit easily on the card tables during her bridge parties. For dinners, those plates appeared as salad plates, ceremoniously brought to the table first, presenting more often than not some variation of a Jell-O-based salad, perched on a leaf of iceberg lettuce, and crowned with a dollop of Miracle Whip. My grandma was the ultimate authority on vegetables and fruit suspended in gelatin.

The salads weren't always gelatin based, although they almost always had Miracle Whip in some form or other. Crunchy pea salad, three-bean salad, and Waldorf salad were just a few of the American classics introduced to me via Grandma's beautiful salad plates.

Despite my years as a professional chef (or perhaps because of them), her salads continue to be some of my favorite recipes. When she moved out of her house into an assisted living facility, I was the recipient of her red-cloth-covered recipe binder. In it were all of the recipes made with Jell-O, soup, Hamburger Helper, and canned tuna that I grew up with. I still refer to it when I am feeling a little retro, or when I need a hug from my grandma. I am dedicating this chapter to her, and in it you will find some of her favorites. There are also salads meant to be served as a meal, and some you can't possibly have a picnic, luncheon, or potluck without.

Greens

There are dozens of lettuces on the market, including baby and heirloom greens, bitter, spicy, salty, green, red, purple, curly, frizzy, and flat. And with all that available, what is it that ends up in most salad bowls? Iceberg, of course. Pale, bland, and devoid of much nutritional value, iceberg lettuce is synonymous with salad to most Americans. And why not? It's crisp, crunchy, and cool. Its texture lends the perfect counterpoint to most salad ingredients. So what if it's not really nutritious? At least it's not bad for you. Pop a multivitamin if you feel guilty.

Kitchen Tips _____

If you're looking for healthier lettuce, look for those with dark colors. Romaine, green and red leaf, Boston, bibb, or butter lettuce, spinach, and chard are all good choices that are readily available. Radicchio, arugula, frissé, or chicory are common, but their strong flavors may be too strong for iceberg eaters. Try mixing them with other lettuces first to see if you like them.

There are several greens called for in this chapter, and it is imperative that you wash and dry them all thoroughly before adding them to a recipe. The best method of washing greens is submerging them in cold water for a couple minutes, then pulling them out of the water, leaving the dirt and sand to sink to the bottom. Dry the greens in a salad spinner, or let them drain in a colander before patting them dry with paper towels. If you don't, your wet greens will water down the salad dressing.

Spinach grows in sandy soil, and must be thoroughly cleaned by repeatedly submerging and rinsing until the water runs clean. In addition, the veins of the larger leaves tend to be more fibrous than is acceptable to the average palate: they need to be deveined. To do this, fold the leaf in half along the vein, and hold it in one hand with the folded, vein edge exposed. Pull the stem up toward the tip of the leaf, and the vein will rip out cleanly.

Listen to Mom!

Many salad greens are now available prewashed and trimmed, ready to pour into the salad bowl. This is super-convenient, but it comes with a price: once the bag is opened, these lettuces deteriorate much quicker than lettuce still attached to a head.

Vegetable Prep

All vegetables need to be washed thoroughly before adding them to a recipe. In most cases, a good rinse will do. But occasionally, a little more is called for.

Most people will agree that, although they may love eating raw onions, they do not love the taste and smell of their breath afterward. Soaking sliced raw onions in cold water reduces the offensive onion oils that make eating onions a bummer for you and those around you. Soak them as long as you can, overnight if possible. Even if you can only soak them for 30 minutes, you'll be amazed at the difference in taste and aftertaste.

Potatoes cook better and retain more nutrients when cooked in their skin. But be sure they are scrubbed of dirt before they are cooked. Mushrooms, too, have a lot of dirt, and should be washed thoroughly. Some chefs maintain that a mushroom should be brushed clean, and never washed. While it is true that they act like a sponge and soak up water, this is pronounced in older mushrooms, in which the underside of the cap is exposed. Fresh mushrooms are still closed under the cap, and will absorb much less moisture. So considering what mushrooms grow in—poo, to put it delicately—I prefer to choose fresh ones and wash them.

Taco Salad

This main-dish salad contains all the ingredients you find in a good taco. The taco shell portion of the recipe can include name-brand tortilla or corn chips, hand-crushed crisp taco shells, or crispy fried flour tortilla strips.

Serves 4
Prep time: 15 minutes
Cook time: 10 minutes

1 lb. ground beef

1 (1-oz.) package taco seasoning mix

1 (15-oz.) can kidney beans, black beans, or pinto beans

1 cup sour cream

1 cup salsa

3 scallions, chopped

½ head iceberg lettuce, shredded

1 ripe tomato, chopped

1 cup grated cheddar cheese

1 (6-oz.) can sliced black olives

1 (4-oz.) can diced green chilies

4 cups tortilla chips

1. In a large sauté pan, brown the ground beef over medium heat. Drain off excess fat, add taco seasoning and beans. Remove from heat and set aside.

2. In a small bowl stir together sour cream and salsa. Set aside.

3. In a large bowl, combine scallions, lettuce, tomato, cheese, olives, and chilies. Mix in ground beef and beans, and salsa dressing. Top salad with tortilla chips before serving.

 Tidbits

Taco seasoning can be bought ready made, or you can mix your own. Recipes vary, but they generally contain ground cumin, chili powder, garlic powder, onion powder, and oregano.

Dress It Up: Tortilla Bowls

Few things are as fun as eating your dishes. Follow the recipe as written, or use colorful flavored tortillas for a fun change of pace. You can even make some unforgettable mini-appetizer cups using wonton wrappers.

1 quart canola oil	4 extra large flour tortillas

Serves 4	
Prep time: 10 minutes	
Cook time: 15 minutes	

1. Heat oil in a saucepan (at least 6 inches deep) to 375°F. Drop the tortilla onto the surface of the hot oil, and press it in the middle with a ladle to completely submerge it.

2. Hold the tortilla under the hot oil until it turns golden brown, about 3 minutes. Remove it with tongs to drain on paper towels. Blot off any excess oil and allow the tortilla to cool. Repeat with remaining tortillas. Before filling your tortilla shell, use a dollop of sour cream to anchor the tortilla bowl to the plate you place it on.

Kitchen Tips

To make this restaurant-quality tortilla bowl, you'll need to do a little deep-frying. If you don't own a deep fryer, get yourself a deep saucepan or pasta pot. I like frying in canola or salad oil, as it has the least flavor. Deep-frying can be a little stinky and messy, so don't wear anything fancy, and open a window. You can check the temperature of frying oil using a deep-fry thermometer, or you can simply drop in a small bit of food. If it sizzles immediately, you're ready to rock. If the food just floats, the oil is too cool, and if it instantly burns to a crisp, the oil is too hot.

Chinese Chicken Salad

In this recipe the crunchy element is fried *rice noodles*. I have also seen crispy chow mien noodles, and fried wonton strips used in the same way. I have even heard of a version that uses raw, crunched-up ramen noodles. Try that one at your own risk.

Serves 4
Prep time: 30 minutes (plus 30–60 minutes for refrigeration)

2 TB. canola oil

1 TB. sesame oil

1 tsp. grated lemon zest

3 TB. lemon juice

2 TB. honey

¼ cup soy sauce

2 cups cooked chicken, diced or shredded

2 cups iceberg lettuce, shredded

2 cups Napa cabbage, shredded

2 medium carrots, sliced thin on an angle

2 scallions, sliced thin on an angle

1 (8-oz.) can sliced water chestnuts, drained

2 cups rice noodles, fried

¼ cup cashews, chopped

1. In a large bowl, whisk together the oils, lemon zest, lemon juice, honey, and soy sauce. Add the chicken, lettuce, cabbage, carrots, scallions, and water chestnuts. Toss thoroughly to coat all ingredients with the dressing. Chill for 30 to 60 minutes.

2. Just before serving, toss in the rice noodles and the cashews.

Chefspeak

Rice noodles (also called rice stick noodles or cellophane noodles) look like thin threads of plastic or fishing line. They are most often soaked in hot water and added to soups, and stir-fries. If they are fried, they puff up into airy, crunchy noodles. Fry small chunks of the rice noodles in 1 inch of canola oil heated to 375°F. When they hit the hot oil they puff up quickly, so be prepared.

Crab Louie

This recipe was passed down from my grandmother, who got it from the chef of *The City of San Francisco*, which ran between Chicago and Oakland. The train was famous for being buried under a snow drift in the Sierra Nevada Mountains for 6 days in the 1950s. Thankfully, Grandma wasn't on board then.

2 cups mayonnaise

2 TB. chili sauce

1 hard-boiled egg, chopped fine

½ green bell pepper, chopped fine

1 (4-oz.) can chopped pimento

2 TB. flat-leaf parsley, chopped

2 scallions, chopped

2 cups cooked crab meat

2 cups shredded iceberg lettuce

2 TB. chopped chives

Serves 4
Prep time: 20 minutes (plus time for refrigeration)

1. In a large bowl, combine the mayonnaise, chili sauce, egg, bell pepper, pimento, parsley, and scallions.

2. Mix well, then add crab meat. Serve chilled, on a bed of lettuce, and sprinkle with chopped chives.

Shrimp Louie: Replace crab with an equal amount of cooked shrimp.

Avocado Louie: Serve Crab or Shrimp Louie in half of a ripe avocado; squeeze a little lemon juice on the avocado before stuffing it with salad, and anchor it on a bed of shredded lettuce to keep it from rocking around.

Potato Salad

The ancient Incas cultivated, ate, and worshipped the potato 2,500 years ago. Spanish conquistadors brought it back to Europe in the 1500s, when we begin to find potato recipes, including what may be the first potato salad, cold and dressed in oil and vinegar.

Serves 4
Prep time: 40 minutes (plus 60 minutes for refrigeration)
Cook time: 20 minutes

2 lb. red new potatoes

1½ cups mayonnaise

2 TB. Dijon mustard

¼ cup cider or vinegar

½ tsp. grated nutmeg

Salt and pepper

1 cup celery, chopped

1 cup yellow onion, chopped and soaked in cold water for 15–30 minutes

1. Cover potatoes with cold water and bring to a boil over high heat. At the boil, turn the heat down to medium, and simmer until tender, about 20 minutes. Drain potatoes and submerge in a bowl of ice water until cool. Cut cooled potatoes into quarters.

2. In a large bowl, combine mayonnaise, mustard, vinegar, nutmeg, and salt and pepper to taste, mixing thoroughly. Add potatoes, celery, and onion, and toss to coat vegetables evenly with dressing.

3. Chill potato salad for 1 hour before serving. Store refrigerated for up to 2 days.

Tidbits

The most important ingredient in a potato salad is, of course, the potato. The common wisdom regarding potato choice is based on the assumption that the potato should be in firm chunks, and not a mealy mash. If you agree, then your choice should be a potato with low starch, also known as waxy potatoes. Waxy potatoes include among their ranks the new potato, red-, yellow-, white-, and purple-skinned potatoes, as well as the heirloom-variety fingerlings. Baker, russet, Idaho, and Burbank potatoes are all mealy, and are more suited to baked potatoes and French fries than potato salad.

Dress It Up: Warm German Potato Salad

Warm vinegar and bacon dressing served over vegetables is an old German tradition. When immigrants from Germany arrived here, they adapted these recipes for the ingredients abundant here. During both world wars this recipe was known simply as warm potato salad.

2 lb. red new potatoes

6 slices uncooked bacon, diced

1 medium yellow onion, chopped

1 cup celery, chopped

2 cloves garlic, minced

1 tsp. dill seed

½ cup cider vinegar

2 TB. seeded spicy mustard

1 TB. sugar

Salt and pepper

Serves 4
Prep time: 30 minutes
Cook time: 20 minutes

1. Cover potatoes with cold water and bring to a boil over high heat. At the boil, turn the heat down to medium, and simmer until tender, about 20 minutes. Drain potatoes and submerge in a bowl of ice water until cool. Peel and slice cooled potatoes.

2. Cook bacon in a large sauté pan over medium heat until crisp. Remove bacon. Add the onion and celery to the bacon fat and continue cooking until translucent, about 5 minutes. Add garlic, dill seed, vinegar, mustard, sugar, and sliced potatoes. Cook gently until all ingredients are warmed. Add bacon, and season with salt and pepper. Serve warm.

Spinach Salad

Spinach packs a hefty nutritional punch. Popeye knew it was loaded with iron, but it's also got vitamins, calcium, magnesium, potassium, and many other nutrients that not only make you strong, but also fight cancers, heart disease, osteoporosis, and arthritis.

Serves 4

Prep time: 30 minutes

---

1 bunch spinach, washed, dried, and deveined

3 hard-boiled eggs, sliced

8 oz. white mushrooms, washed and sliced

1 purple onion, sliced and soaked in cold water for 15–30 minutes

6 slices bacon, fried crisp and crumbled

1 clove garlic, minced

1 tsp. Dijon mustard

½ cup olive oil

3 TB. red wine vinegar

Salt and pepper

1 cup chopped toasted pecans

1. In a large bowl, combine the spinach, egg, mushrooms, onion, and bacon. Set aside.

2. In another bowl, combine garlic, mustard, olive oil, and vinegar. Mix well, season with salt and pepper, and drizzle over the salad to lightly coat the greens. Top with pecans and serve immediately.

Smoked Duck Spinach Salad: Omit the eggs, and replace with 2 cups of shredded smoked duck. Replace the red wine vinegar with an equal amount of rice vinegar, and add to the dressing 1 tablespoon of soy sauce, 1 teaspoon of sesame oil, and 1 tablespoon of sesame seeds. Replace the pecans with cashews.

Spinach and Shrimp Salad: Replace the eggs with 1 pound of cooked bay shrimp. Add chopped scallions, tomatoes, and avocados. Dress with Green Goddess dressing made in a blender with 1 cup mayonnaise; ½ cup sour cream; one bunch each of scallions, tarragon, parsley, and thyme; six anchovy filets; one clove garlic; 2 tablespoons tarragon vinegar; and salt and pepper to taste.

Kitchen Tips

Smoked duck may seem like an exotic ingredient, but if you have a Chinese restaurant in your town, you've got smoked duck. Most restaurants will happily sell you a half or whole duck. They may even deliver.

Dress It Up: Warm Bacon Dressing

This dressing turns fresh spinach leaves into more of a side dish than a salad. Who cares what you call it? It's delicious!

1 lb. uncooked bacon, diced

2 TB. Dijon mustard

2 TB. balsamic vinegar

2 TB. honey

Salt and pepper

Serves 4
Prep time: 10 minutes
Cook time: 5 minutes

1. Sauté bacon over high heat until crispy.

2. Remove from heat and stir in mustard, vinegar, honey, and salt and pepper to taste. Pour over spinach salad and serve immediately. Leftover dressing can be refrigerated for up to 2 days, and must be rewarmed before serving.

Cole Slaw

Shredded cabbage salad with vinegar dressing was served in ancient Rome, but the term *cole slaw* is an American corruption of the Dutch word *koolsla*, meaning cabbage salad.

1 cup sour cream

2 tsp. celery seed

½ tsp. salt

2 TB. lemon juice

1 white onion, grated

1 cup Italian flat-leaf parsley, chopped

¼ cup chives, chopped

½ head green cabbage, shredded

½ head purple cabbage, shredded

1 carrot, grated

Serves 4
Prep time: 15 minutes (plus time for refrigeration)

1. In a large bowl, combine sour cream, celery seed, salt, lemon juice, and onion.

2. Mix thoroughly, then add parsley, chives, cabbages, and carrot. Toss to coat vegetables thoroughly with dressing. Serve chilled, and store in refrigerator for up to 2 days.

Caesar Salad

This salad, invented in the 1920s by Caesar Cardini at his restaurant in Tijuana, was traditionally tossed together table-side.

Serves 4
Prep time: 20 minutes

1 egg yolk

1 clove garlic, minced

4 anchovy filets, minced

3 TB. lemon juice

¼ cup olive oil

Salt and pepper

1 head romaine lettuce, washed, dried, and chopped

½ cup freshly grated Parmesan cheese

1 cup garlic croutons

12 anchovy filets

1. In a large bowl, whisk together the egg yolk, garlic, anchovies, and lemon juice. Slowly drizzle in the olive oil while whisking, taking 3 to 4 minutes to add all the oil. Season with salt and pepper, then set aside.

2. Add to the dressing the lettuce, Parmesan cheese, and croutons. Toss well to evenly coat, and divide evenly between four plates. Top each salad with three anchovy filets and serve.

Listen to Mom!

Don't be alarmed by the appearance of egg yolk in this recipe. Yolks are necessary to create all emulsified dressings, which are oil-and-acid-based dressings that do not separate after being well mixed. If your eggs are chilled, and you, your equipment, and your kitchen are clean, there is no danger. Most people worry that raw eggs will give them salmonella, but the majority of salmonella cases are caused by unwashed fruit, not raw eggs or meat.

Three-Bean Salad

This recipe is a great choice for pool parties, because it has no mayonnaise, and can therefore sit out in the sun all day. It actually tastes better when it's at room (or patio) temperature.

½ **cup sugar**

⅓ **cup canola oil**

½ **cup tarragon vinegar**

½ **cup white wine vinegar**

Salt and pepper

1 red, yellow, or green bell pepper, chopped

1 (15-oz.) can kidney beans

1 (15-oz.) can yellow wax beans

1 (15-oz.) can green string beans

1 small purple onion, chopped and soaked in cold water for 15–20 minutes

2 scallions, chopped

Serves 4
Prep time: 10 minutes (plus time for refrigeration)

1. In a large bowl, combine the sugar, oil, vinegars, and salt and pepper to taste, mixing well to combine.

2. Add the bell pepper, kidney beans, wax beans, string beans, onions, and scallions. Toss well to coat the vegetables with dressing.

3. Cover the salad with plastic wrap and refrigerate for 2 hours, or overnight.

More Than Three-Bean Salad: I simply cannot be tied down to just three beans. This recipe is not the boss of me, and if I want to use more beans, I will. In addition to the original three, try adding black beans (rinse them first to keep the entire salad from turning gray), garbanzo beans, pinto beans, navy beans, or black-eyed peas.

Southwestern Bean Salad: Add to the dressing one (4 oz.) can of chopped green chilies, 1 cup chopped fresh cilantro, 1 tablespoon ground cumin, and 1 teaspoon chili powder. Omit the tarragon vinegar, and add ¼ cup fresh lime juice. In addition to the original three beans, add one (15-oz.) can of pinto beans and one (15-oz.) can of corn. Garnish with a dollop of sour cream and crispy fried corn tortilla strips.

Grandma's Jell-O Salad

Here's just the thing to serve when you're feeling nostalgic.

Serves 6
Prep time: 45 minutes (plus at least 6 hours for refrigeration)

1 (3-oz.) pkg. lime gelatin

1 (3-oz.) pkg. lemon gelatin

2 cups boiling water

1½ cups cold water

¼ cup prepared horseradish

1 tsp. salt

3 TB. lemon juice

1 cup cucumber, peeled and grated

1 cup carrot, peeled and grated

½ cup diced radish

½ cup diced celery

1 cup grated sweet white onions

1 (8-oz.) can crushed pineapple, drained

1. In a large bowl, dissolve the lime and lemon gelatin in the boiling water. Add the cold water, and chill until partially set, about 30 minutes.

2. Meanwhile, in a separate bowl combine the horseradish, salt, lemon juice, cucumber, carrot, radish, celery, onion, and pineapple. Stir this mixture into the partially set gelatin. Pour into a mold and chill for at least 6 hours, or overnight.

3. Unmold the salad by dipping the bottom of the mold into hot tap water for about 5 seconds. Turn it out onto a platter, tap once or twice, and lift up the mold. Serve wedges of salad on a lettuce leaf with a dollop of cottage cheese.

Kitchen Tips

Only canned pineapple can be added to gelatin. Fresh pineapple contains bromelain, an enzyme that prevents gelatin from setting by breaking down the protein structure. The same enzyme is used as a meat tenderizer. It is bromelain that makes your mouth sore when you've eaten too much pineapple. It's tenderizing your mouth. Bromelain is destroyed by heat, such as that used in the canning process. Therefore, canned pineapple can be added to the gelatin without fear.

Seven-Layer Salad

This salad goes by several different names (layered salad, Swiss layered salad, summer layered salad, 24-hour salad), and has varied ingredients. But it always has peas, and a sweet, simple mayonnaise-based dressing.

2 cups mayonnaise

¼ cup Dijon mustard

1 tsp. grated nutmeg

Salt and pepper

1 medium-size head of lettuce, shredded

2 cups fresh or 1 (8-oz.) package frozen peas, thawed and drained

1 large tomato, diced

1 cup grated Swiss, cheddar, or jack cheese

1 medium purple onion, sliced and soaked in cold water for 15–20 minutes

2 tsp. sugar

8 slices of crisp, cooked bacon, crumbled

Serves 4
Prep time: 30 minutes (plus 2–24 hours for refrigeration)

1. In a small bowl, combine the mayonnaise, mustard, nutmeg, salt, and pepper. Set aside.

2. In a clear salad bowl, evenly layer half the lettuce, half the peas, half the tomatoes, and half the cheese. Spread half the dressing on top of the cheese as evenly as possible. Top the dressing with half the onions, and sprinkle on 1 teaspoon of sugar. Repeat the layering with the remaining ingredients.

3. Cover the salad tightly with plastic wrap and refrigerate for 2 hours, or overnight. Before serving, sprinkle the top of the salad with crumbled bacon.

Multilayered Salad: There is no rule that says there can only be seven layers. Make it 10 or even 15. I love adding lots of crunchy layers, including chopped celery, radishes, water chestnuts, or sweet red and yellow bell peppers. And why not make it a meal with a couple of sliced hard-boiled eggs?

Dilly Seafood Layered Salad: When making the dressing, omit the nutmeg, and add 1 tablespoon of dried dill, or one bunch of chopped fresh dill. Include in the layers 8 ounces of cooked bay shrimp, 8 ounces of cooked crab meat, one diced avocado, and one peeled and sliced cucumber.

Kitchen Tips

The most important factor in creating a successful layered salad is the presentation. Use a large clear glass or plastic bowl so the layers show. If it gets tossed before it's served it's no longer layered, so serve the salad with big salad spoons and dig deep so that each guest gets a bit of each layer.

Chef Salad

It's uncertain where this salad began, although recipes for it appeared in print as early as the 1930s. It is known in the food business as a composed salad because it is not tossed, but arranged.

Serves 4
Prep time: 30 minutes

4 cups mixed salad greens, washed and dried

1 carrot, sliced into strips

1 stalk celery, sliced into strips

1 red bell pepper, sliced into rings

½ cup radishes, sliced

¼ lb. cooked turkey breast, sliced into strips

¼ lb. ham, sliced into strips

¼ lb. Swiss cheese, sliced into strips

2 hard-boiled eggs, sliced

1 ripe tomato, cut into wedges

1 cup salad dressing of your choice

1. Divide the greens evenly between four plates.

2. For each salad divide evenly the carrot, celery, bell pepper, and radishes, and sprinkle over the lettuce.

3. On the top of each salad, arrange a section of turkey, ham, cheese, egg, and tomato. Serve chilled with a small dish of dressing on the side.

Dress It Up: Salade Niçoise

This salad contains ingredients that are indigenous to the Mediterranean region, and are readily available in Nice, France, hence the name. One bite and you can taste the sun along the Côte d'Azure.

½ lb. red new potatoes

½ lb. green beans or haricot vert, trimmed

1 cup extra virgin olive oil

3 TB. red wine vinegar

1 TB. lemon juice

1 clove garlic, minced

¼ cup flat-leaf parsley, chopped

Salt and pepper

4 cups mixed salad greens, washed and dried

1 ripe tomato, cut into wedges

2 hard-boiled eggs, quartered

1 (6-oz.) can tuna, drained

½ cup black Niçoise olives, pitted

12 anchovy filets

Serves 4
Prep time: 30 minutes
Cook time: 20 minutes

1. Cover potatoes with cold water and bring to a boil over high heat. At the boil, turn the heat down to medium, and simmer until tender, about 20 minutes. Drain potatoes and submerge in a bowl of ice water until cool. Cut cooled potatoes into quarters, leaving the skin on.

2. Cover the green beans with cold water and bring to a boil over high heat. Boil for 3 minutes, then drain and immediately submerge in a bowl of ice water until cool.

3. In a small bowl, combine the oil, vinegar, lemon juice, garlic, and parsley; season with salt and pepper. Mix well, then add the potato and green beans, toss to coat evenly, and set aside.

4. Divide the salad greens evenly between four plates. For each salad divide evenly the tomato, eggs, tuna, potato, green beans, and olives, and arrange in sections on top of the lettuce. Drizzle remaining dressing on top and garnish each salad with three anchovy filets. Serve immediately.

Cobb Salad

This *chopped salad* originated at the world-famous Brown Derby Restaurant in Hollywood. (A lot of good food sprang from that iconic place.) Supposedly, owner Bob Cobb and his Hollywood buddies went grazing through the kitchen late one night. They threw this salad together with what was laying around (a common scenario in the history of culinary arts).

Serves 4

Prep time: 30 minutes (plus time for refrigeration)

---

1 cup extra virgin olive oil

3 TB. red wine vinegar

1 TB. lemon juice

1 TB. Dijon mustard

1 TB. Worcestershire sauce

1 clove garlic, minced

1 tsp. sugar

Salt and pepper

4 cups mixed salad greens, washed and dried

2 cups cooked chicken, diced

1 ripe tomato, diced

2 hard-boiled eggs, chopped

6 slices bacon, cooked crisp and crumbled

1 ripe avocado, diced

1 cup Roquefort cheese, crumbled

1. In a large bowl, combine the olive oil, vinegar, lemon juice, mustard, Worcestershire, garlic, and sugar; season with salt and pepper. Whisk together thoroughly. Add the chopped lettuce and toss to coat. Divide lettuce evenly between four plates.

2. Arrange the chicken, tomato, eggs, bacon, avocado, and Roquefort in sections on top of the lettuce. Serve chilled.

Chefspeak

A **chopped salad** is one in which all the ingredients are cut to the same size, usually about ½- to ¾-inch dice. The ingredients can be tossed together, or, as in the case of the Cobb Salad, arranged in sections or strips on top of a bed of chopped lettuce.

Waldorf Salad

Named for the super-deluxe Waldorf Astoria hotel in New York City, this salad was the brainstorm of the maître d'hôtel, Oscar Tschirky. The original version, dated to the 1890s used only apples, celery, and mayonnaise. Nuts and grapes were added in the 1920s.

2 red apples, diced, skin on

4 stalks celery, diced

1 cup walnuts, toasted and chopped

1 cup green or red grapes, halved

1 cup mayonnaise

Serves 4
Prep time: 15 minutes (plus time for refrigeration)

1. In a large bowl combine the apples, celery, walnuts, and grapes.

2. Toss with mayonnaise to coat, and serve chilled.

Waldorf Gelatin Salad: Dissolve lemon gelatin in 2 cups of boiling water, and chill. When partially set, about 30 minutes, fold in 2 cups diced apples, 1 cup diced celery, 1 cup halved grapes, 1 cup chopped walnuts, 1 tablespoon cider vinegar, 1 teaspoon salt, and 1 cup mayonnaise. Chill to set.

Chapter 5

Souper Soups and Chilis

In This Chapter

- Stocks as the basis for any soup
- Classic feel-better soups
- Chowders and puréed soups
- Fancy company-worthy soups
- Chill-chasing chilis

Soups are warm and satisfying, and about as cozy as food gets. And while most of America gets their soup out of a can, soup is actually very simple to make. There are a few specific techniques you need to know, but they are not at all complicated. They do take a little more time than simply using the can opener, which is why many home cooks with busy lives opt out of it. But with a little planning, good soup can be made at home with ease.

There are two basic families of soups: thick and thin. Thin soups use meat or vegetable stocks as a base into which float a variety of foods. Thick soups can be a purée of foods, like potatoes or tomatoes, or they can be thinner stock-based soups thickened with a roux, milk, or cream.

One great thing about soup making is its ability to use, and even showcase, leftovers. Almost any leftover vegetable from a salad or side dish can be added to a soup or stock to increase flavor and nutrition. Leftover bones and meat scraps can be added to enrich a stock. Meats and grains are commonly chopped and added near the end of cooking in bean soups, chowders, and clear soups like chicken noodle. Soups are also a great way to utilize less than perfect vegetables. A little bruising will keep a tomato on the sidelines of salad making, but it's perfect for soup. In fact, less perfect vegetables are usually less expensive, which makes them perfect choices for soup making.

The Foundation: Stock

Making homemade soup stock is not hard. The main ingredients are aromatic vegetables and bones. The typical vegetables are what the chefs call *mirepoix*, which include carrots, onions, and celery. You can definitely add other vegetables if you'd like. The more you add, the more nutritious your soup will be. Be wary of excessively strong flavors (fennel, for instance, can overpower a soup if too much is added) and strong colors (beets will make your soup red). As far as bones go, you can buy them cheap from a butcher, or do what I do and save them after serving a large roast. The bones of young animals and joints are the best choice for stock because the cartilage and connective tendons release collagen into the stock, making it rich, flavorful, and thick.

Kitchen Tips _____

One trick of mine is to save scraps of meat, bones, and vegetables in an empty paper milk carton in my freezer. I add scraps to it throughout the week, and when it's full, I peel the paper off the frozen block of stock scraps, toss the block into the stockpot and cover it with water. Voilà! Instant stock ingredients.

Purées

Puréed soups can be made in several ways. Blenders make the finest purée. Food processors produce a slightly chunkier result, as do hand-held *immersion blenders*. Food mills are an old-fashioned manual option that work really well but take a little extra elbow grease. Regardless of the purée method you choose, it's a good idea to cool the food as much as possible once it is cooked before you purée it. The splatter potential is real, and the results can be scorching. Use caution. Many cooks forget that steam is hot, and hurts just as much as boiling water, if not more.

Once your purée is finished, you may wish to strain it to remove any oversized chunks. This is how the smoothest possible purées are made. Use a fine mesh strainer, and strain it back into a saucepan to finish and warm the soup.

Chefspeak _____

Immersion blenders are basically blenders on a stick. A little propeller is inserted into a pot of food, and as it whizzes around, the food is drawn into the blade. The advantage is that the soup does not have to be transferred out of the pot, and only the blade of the immersion blender needs to get cleaned. The downside is that it is a little harder to get a really thin, fine purée.

Roasted Peppers

A few recipes call for some precooked vegetables, including roasted peppers. A roasted pepper has a much different flavor than one that is merely sautéed or baked. The charred skin adds a smoky, grilled quality, and it removes the papery, tough skin. This method can be used for any pepper, including bell peppers and chili peppers. Place the whole raw pepper directly onto the burner of a gas stove. Turn the flame on high (don't forget to ventilate!) and let the pepper sit over the flame until it blackens. Use tongs to turn the pepper to blacken all sides. Drop the blackened pepper into a plastic or paper bag, and seal it tight. As it cools, the pepper will generate steam, which helps the skin slide off. When it's cool, rub off the skin, open it up, remove the seeds and stem, then add to your recipe. If you do not have a gas stove, the same results can be had using a broiler, an oven at 500°F to 550°F, or an outdoor grill.

Flavorful Stock for Soup

Stock is a basic ingredient for most soup recipes. And while it is readily available in your supermarket, it is an easy thing to make yourself. It just requires time.

> *Makes 4 quarts*
>
> **Prep time:** 1 hour
> **Cook time:** 4–6 hours

4 lbs. meat parts: poultry carcass, especially wings and joints; or beef, veal, lamb bones, especially joints and meat scraps

2 carrots, chopped

4 stalks celery, chopped

1 large yellow onion, chopped

1 bay leaf

1 tsp. black peppercorn

1 clove

1 sprig fresh parsley (or 1 tsp. dried)

1 sprig fresh thyme (or 1 tsp. dried)

About 4 quarts cold water

1. Preheat oven to 500°F. Wash meat and spread into a roasting pan in one layer. Bake until well browned, about 30 minutes. Remove from oven and place in stockpot.

2. Add the remaining ingredients to the stockpot. Cover with cold water, bring to a boil over high heat, then reduce heat and cook at a bare simmer for 4 to 6 hours. Skim the top of the stock periodically to remove any residue.

3. Drain stock by pouring it into a colander placed over a large bowl, and then let it cool. If there is meat left on the bones, let them cool and pick the meat off for use in soups and stews.

4. To degrease the stock, refrigerate overnight, then remove the fat that has solidified on top. Good stock will have a jellied consistency when chilled. Store refrigerated for up to 4 days, or frozen for 1 month.

Kitchen Tips

Many chefs brown the vegetables in addition to the bones for a rich, dark brown stock. If you want to try it, use caution. Small vegetables burn easily. Add them toward the end of cooking to avoid a bitter flavor. Tomato paste is another common ingredient to the brown stock roasting pan. It adds a little acidity and color. Add one (6-oz.) can with the vegetables toward the end of roasting.

Vegetable Stock: Omit the meat, and replace with a variety of vegetables. Choose an even assortment, as too much of one vegetable will overpower the stock.

Light Stock: Instead of browning the bones in the oven, put them directly in the pot with the vegetables. The stock will be slightly less rich in flavor, and lighter in color. It's a good choice when you want the other soup and sauce ingredients to shine.

Fish Stock: Fish meat and bones have strong flavors, and do not need browning or prolonged cooking. Combine fish bones, heads, tails, skins, shells, and meat scraps with vegetables, fresh herbs such as thyme or parsley, and the juice of one lemon. Cover with water and simmer for only 30 minutes.

Chicken Soup

You can use this same method to make turkey or beef soup. You can simply change the bones and meat, or go all-out and add tomatoes, garlic, and mushrooms. Yum!

Serves 6
Prep time: 10 minutes
Cook time: 30 minutes

6 cups chicken stock

1 carrot, diced

1 stalk celery, diced

2 cups cooked chicken meat, diced

1 cup fresh or frozen peas

Salt and pepper

1. Combine the stock, carrot, and celery in a saucepan and simmer until the vegetables are tender, about 15 minutes.

2. Add chicken and peas, and cook until they are warmed through, about 5 minutes more. Season with salt and pepper.

Extra-Hearty Chicken Soup: Add 2 cups of cooked noodles, cooked rice, cooked barley, or dumplings. To make dumplings, in a medium bowl, combine 1 cup of all-purpose flour, 2 teaspoons baking powder, ½ cup grated cheese, and a pinch of salt. Combine 1 egg and ¾ cup milk, then add it in and mix into a dough. Drop dumpling dough on top of the simmering soup, cover, and cook for 10 minutes.

Matzo Ball Soup: Brown ¼ cup chopped onion in 2 tablespoons of chicken fat. Remove from heat and beat in two eggs, 2 tablespoons of chicken stock, ½ cup matzo meal, and a pinch of salt and pepper. Chill completely, then roll into balls and simmer in soup for 30 minutes.

Tortilla Soup: Add to your chicken soup three chopped tomatoes, one (4-oz.) can diced green chilies, and 1 teaspoon each chili powder, ground cumin, and hot sauce. Simmer 10 minutes, then mix in 1 cup sour cream and ¼ cup chopped fresh cilantro. Garnish with fried corn tortilla strips.

Vegetable Soup

You can add more vegetables to this recipe, but beware! Too many strong flavors and colors tend to overpower an otherwise charming soup. Balance is the key.

1 small yellow onion, chopped

2 stalks celery, chopped

1 carrot, chopped

2 parsnips, chopped

2 TB. butter

6 cups vegetable stock or water

2 cups fresh or canned tomatoes, chopped

1 cup fresh or frozen peas

1 cup fresh or frozen green beans

1 cup fresh or frozen chopped broccoli

Serves 4	
Prep time: 10 minutes	
Cook time: 40 minutes	

1. In a large saucepan, sauté the onion, celery, carrot, and parsnips in butter until translucent. Add the stock and tomatoes and simmer until carrots and parsnips are tender, about 30 minutes.

2. Add peas, beans, and broccoli, and simmer another 5 minutes before serving.

Minestrone Soup: Add to the sautéing onions 2 tablespoons dried oregano. Add into the simmering soup 2 cups cooked cannellini beans and 2 cups of uncooked macaroni. Cook until the pasta is tender. Replace the green beans and broccoli with chopped zucchini and shredded green cabbage. Serve with a generous topping of freshly grated Parmesan cheese.

Tidbits _____

In Italian *minestrone* means "big soup," and that's just what this is. It's got a boatload of nutrition, and makes a satisfying meal in itself.

Vegetable Bean Soup: Add to the sautéing onions 2 tablespoons dried thyme. Add to the simmering soup 2 cups of cooked navy, kidney, black, pinto, or cannellini beans.

Vegetable Barley Soup: Add to the sautéing onions 2 tablespoons dried sage. Add into the simmering soup 1 cup of barley and cook until tender, about 30 minutes.

Creamy Tomato Soup

This soup is perfect served up with a grilled cheese sandwich on a rainy day, or one that just feels rainy.

Serves 6
Prep time: 10 minutes
Cook time: 30 minutes

1 medium onion, chopped

2 stalks celery, chopped

1 carrot, chopped

2 cloves garlic, chopped

1 bay leaf

1 TB. dried oregano

1 TB. dried basil

4 TB. olive oil

4 TB. all-purpose flour

4 cups ripe tomatoes, chopped

1 (6-oz.) can tomato paste

4 cups vegetable stock or water

2 cups heavy cream

Salt and pepper

1. In a large saucepan, brown onion, celery, carrot, garlic, and herbs in olive oil over medium heat. Add flour and stir until all the oil is absorbed.

2. Add tomatoes, tomato paste, and stock, and simmer for 30 minutes. Remove from heat and let cool for at least 15 minutes.

3. Working in batches, purée the soup in a blender. Strain back into a saucepan, and return to the stove.

4. Bring soup back to a simmer, add cream, season with salt and pepper, and serve. Be careful not to boil the soup once cream has been added or it will curdle.

Kitchen Tips

Fresh tomatoes are wonderful. Unfortunately, they are not grown everywhere, and are not in season year-round.

Unless the season is at its peak, I usually opt for canned tomatoes. They are picked and processed at the height of ripeness, so they are of good and uniform quality. When the tomato season does arrive, I not only eat my fill, but preserve some chopped and stored in freezer bags for later in the year.

Quick Cream of Tomato Soup: If you look carefully at this recipe you may notice that tomato soup is basically tomato sauce with stock and cream. You can make it in a jiffy by combining equal amounts of canned tomato sauce, canned stock, and heavy cream.

Dress It Up: Gazpacho

Gazpacho was traditionally puréed by hand in a mortar. Today, a blender makes quick work of it, as does a food mill.

2 dinner rolls, soaked in 1 cup of water for 10 minutes

6 ripe tomatoes, chopped

1 cup cucumber, peeled, seeded, and chopped

1 cup red bell pepper, chopped

3 scallions, chopped

2 cloves garlic, chopped

2 TB. red wine vinegar

½ cup olive oil

1 TB. salt

1 TB. ground cumin

1–2 TB. hot pepper sauce

2–4 cups tomato juice

Serves 6
Prep time: 10 minutes (plus time for refrigeration)

1. In a large bowl, combine all ingredients, mix well, and refrigerate for at least 1 hour or overnight to mingle flavors.

2. Working in batches, purée in a blender to desired consistency. Serve chilled with a dollop of sour cream.

Tidbits _____

Gazpacho comes from Andalusia in southern Spain. It was originally made without tomatoes, which weren't introduced until the discovery of the New World. There are several regional varieties, including a green version made with lettuce, parsley, cucumbers, and mint, and *ajo blanco*, a white gazpacho made with olive oil, bread, garlic, and nuts.

New England Clam Chowder

The term chowder is derived from the French word for a big soup pot, *chaudiere*. Fishermen would throw a bit of seafood into these communal pots, creating a hearty fish stew. The practice probably migrated down to New England from Newfoundland.

Serves 6
Prep time: 10 minutes
Cook time: 45 minutes

6 slices uncooked bacon, diced

1 medium yellow onion, diced

2 TB. all-purpose flour

2 (6.5-oz.) cans chopped clams in their juice

2 cups water or fish stock

½ lb. red new potatoes, diced

2 cups milk

½ cup heavy cream

Salt and pepper

1. In a large saucepan, cook bacon to render fat. Add onion and cook over medium heat until golden brown. Add flour and cook until fat is absorbed. Add clams, clam juice, and water while whisking. Increase heat and bring liquid to a boil, stirring periodically.

2. At the boil, add potatoes and reduce heat. Simmer until potatoes are tender, about 15 to 20 minutes. Add milk and cream, and season with salt and pepper. Simmer another 5 minutes before serving. Do not return to a boil after milk is added, or the soup will curdle.

Kitchen Tips

Don't forget the oyster crackers. These crispy little cracker nuggets add just the right touch to a well-made chowder.

Manhattan Clam Chowder: Omit the flour, and add instead 1 cup chopped celery, 1 cup chopped carrot, 3 cloves chopped garlic, 4 cups chopped tomatoes (fresh or canned), and 1 tablespoon each dried oregano and basil. Omit the milk and cream.

Corn Chowder: Omit the clams and clam juice and water, and replace with 2 cups of corn kernels (fresh, canned, or frozen) and 2 cups chicken or vegetable stock. Garnish with chopped chives.

Dress It Up: Southwestern Chicken Chowder

Chowders do not have to have fish. Today, the term denotes any soup that is thick and chunky.

6 slices uncooked bacon, diced

1 large yellow onion, diced

3 cloves garlic, chopped

1 TB. ground cumin

2 TB. all-purpose flour

2 cups chicken stock

½ lb. red new potatoes, diced

2 poblano chilies, roasted, seeded, and chopped

2 red bell peppers, roasted, seeded, and chopped

2 cups chopped grilled chicken

2 cups milk

½ cup heavy cream

Salt and pepper

1 cup canola oil

2 flour tortillas, cut into thin strips

Serves 6	
Prep time: 30 minutes	
Cook time: 45 minutes	

1. In a large saucepan, cook bacon to render fat. Add onion, garlic, and cumin, and cook over medium heat until golden brown. Add flour and cook until fat is absorbed. While whisking, slowly add chicken stock. Increase heat and bring liquid to a boil, stirring periodically.

2. At the boil, add potatoes and reduce heat. Simmer until potatoes are tender, about 15 to 20 minutes. Add the roasted chilies, peppers, and chicken, and simmer 10 minutes. Add milk and cream, and season with salt and pepper. Simmer another 5 minutes. Do not return to a boil after milk is added, or the soup will curdle.

3. In a separate pan, heat oil to 375°F. Fry tortilla strips until golden, and drain on paper towels. Serve soup with a handful of tortilla strips and garnish with chopped avocado, a dollop of sour cream, and a sprinkling of fresh chopped cilantro.

Creamy Potato Soup

Potato soup is really just a flavorful, thinned-down version of mashed potatoes. With that in mind, choose the same potato that you would for any good mash. Avoid the waxy new potatoes, and stick with the bakers: russet, Burbank, and Idaho.

<table>
<tr><td>

Serves 6

Prep time: 15 minutes
Cook time: 45 minutes

</td></tr>
</table>

1 large yellow onion, diced

2 stalks celery, chopped

2 TB. butter

2 TB. all-purpose flour

4 cups chicken or vegetable stock

2 lb. russet potatoes, peeled and chopped

2 cups milk

½ cup heavy cream

Salt and pepper

1. In a large saucepan sauté the onion and celery in butter over medium heat until golden brown. Add flour and cook until fat is absorbed. While whisking, slowly add chicken stock. Increase heat and bring liquid to a boil, stirring periodically.

2. At the boil, add potatoes and reduce heat. Simmer until potatoes are tender, about 15 to 20 minutes.

3. Allow soup to cool for 15 to 20 minutes, then purée. Return to the heat, add milk and cream, season with salt and pepper, and simmer another 5 minutes before serving. Do not return to a boil after milk is added, or the soup will curdle.

Cheese and Potato Soup: Add to the butter one chopped carrot and three cloves chopped garlic. After the milk is added and simmered for 5 minutes, stir in 1 cup of grated cheddar cheese, and stir until melted and thoroughly incorporated. Garnish with some fresh chopped dill.

Butternut Squash Soup: Add 3 cloves of chopped garlic and 1 TB. dried rosemary to the butter, and replace the potatoes with an equal amount of peeled, chopped butternut squash.

Dress It Up: Vichyssoise

This soup is properly pronounced *vee-she-swahz*. Don't get caught dropping the Z sound. It is named for the French spa town of Vichy, although it is supposedly an American creation. Certainly potato leek soup made in this same manner, but served hot, is a well-documented French recipe. C'est la vie!

1 large yellow onion, diced

3 *leeks*, sliced

4 russet potatoes, peeled and sliced

2 TB. butter

2 cups chicken stock, vegetable stock, or water

2 cups heavy cream

Salt and white pepper

Serves 4
Prep time: 20 minutes
Cook time: 30 minutes (plus 4 hours or overnight for refrigeration)

1. In a large saucepan over medium heat, sauté onion, leeks, and potatoes in butter until tender, but not browned. Cover with stock and simmer for 20 minutes.

2. Allow soup to cool for 15 to 20 minutes, then purée. Return to the heat, add cream, season with salt and pepper, and simmer another 5 minutes. Cool, then chill completely before serving. Garnish with chopped chives or watercress.

Chefspeak

Leeks are in the lily family, along with all the other onions. They grow in sandy soil, and should be washed thoroughly before using. To be sure you wash out all the sand, slice the leeks in half lengthwise to expose the inner layers.

Split Pea Soup

Legumes are edible seeds inside of a seed pod. When the seeds are dried, they are called pulses. This same recipe can be made with any pulse, including lentils.

Serves 4
Prep time: 24 hours (includes overnight soaking)
Cook time: 1–2 hours

6 slices uncooked bacon, diced

1 large yellow onion, chopped

2 stalks celery, chopped

1 carrot, chopped

3 cloves garlic, chopped

1 bay leaf

1 tsp. dried thyme

2 cups split peas, soaked in 8 cups water overnight, then rinsed

Water to cover

Salt and pepper

1. In a large saucepan cook bacon over medium heat to render fat. Add onion, celery, carrot, and garlic, and cook until tender and light brown.

2. Add bay leaf, thyme, and peas to the pot, and cover with cold water. Bring to a boil, and simmer for 1 to 2 hours, until peas are tender. Season with salt and pepper.

Kitchen Tips

I love cooking dried beans, but I often forget to do the overnight presoak. Fortunately, there is a quick(ish) method. Bring the dried beans to a boil for 5 minutes, then cover and set them aside off the heat for 1 hour. You can cut a bean in half to see if it is fully soaked. If it is, there will be an even color throughout. If not, there will be a dry core.

Split Pea with Ham: Add a ham bone to the simmering peas. Remove before serving, and stir in 2 cups chopped ham meat.

Navy Bean Soup: Replace peas with an equal amount of navy beans. Add 2 cups chopped, fresh or canned tomatoes and 2 cups chopped ham.

Beef and Bean Soup: Replace split peas with an equal amount of white, navy, pinto, kidney, or lima beans. In addition to browning the bacon, brown 1 pound of ground beef or stew beef. Replace water with beef stock, and add 2 cups chopped fresh or canned tomatoes.

Dress It Up: Minted Pea Soup

Aromatic mint is in the same herb family as rosemary, basil, oregano, and sage. There are many varieties, but the two most readily available are spearmint and peppermint. Peppermint is the stronger of the two, with an almost peppery heat.

1 large yellow onion, chopped

2 stalks celery, chopped

2 cloves garlic, chopped

2 TB. butter

2 lb. fresh, canned, or frozen green peas

1 cup chopped fresh mint (or 2 TB. dried)

4 cups vegetable stock or water

2 cups heavy cream

Salt and pepper

Serves 6		
Prep time: 10 minutes		
Cook time: 60 minutes		

1. In a large saucepan, sauté onion, celery, and garlic in butter over medium heat until tender, but not browned. Add peas, mint, and stock, and simmer for 30 minutes.

2. Allow soup to cool for 15 to 20 minutes, then purée. Return to the heat, add cream, season with salt and pepper, and simmer another 5 minutes. Serve warm or chilled with a dollop of sour cream and a mint sprig.

French Onion Soup

The key to this soup is the slow-cooked onions and the Gruyere cheese. Named for the medieval Swiss town, Gruyere is a Swiss-style semifirm cheese with a nutty, buttery flavor. If you can't find it in your market, drive around a little more before you give in and use any old Swiss cheese. It's worth the effort.

Serves 4
Prep time: 10 minutes
Cook time: 90 minutes

1 lb. yellow onions, thinly sliced

4 TB. butter

4 cups beef stock

½ cup sherry

Salt and pepper

4 slices French baguette, toasted

8 oz. Gruyere cheese, grated

1. In a large sauté pan over low heat, cook the onions in butter, stirring frequently, until tender and golden brown, about 45 minutes. Don't cook them too fast, or they will be bitter rather than sweet.

2. Add beef stock, sherry, season with salt and pepper, and simmer 15 minutes.

3. Divide soup between serving bowls, top with one slice of baguette and a handful of grated cheese. Brown under a broiler for 5 minutes, or until golden and bubbly. Serve immediately.

Listen to Mom!

Onions have a lot of sugar, which can easily burn and become bitter. But it can also be turned into sweet caramel if cooked slowly. This process takes some patience, but it is totally worth it. It is the difference between a well-made onion soup and an amateur one. Plan ahead and set aside enough time to slow-cook your onions. *Tres magnifique!*

Chili con Carne

Con carne means with meat, and real Texas chili is full of it. The real thing also has chili powder (dried ground chiles with added herbs and spices) or chile paste (made by rehydrating dried chiles, then puréeing them). For some good Texas-worthy powders and pastes, try GourmetSleuth.com.

6 slices uncooked bacon, diced

1 yellow onion, chopped

1 green or red bell pepper, chopped

4 cloves garlic, minced

1 lb. ground beef

2 TB. ground cumin

2 TB. dried oregano

2–4 TB. chili powder or paste

2 cups fresh or canned tomatoes, chopped

1 (15-oz.) can kidney beans

2 cups beef stock

½ cup red wine

2 TB. masa harina (corn flour used for tortillas; available in the flour aisle of most supermarkets and Latin American grocers)

Salt and pepper

Serves 6
Prep time: 10 minutes
Cook time: 90 minutes

1. Cook the bacon in a large saucepan over medium heat to render fat. Add onion, bell pepper, and garlic, and cook to golden brown. Add beef and spices and cook until browned.

2. Add tomatoes, beans, stock, and wine and simmer over medium heat for 1 hour. Fifteen minutes before serving, add masa harina and season with salt and pepper. Serve with a dollop of sour cream, grated cheddar cheese, and diced raw onion.

Turkey Chili: To reduce the fat in this recipe, replace the ground beef with an equal amount of ground turkey, and replace the beef stock with turkey, chicken, or vegetable stock.

Vegetarian Chili: Replace the bacon with 3 tablespoons olive oil. Replace the ground beef with an additional can of kidney, black, or pinto beans. Replace the beef stock with an equal amount of vegetable stock or water.

Five-Can Chili: This is a classic campout meal. Combine in a pot one can each of prepared chili, corn, chopped tomatoes, kidney beans, and diced green chilies. Warm together over the campfire, then add 1 cup barbecue sauce, 1 tablespoon chili powder, and hot pepper sauce to taste. Serve on a tin plate, and use your bandana as a napkin.

Dress It Up: Chili Verde

Verde means green, and that's just what the ingredients of this recipe are. Put those tomatoes away!

<table>
<tr><td>

Serves 6

Prep time: 10 minutes

Cook time: 3 hours

</td></tr>
</table>

1 yellow onions, chopped

1 *Anaheim* chili, chopped

1 *poblano* chili, chopped

8 oz. *tomatillos*, chopped

2 stalks celery, chopped

1 bunch scallions, chopped

1 bunch fresh cilantro, chopped

1 head romaine lettuce, chopped

4 TB. olive oil

3-lb. pork butt or shoulder roast

1 cup hulled, toasted pumpkin seeds

4 cups chicken or beef stock

2 TB. ground cumin

2 TB. dried oregano

2 TB. masa harina

Salt and pepper

1. Combine onions, chilies, tomatillos, celery, scallions, cilantro, and lettuce in a large bowl, and stir to combine. In batches, purée the mixture in a blender.

2. Heat olive oil in a large saucepan over medium heat. Brown the pork roast on all sides, then add the pumpkin seeds and the puréed vegetables and cook to warm through, about 10 minutes. Add stock and spices, reduce heat and simmer covered for 2 hours over low heat, until the pork is very tender and easily falls apart. Check periodically to be sure there are at least 2 inches of liquid in the pan, and add more if necessary.

3. Remove the roast from the pot, cool for 15 to 20 minutes, then shred or chop. Return the meat to the pot, add masa harina, season with salt and pepper, then simmer another 10 minutes before serving with warm tortillas and crumbled ranchero cheese.

Chefspeak

The **Anaheim** chili is the most mild fresh green chili. The **poblano** is a bit hotter. They can be used in this recipe interchangeably with other chilies if you prefer, as long as they're green. **Tomatillos** are not green tomatoes. They are actually in the gooseberry family. Remove their paper husks and wash well to remove the naturally occurring soapy film.

Part 3

Supper Time

There was a time, not too long ago, when every American family sat down and ate together. Today, it is more common to see fast food being scarfed in the car on the trip from piano lessons to soccer practice. Not only is it terribly bad for us, it's not nearly as fun.

If you qualify as one of those busy families, use this section as motivation to get everyone together around an actual table, at least once a week. You may find that staring each other in the face is more comforting than the food.

There is a recipe for everyone in this section. The meat and fish lovers, the vegetarians, and the just plain hungry are sure to find a comforting recipe that whisks them away to their happy place. Sunday dinner, church socials, potluck picnics, and tailgate parties are all represented. So turn off the TV and set the table.

Chapter 6

A Bird in the Hand

In This Chapter

- ◆ High-heat roasting
- ◆ Home-style favorites
- ◆ Slow simmers
- ◆ An international flavor

When the Republicans promised a chicken in every pot during Herbert Hoover's 1928 presidential campaign, they were making quite a promise. That bird was hard to come by back then. It wasn't until after World War II that chickens were readily available to the masses. Now they are everywhere, and in America we each eat over 30 pounds of chicken a year. And why not? It's a carb-free, low-fat source of protein that happens to taste pretty good. So good, in fact, that it is the description of choice for other, somewhat questionable meats. (Rattlesnake? Possum? Frogs' legs? They taste just like chicken!)

All Birds Are Not Created Equal

There are a lot of birds out there on the market. Which one should you pick? Whole chickens are always less expensive than cut up parts, but unless you possess good butchering skills, it's worth paying a little more. Most of the recipes in this chapter can be made with any of the prefabricated chicken pieces in your supermarket.

When buying whole birds, there are two main options, broiler/fryer or the plumper, fattier roaster. They are interchangeable for these recipes. Free-range chickens can be used as well. These birds have more flavor because they are allowed to exercise a bit more. There are natural birds that contain nothing synthetic, no preservatives or artificial flavoring or colorings. (USDA standards do permit antibiotics and hormone use in natural birds.) Organic birds are fed grains that have not been exposed to chemicals and pesticides. They may not be treated with antibiotics or drugs, and must be allowed to go outside and play.

Kosher chickens are organic and free range, and are processed under strict supervision of a rabbi. They are also soaked in salty brine, which gives them a unique flavor.

Carving How-To's

Carving up a whole roasted bird at the table is a time-honored family tradition that I always avoid. Never have I allowed this Norman Rockwell moment at my table, because it never looks like that. Nobody wants to witness the carnage. Nobody wants to see a half-mangled carcass in the middle of the table. They just want to eat! So I carve in the kitchen, where I can use tongs, scissors, and rubber gloves if necessary to cut that bird up into delicious-looking pieces, without an audience.

To carve a whole chicken, use a set of tongs in one hand and a good sharp boning knife in the other. Start first with the breast meat, which should be facing up. Slice down the breast bone, then taking little swipes between the meat and the ribs with the tip of the knife, remove the entire breast. Then repeat on the other side.

Next comes the leg and thigh. Slice through the skin that connects the leg to the body. Grab hold of both legs (use tongs or gloves if it is hot), and lift the bird by the legs, bending them away from the carcass until the thigh joints break. Trim the rest away with the tip of a knife. Detach the leg from the thigh by cutting down at the joint and bending it backward until it breaks so you can cut through the joint. Remove the wings in the same manner, bending them backward to break the joints, then cut right through.

A bird will yield eight pieces; two wings, two thighs, two legs, and two breasts. But for most dishes, the breasts (and sometimes the thighs) are too big for a single portion. And when frying or braising, those larger pieces will take longer to cook than everything else. For that reason, I cut the breast in half crosswise, using a large chef knife, focusing the pressure on the rear of the blade to cut through the bone. A cleaver works, too, although it is a bit dramatic.

High Roasting

By far, the best method for roasting birds is what I call high roasting, or roasting at high temperatures. I cook all big hunks of meat in ovens well above 450°F, and they are always good. The best part, though, is the speed in which you can whip up a hearty meal. It's definitely impressive.

Kitchen Tips

Read all about high roasting in Barbara Kafka's book *Roasting, A Simple Art* (Morrow Cookbooks, 1995).

The downside to high roasting is the heat it generates in the kitchen (be sure to ventilate), and the smoke that can occur from dripping fat. To combat this last problem, I always fill the roasting pan with an inch or two of water. The fat drips into the water, not onto a scalding hot pan.

Speaking of pans, a nice roasting pan with a rack is ideal, but by no means necessary. I have made roasts on cookie sheets and brownie pans, with cake racks jerry-rigged in place. No rack? No problem. While it's best not to have the meat resting in the water at the base of the pan, anything can be used to elevate it. A bed of new potatoes, or a couple russets cut in half and laid flat side down work great. And you have the added bonus of yummy potatoes. I have even resorted to wads of tin foil. No one will see it, and you're not getting graded, so use whatever works.

Frying

Cast iron is the pan of choice when frying chicken. The heat distributes slowly and evenly, better than any other type of cookware. Cast-iron pans are easy to find, and can be had for a song at flea markets and garage sales. (Read about seasoning cast iron in Chapter 1.) If you don't have cast iron, heavy aluminum is the next best choice. A countertop deep fryer works, too.

Marinating

Marinating meat is an ancient form of tenderizing. Wine and vinegar soften tough meat, and the spices help disguise less than agreeable flavors that were common in the days before refrigeration.

The best marinated meats soak with as much of the meat submerged for as long as possible. It can be done in a bowl or a pan, or for really good results, use large plastic zipper bags. The plastic helps the marinade cling to the meat.

Chicken à la King

This dish is an excellent use for leftover chicken. Or why not make it turkey? In many households it's a day-after-Thanksgiving tradition.

1 small yellow onion, chopped

8 oz. mushrooms, sliced

2 TB. butter

2 TB. all-purpose flour

1½ cup chicken stock

½ cup milk

¼ cup sherry

3 cups cooked chicken meat, diced

1 (4-oz.) can chopped pimentos

Serves 4
Prep time: 30 minutes
Cook time: 30 minutes

1. In a large sauté pan, brown the onion and mushrooms in butter over high heat.

2. Add the flour and cook until the fat is absorbed. Slowly add the chicken stock while whisking. Add the milk, sherry, chicken, and pimentos.

3. Reduce heat and simmer for 10 minutes to warm through. Serve over a split biscuit, toast, rice, or use it to fill pastry shells.

Roast Chicken with Gravy

The water at the bottom of the pan keeps your kitchen smoke-free. Roasting at high temperatures causes animal fat to drip into the pan and burn. But the water quickly cools and dilutes the fat.

Serves 4
Prep time: 10 minutes
Cook time: 70 minutes

1 (3–5-lb.) whole chicken, roaster or fryer

1 tsp. salt

½ tsp. pepper

1 small yellow onion, chopped

1 carrot, chopped

1 stalk celery, chopped

2 TB. all-purpose flour

1 tsp. dried sage

Salt and pepper

1. Preheat oven to 500°F. Rinse chicken; remove giblets and reserve. Bend the wings backward and tuck the wing tips behind the chicken's back (like it's being cuffed). Place the roasting rack inside the pan, and set the bird on the rack, breasts facing up. Sprinkle with salt and pepper, then fill the bottom of the pan with 1 inch of water. Bake for 1 hour.

2. Meanwhile, put the giblets into a small saucepan with the onion, carrot, and celery. Cover with 4 cups water and bring to a boil. Reduce heat and simmer until the roasting chicken is done. Strain out the giblets and vegetables, and reserve the broth.

3. When the bird has cooked for 1 hour, remove it from the oven and let it cool, covered in foil for 10 minutes. Using large tongs, transfer the bird to a cutting board. Remove the rack from the pan, then place the roasting pan on a burner over high heat. Reduce most of the water away, then add the flour, whisking until all the fat is absorbed. Slowly add the reserved broth until the gravy reaches the desired consistency. Add the sage, and salt and pepper to taste.

4. Using tongs and a sharp knife, carve the two breasts, the two leg/thigh portions, and the two wings. You can also separate the leg from the thigh if you like. Arrange the chicken pieces on a serving platter, and present to the table with the gravy on the side.

Lemon Chicken: Cut two lemons into quarters. Squeeze one quarter over the chicken before it goes into the oven, and stuff the rest into the chicken's cavity. The oil from the lemon zest will flavor the bird, and the juice will trickle down into the pan. This will make your gravy nice and tangy (see Step 3).

Garlic Chicken: Peel the cloves from two heads of garlic. Stuff a few between the breast meat and skin, and put the rest into the chicken's cavity. The garlic will become tender and sweet in the oven. Remember to scoop the cloves out of the chicken and serve them alongside the meat.

Beer Can Chicken: This is traditionally a recipe for the outdoor grill, but it works great in the oven too. Rub the chicken skin and cavity with your favorite barbecue dry rub. Open a can of beer, take a swig, then slide the chicken down on top of the can, so the bird is sitting upright and the can is in the cavity. Place the whole thing in a pan and roast at 350°F for 90 minutes.

Dress It Up: Turkey and Stuffing

If you've never hosted a holiday meal, you will once you see how easy it is to make this bird.

Serves 8–10

Prep time: 1 hour
Cook time: 20 minutes per pound

---

4 stalks celery, chopped

1 large yellow onion, chopped

4 TB. butter

4 cups day-old bread, cubed

2 tsp. salt

1 tsp. pepper

2 TB. dried sage

1 TB. dried thyme

1 tsp. dried rosemary

2 cups turkey or chicken stock

1 (10–15-lb.) turkey, defrosted

For gravy:

1 large yellow onion, chopped

1 stalk celery, chopped

1 carrot, chopped

1 tsp. dried sage

¼ cup all-purpose flour

Salt and pepper

¼ cup heavy cream

1. Preheat oven to 450°F. In a large sauté pan over medium heat, cook the celery and onion in butter until golden brown. Cool completely. (To rush this step, spread the mixture onto a cookie sheet and refrigerate.)

2. In a large bowl combine the cubed bread, the cooled onions and celery, salt, pepper, and herbs. Toss to combine, then moisten with stock. Stuffing shouldn't be soggy, just moist.

3. Remove giblets and wash turkey inside and out. Bend the wings backward and tuck the wing tips behind the turkey's back (like he's being cuffed). Place the roasting rack inside the pan, and set the bird on the rack, breasts facing up. Loosely fill the cavity with stuffing. Sprinkle the bird with salt and pepper, and fill the bottom of the pan with 1-inch of water.

4. Put the pan in the oven, and reduce the heat to 350°F. (For larger birds, roast at 325°F.) Baste with melted butter or drippings every 10 to 15 minutes throughout roasting time. Cook for 20 minutes for every pound. When you think it's done, insert an instant-read thermometer into the thigh muscle. The meat should be 180°F to 185°F, and the stuffing should be 165°F.

5. Meanwhile, put the giblets into a small saucepan with the onion, celery, carrot, and sage. Cover with water and bring to a boil. Reduce heat and simmer slowly until the roasting turkey is done. Strain out the giblets and vegetables, and reserve the broth.

6. When the bird is done, remove it from the oven and let it cool, covered in foil, for 10 minutes before carving it. Using large tongs, transfer the bird to a cutting board.

7. Remove the rack from the pan, and pour off all but ¼ of the turkey drippings. Place the roasting pan on a burner over high heat. Add the flour, whisking until all the fat is absorbed. Slowly add the reserved broth, whisking, until the gravy reaches the desired consistency. Season with salt and pepper. Just before serving, add the heavy cream.

8. Carve the bird, and scoop the stuffing out of the cavity and into a serving dish.

Listen to Mom!

The stuffing ingredients must be cool before they are put inside the raw bird. Any increase in temperature before roasting increases the likelihood of bacterial growth.

Fried Chicken

My secret to great fried chicken is resting the flour-coated chicken for 10 minutes before frying. This gives the egg a chance to fully absorb the flour, so less coating is lost in the hot oil.

Serves 4–6
Prep time: 30 minutes (plus 4–12 hours for refrigeration)
Cook time: 45 minutes

¾ **cup salt**

½ **cup sugar**

2 **cups water**

1 **whole fryer**

2 **large yellow onions, sliced**

1 **quart buttermilk**

1 **TB. hot pepper sauce**

4 **eggs**

¼ **cup milk**

3 **cups all-purpose flour**

2 **tsp. baking powder**

2 **tsp. salt**

1 **tsp. pepper**

1 **tsp. cayenne pepper**

2 **cups shortening**

1. In a small saucepan, combine salt, sugar, and water. Bring to a boil, then remove from heat and set aside. This is a brine. Rinse chicken and cut into serving-size portions. Cut each breast in half, separate leg and thigh, and tuck wing tip in front of the elbow joint to hold it in a compact form.

2. Add to the brine sliced onions, buttermilk, and hot pepper sauce, and whisk well to combine. Add chicken, making sure it is submerged. Refrigerate for at least 4 hours, or as long as 12.

3. In a medium bowl whisk together eggs and milk. In a second bowl combine flour, baking powder, salt, and peppers. Drain chicken from buttermilk, rinse, and pat dry. Reserve onions. Dredge chicken first in egg, then in flour, making sure each piece is well coated. Shake off excess flour and set chicken aside at room temperature for 10 minutes.

4. Fill the skillet with 2 inches shortening and set over high heat. When the shortening reaches 375°F, add a batch of chicken. Do not crowd the chicken in the pan. Cook until the chicken is browned on both sides, about 10 to 15 minutes. After turning, reduce the heat to 350°F, cover the pan, and cook another 10 minutes. Check the largest pieces for doneness by slicing in and checking the center meat. Remove chicken to a paper towel-lined tray to dry, and repeat with remaining chicken.

When chicken has drained, keep it warm in a 200°F oven until ready to serve. Fry reserved onions in the same manner. Serve chicken and onions with mashed potatoes (see Chapter 9) and gravy and cole slaw (see Chapter 4).

Listen to Mom!

Deep-frying in a skillet on the stove top can be tricky. Be sure to check the chicken periodically and monitor the rate at which it is browning. Turn down the heat if it's getting too dark. You can stick a hot oil thermometer on the side of your pan, but don't rely solely on that. Thermometers are not always accurate. Use your eyes, too.

Cornmeal Coating: Add 1 cup of cornmeal to the flour dredge for a sweet, crunchy coating.

Extra Thick and Crispy Batter: Double-dredge the chicken for a thicker batter: dip it in egg, flour, then egg again, and flour again. Or add to the flour dredge 2 cups of bread crumbs, cornflakes, crushed crackers, or instant potato flakes.

Oven-Fried Chicken: Spread the coated chicken onto a baking sheet coated with pan spray, then bake at 400°F for 30 to 45 minutes.

Chicken Fricassee

A fricassee is a stew, usually of chicken, veal, or rabbit. What shows up in the fricassee is a matter of preference, and in most cases it includes whatever is on hand. What distinguishes it is the meat, first browned in butter before stewing.

Serves 4–6

Prep time: 30 minutes
Cook time: 45 minutes

---

1 (3–4-lb.) chicken, cut into serving pieces

4 TB. butter

1 large yellow onion, diced

1 tsp. dried thyme

2 TB. all-purpose flour

2 cups chicken stock

2 cups white wine or water

1 cup cream

Salt and pepper

1. In a large skillet over high heat, brown the chicken on all sides in the butter. Remove the chicken and add the onion and thyme. Reduce the heat and cook the onion until tender and golden brown, about 30 minutes.

2. Add the flour and cook for 2 minutes, stirring until it is absorbed by the fat. Slowly add the chicken stock and wine while whisking. Increase heat and bring to a boil. Add the chicken, reduce heat, and cover. Simmer for 20 to 30 minutes, until chicken is cooked through. Remove from heat, stir in cream, and season with salt and pepper. Serve with buttered noodles or rice.

Creole Fricassee: Add with the onions one diced green bell pepper, three chopped cloves garlic, and 1 teaspoon cayenne pepper. Add with the chicken ½ pound *andouille sausage.* For the last 5 minutes of cooking add ½ pound chopped raw shrimp.

 Chefspeak _____

Andouille sausage is a spicy smoked pork sausage. It is a specialty of France, and a common ingredient in the Cajun and Creole cuisines of Louisiana.

Turkey Mushroom Fricassee: Replace the chicken with chunks of turkey breast. Add with the onions 1 pound of chopped mushrooms. In addition to the regular white button variety, try using shitake, portobello, morels, or chanterelle mushrooms.

Arroz con Pollo

This dish originated in Spain, but took root in every Latin American country. You can guess its origin by the use of saffron, which is common in another Spanish rice dish, *Paella*.

2 TB. olive oil

1 (3–4-lb.) chicken, cut into serving pieces

1 large yellow onion, chopped

1 Anaheim chili pepper, chopped

1 red bell pepper, chopped

1 (4-oz.) can diced green chilies

3 cloves garlic, chopped

3 threads of *saffron* or 1 TB. annatto oil or 2 tsp. turmeric

1 tsp. cumin

1 cup rice

2 cups ripe chopped tomatoes

2 cups chicken stock

Serves 4–6	
Prep time: 30 minutes	
Cook time: 30 minutes	

1. In a large skillet over high heat, brown the chicken on all sides in the olive oil. Remove browned chicken from the pan and add the onion, peppers, chilies, garlic, spices, and rice. Stir well to coat all ingredients with oil. Cook until the onions and peppers are translucent.

2. Add the tomatoes and stock and stir. Bring to a boil, then reduce the heat to a bare simmer. Add the chicken back in on top of the rice, cover the pan and simmer 20 minutes, until the rice is tender and the liquid is absorbed.

Chefspeak

Saffron is the *stigma* (part of the flower's reproductive system) of a low-growing crocus. It was used as a fabric dye before it was coveted for its culinary value. The red threads of the stigma must be harvested by hand, hence the exorbitant price. The good news is, a little goes a long way.

Teriyaki Chicken

This Japanese recipe dates back to the 1600s. *Yaki* means grill, and *Teri* means glaze or gloss. Any type of meat or fish can be prepared in this manner prior to baking, grilling, barbecuing, or frying.

Serves 4–6

Prep time: 10 minutes (plus 1–6 hours for refrigeration)

Cook time: 45 minutes

---

2 cups soy sauce

¼ cup sesame oil

¼ cup rice vinegar

2 scallions, chopped

3 cloves garlic, chopped

1 (3–4-lb.) chicken, cut into serving pieces

1. In a large bowl, combine the soy sauce, sesame oil, rice vinegar, scallions, and garlic. Mix well. Add the chicken pieces and coat well. Be sure chicken is submerged in marinade. Refrigerate for 1 to 6 hours.

2. Drain chicken from marinade, spread out onto a baking sheet coated with pan spray, and bake in a 400°F oven for 30 to 45 minutes. Serve with steamed rice and stir-fried vegetables.

Grilled Teriyaki: Cook the same meat on an outdoor grill, barbecue, or under a broiler for a more authentic flavor.

Thai Marinade: Replace the soy sauce with Thai fish sauce. Add 1 can coconut milk, ¼ cup each chopped kaffir lime leaves and lemongrass, and 1 tablespoon each ground coriander, ground cumin, and fresh grated ginger.

Jerk Chicken: Reduce the soy sauce to ¼ cup, and increase the vinegar to ¾ cup. Add ½ cup each orange juice and lime juice. Add 1 tablespoon each of sugar, allspice, thyme, cayenne, and black pepper. Add 1 teaspoon each of sage, nutmeg, cinnamon, cumin, and garlic powder. Add a chopped hot chile pepper if you dare. A scotch bonnet is the classic, but a jalapeño will do.

Chapter 7

Meaty Traditions

In This Chapter

◆ One-pot meals for the common man

◆ Classic dishes fit for a king

◆ Meats flavored with herbs and spices

◆ Low-slow cooking methods to tenderize meat

Meat is the staple of the American dinner table. (Unless you're a vegetarian. But I guess vegetarians probably aren't reading this chapter.)

While *meat* generally describes the skeletal muscle (and sometimes glands, organs, and flesh) of all animals, including fish and birds, in the culinary world it specifically refers to four-legged domesticated animals. Chickens are classified more specifically as *poultry*, as are turkeys, ducks, and geese. Venison, buffalo, boar, possums, and animals that were traditionally hunted are referred to as *game*.

Most of the meat dishes we love were born of necessity as ways to use up leftovers, stretch a little into a lot, or utilize the cheaper cuts of meat. The cooks of yesteryear discovered cooking methods that made these meats palatable, and even delicious.

Marinades

Today, a marinade is a delicious method of seasoning that requires forethought and planning. It is nothing that can happen on the spur of the moment. But marinating was not originally designed to add interest to an otherwise boring chicken breast. It was the only way certain cuts of meat were made edible. Before crock pots and Ac'cent, meat was tenderized by pounding it or marinating it. Acidic vinegars and citrus juices help break down the meat, making it better able to absorb moisture, which results in a more tender piece of meat.

But marinades didn't just tenderize the meat; they made it easier to stomach. After all, there weren't always refrigerators or ice boxes. Wine, vinegar, and spices were helpful in masking some pretty bad flavors.

Braising and Stewing

Skeletal muscles that are used often by the animal are referred to as tough cuts (for example, cuts from the legs and neck). These cuts are tougher because the muscle and its connective tissue are more developed to support the animal's movements. So shanks, briskets, flanks, and round cuts (all on the lower half of the body), and chucks (by the neck) have more tough connective tissues. The loin, which runs down the animal's back, sees little if any movement, and is therefore super tender and lean.

If the connective tissues laced through these tough cuts of meat get cooked too hot and fast, they will toughen. But if they are heated gently, they will soften and melt. This is where stewing and braising work wonders. Some liquid and moist heat softens those tough fibers, allowing added flavorings to be absorbed and distributed throughout the cut. The key is to take your time, and regulate the heat. Oven and burner settings should be low enough that the liquid is barely simmering. Covered pots will quickly heat up, so check them periodically, and adjust the temperature if necessary. You can cool them down by removing the lid partially or taking the pot partially off the burner.

Fat

Marbled meat describes meat (most often red) that contains various amounts of fat within the muscle, giving it a marbled appearance. Marbled cuts of meat are more tender and flavorful than less and nonmarbled meats. Even if a piece of meat is tough, if it is marbled, slow heat will soften the fat, enabling it to penetrate and flavor the meat. Because fat carries the flavor of the other ingredients, the smallest amount of flavor is intensified and evenly distributed wherever the fat goes.

Despite the fact that fat adds flavor, we all know that saturated fat (which comes mainly from animal sources) contributes to coronary artery disease by elevating cholesterol levels. For that reason, it is advised that we eat leaner cuts of meat. But meats with lower amounts of fat or no fat are not as tasty, so their flavor must be enhanced by other foods. A great example of this is the pork loin. While *porky* is traditionally a synonym for *fatty*, the pork industry has succeeded in drastically reducing the fat in pork. Today's pork contains over 30 percent less fat than it did 20 years ago. But how do you cook that other white meat? Many recipes include bacon or other oils to help moisten and flavor the lean cuts. Creamy, spicy, or fruity sauces and stuffings are commonplace, all used regularly to make up for shortcomings.

Kitchen Tips

When shopping for slow-cooking roasts of pork, look for pork butt, Boston butt (which is a portion of shoulder), or picnic roast (another shoulder cut).

So which is better? A nicely marbled steak or a doctored-up pork loin? The key is balance and moderation. A leaner diet is healthier overall, but don't deprive yourself of the occasional meatloaf. That would be un-American.

Yankee Pot Roast

There are numerous renditions of this recipe, including one with a red broth. Red wine and tomatoes are added to the cooking liquid, as well as additional root vegetables, like parsnips and turnips.

Serves 4–6
Prep time: 30 minutes
Cook time: 3 hours

6 slices uncooked bacon, diced

1 (3–4-lb.) beef chuck roast

1 cup all-purpose flour

1 large onion, chopped

1 bay leaf

¼ cup fresh parsley, chopped (or 1 TB. dried)

4 carrots, diced

4 new potatoes, quartered

Salt and pepper

1. In a large pot, brown the bacon until crisp and the fat is rendered. Remove the bacon. Coat the chuck roast evenly with flour, shake off the excess, and brown in the bacon drippings. Add the onion, bay leaf, and parsley and cook over high heat until translucent.

2. Add 2 cups water and bring to a boil. Reduce the heat to low, cover, and cook at a bare simmer for 3 hours. During the last 30 minutes of cooking, add the carrots and potatoes and continue cooking until tender. Remove the meat and vegetables and reduce the cooking liquid to gravy consistency. Season with salt and pepper. Slice the meat and arrange on serving plate with vegetables and gravy.

Kitchen Tips

Pot roast is a braised meat dish in which tougher, less expensive cuts of meat are cooked very slowly until tender. The long, low heat breaks down tough connective tissues and loosens the marbled fat, which in turn adds flavor and moisture to the meat. The best cuts for such a dish include chuck and round roasts.

Dress It Up: Pot au Feu

Pot au feu means *pot with fire*, and it refers to a stewed one-pot meal. There are several variations of this dish throughout the world, including the Flemish *hochepot*, the Italian *bollito misto*, and the New England boiled dinner.

2–3 lb. beef short ribs

1 (2–3-lb.) beef chuck roast

1 large yellow onion, chopped

2 carrots, chopped, plus 4 carrots, diced

3 stalks celery, chopped

2 bay leaves

1 sprig fresh parsley

1 sprig fresh thyme

½ tsp. black peppercorns

1 tsp. salt

8 small new potatoes

3 leeks, sliced in quarters lengthwise

2–3 marrow bones

8 diagonal slices French baguette, toasted

Serves 4–6	
Prep time: 30 minutes	
Cook time: 3½ hours	

1. Tie each piece of meat securely with twine to hold it together. Place the meat in the pot with the onion, chopped carrots, celery, bay leaves, parsley, thyme, and peppercorns. Cover completely with 3 to 4 quarts cold water and bring to a boil over high heat. At the boil, reduce the heat to low, and cook at a bare simmer for 3 hours.

2. After 3 hours, remove the meat to an oven-proof dish, cover, and keep warm in a 200°F oven. Strain the broth to another large saucepan. Add the salt and potatoes, and bring it to a boil over high heat. Cook for 15 minutes then add the diced carrots and leeks. Cook another 15 minutes until vegetables are tender.

3. Thinly slice the chuck roast and divide the short ribs into serving portions. Arrange on a platter with the potatoes, carrots, and leeks. Remove the marrow from the bones and spread it on the toast. Serve the broth and toast as a first course, and the meat and vegetables second, with an assortment of condiments, including horseradish, mustard, and cornichons.

Listen to Mom!

Why does the recipe call for sprigs of fresh herbs? It's to keep the broth clear. Dry herbs make a speckled broth, even after straining. Some chefs use a *bouquet garni*, a sachet of herbs tied in cheesecloth, which can be easily retrieved. We tie the meat up in twine for the same reason. These cuts of meat will easily fall apart in such prolonged cooking, which can cloud up the broth, and make them hard to fish out for slicing.

Beef Brisket

A brisket is a cut of beef from down around the rib cage. It's full of connective tissue, which makes it bad for grilling, but perfect for long, slow, moist cooking such as braising.

Serves 4–6
Prep time: 30 minutes
Cook time: 3 hours

1 (2–3-lb.) beef brisket

2 large yellow onions, sliced into rings

3 cloves garlic, chopped

¼ cup olive oil

2 cups chopped fresh or canned tomatoes

2 cups red wine

1 tsp. dried thyme

1 tsp. black pepper

1. Preheat oven to 300°F. Place the brisket at the bottom of the pot and cover with onion rings. In a separate bowl combine the rest of the ingredients and pour over the brisket. Cover and bake 2 hours.

2. After 2 hours, turn the brisket over, stir the sauce and baste the meat. Cover and continue cooking another hour. To serve, remove meat from sauce, thinly slice against the grain, arrange on a platter, and cover with pan sauce.

Barbecue Brisket: Before baking, combine and pour over the brisket and onions 1 cup chili sauce, 1 cup ketchup, 1 cup brown sugar, one can dark beer, 1 tablespoon Worcestershire sauce, 1 tablespoon hot pepper sauce, four cloves crushed garlic, salt, and pepper.

Coke Brisket: I know it sounds weird, but trust me. Before baking, combine and pour over the brisket and onions one can cola, one package dry onion soup mix, one (15-oz.) can tomato sauce, four cloves crushed garlic, salt, and pepper. Don't try tasting this sauce until it's cooked. (Again, trust me.)

Chuck Wagon Brisket: Before baking, combine and pour over the brisket and onions a (4-oz.) can green chilies, a (15-oz.) can corn, ¼ cup cider vinegar, 1 cup strong black coffee, four cloves crushed garlic, 3 cups beef stock, salt, and pepper.

Tidbits

There are several varieties of chili sauce on the market. They are usually tomato based, with chili powder, sugar, vinegar, and other spices. It is thick, like ketchup, and should not be confused with the thinner, hotter pepper sauce.

Beef Stew

What's the difference between stew and a pot roast? Pot roast is a braised dish in which the meat is cooked with a clear liquid. In a stew the meat is first floured and browned before the liquid is added, which turns the broth into gravy.

1 TB. olive oil	1 bay leaf
2 lb. stew beef, cut into 1-inch cubes	6 cups beef stock
2 cups all-purpose flour	2 large russet potatoes, peeled and diced
2 cloves garlic	2 carrots, diced
1 onion chopped	Salt and pepper
2 TB. tomato paste	2 TB. fresh parsley, chopped
1 TB. dried thyme	

Serves 4–6

Prep time: 30 minutes
Cook time: 2½ hours

1. In a large stew pot, heat the oil over high heat. Toss beef in flour to coat evenly, and shake off excess. Brown floured meat in the hot oil until brown on all sides. Work in batches if necessary so as not to crowd beef in pot.

2. Add garlic and onion to the beef, and sauté for 5 minutes. Add tomato paste, thyme, bay leaf, and stock. Bring to a boil, then reduce heat to low. Cover and cook at a bare simmer for 1 hour, or until the meat is tender. After 1 hour, add the potatoes and carrots, cover, and continue cooking for another 30 minutes, until vegetables are tender. Season with salt and pepper before serving with a sprinkle of fresh parsley on top.

Irish Stew: Replace the beef stock with 3 cups each of red wine and Guinness Stout (a dark Irish beer).

Vegetable Beef Stew: In the last 30 minutes of cooking add more vegetables, including mushrooms, peas, green beans, parsnips, and turnips.

Goulash: Omit the potatoes and carrots, reduce the beef stock to 4 cups, and add in ¼ cup white vinegar, ¼ cup Hungarian paprika, the zest of one lemon, and 1 teaspoon oregano. Serve on buttered noodles.

Dress It Up: Boeuf Bourguignon

Translated from French, this recipe is *beef in the style of Burgundy*. Burgundy is a region of eastern France that produces several well-known wines.

Serves 4–6
Prep time: 30 minutes
Cook time: 2½ hours

6 slices uncooked bacon, diced

4 *shallots*, chopped

2 cups pearl onions, peeled

8 oz. small button mushrooms

2 cups all-purpose flour

2 lb. stew beef, cut into 1-inch cubes

1 TB. dried thyme

1 bay leaf

6 cups red burgundy wine

¼ cup cognac or brandy

Salt and pepper

1. In a large stew pot, cook the bacon over high heat. Add the shallots, onions, and mushrooms, and sauté 1 minute. Toss beef in flour to coat evenly, and shake off excess. Add to the pot and brown floured meat in the hot oil until brown on all sides. Work in batches if necessary so as not to crowd beef in pot.

2. Add the thyme, bay leaf, and wine. Bring to a boil, then reduce heat to low. Cover and cook at a bare simmer for 2 hours. Ten minutes before serving, add cognac and simmer for 10 minutes. Season with salt and pepper. Serve with buttered noodles and French bread.

Chefspeak _____

Shallots are a milder cousin of the onion. They consist of a few small bulbs that grow together, with a brown papery skin.

Beef Stroganoff

Stroganoff was probably named after a late-nineteenth-century Russian diplomat, Count Pavel Stroganoff. But similar recipes appear in print decades earlier, so it's likely that the count's chef stole it from someone and added his boss's name to it.

1 large yellow onion, chopped	**½ tsp. grated nutmeg**
2 TB. butter	**Salt and pepper**
2 lb. beef filet, cut in thin strips	**½ cup dry white wine**
	1 cup sour cream
8 oz. button mushrooms, sliced	

Serves 4–6

Prep time: 10 minutes

Cook time: 20 minutes

---

1. In a large sauté pan, brown the onions in melted butter over high heat.

2. Add the beef and sauté for 5 minutes. Add the mushrooms, nutmeg, and salt and pepper to taste, and sauté another 5 minutes to brown mushrooms. Add white wine and stir to *deglaze* pan. Remove from heat and stir in sour cream.

3. Serve over buttered noodles.

Chefspeak

To **deglaze** means to heat a liquid in a pan that has just been used to brown or sauté food while scraping off the brown crusty bits from the bottom of the pan. The process releases rich flavors that would otherwise be lost and incorporates them into a sauce.

Meatloaf

It's called meatloaf because it's typically baked in a loaf pan or on a baking sheet in the shape of a loaf. But you can also bake meatloaves individually in muffin pans, use a cake pan and cut the meatloaf into wedges, or double the recipe and bake it in a brownie pan if you're feeding a crowd.

Serves 4–6
Prep time: 15 minutes
Cook time: 45 minutes

2 slices sandwich bread or 1 cup bread scraps or crumbs

½ cup milk

1 egg

1 (1-oz.) pkg. onion soup mix (or ¼ cup of your own blend of dried herbs and spices—try mixing 2 tsp. each of dried oregano, thyme, basil, celery seed, coriander, and onion powder)

1½ lb. ground beef

4 strips uncooked bacon

1. Preheat oven to 350°F. Place bread in a large bowl and pour the milk on top of it. Set aside to soften for 15 minutes. Stir in the egg and soup mix to form a paste. Add the meat and mix well.

2. Pack the meat into the loaf pan, rounding the top like a loaf of bread. Cover the top of the loaf with bacon strips laid lengthwise. Bake until brown and bubbly, about 45 minutes.

Tidbits

Although meat has been mixed with grains and vegetables for centuries as a means of stretching and economizing, it wasn't until the 20th century that we find meatloaf as we know it today. Recipe booklets were offered to the home cook in an effort to sell meat grinders. From these we see some of the first molded ground meat dishes. But it was not until refrigeration became commonplace that the loaf of meat turned into the all-American dish it is today.

Flavor Variations: There are dozens of meatloaf recipes that include the favorite flavors of any given family. Common renditions include ketchup, barbecue sauce, or chili sauce, both mixed into the meat as well as smothered on top. Chopped pickles, carrots, tomatoes, and onions are also common additions to the meat mix, as well as cooked rice or barley. Spices vary too, often including powdered garlic, onion, dried oregano, basil, sage, rosemary, parsley, cumin, or chili powder.

A Lighter Loaf: Replace the ground beef with ground turkey, chicken, or veal for a low-fat version of this classic.

Cheeseburger Meatloaf: Stir into the meat mixture 2 cups grated cheddar cheese.

Corned Beef and Cabbage

Corned beef is a brisket that has been preserved by curing in salt and spices. The term *corn* is a reference to the chunky salt pellets used in the process.

Serves 4–6
Prep time: 10 minutes
Cook time: 2½ hours

1 (3–4-lb.) corned beef brisket

3 large yellow onions, chopped

1 sprig fresh thyme

2 carrots, peeled and chopped into 2-inch pieces

8 whole new potatoes

1 green cabbage, washed and cut into quarters

1. Place the corned beef in a large pot with the onions and thyme. Cover with cold water and bring to a boil over high heat. Reduce the heat and cook at a bare simmer for 2 hours. Skim off residue as necessary.

2. Add the carrots, potatoes, and cabbage, and continue to cook another 30 minutes, until vegetables are tender. Remove meat from the pot and thinly slice it against the grain. Arrange meat on a platter with vegetables, and serve with grainy mustard and horseradish sauce.

Tidbits

While corned beef is generally associated with the Irish, it is not nearly as common in Ireland as it is here in America. Historically it was pork that was preserved in salt and spices. But the immigrants brought their cooking traditions with them and used them on the products available here. Most corned beef made in Ireland today is made for tourists.

Sausage and Peppers

What makes Italian sausage Italian? It's the seasoning, which includes fennel seed and garlic.

3 TB. olive oil

1 lb. hot or mild Italian sausage, sliced into 1-inch diagonal pieces

2 large yellow onions, sliced

4 cloves garlic, minced

2 green bell peppers, seeded and sliced

2 red bell peppers, seeded and sliced

1 tsp. dried oregano, or ¼ cup fresh oregano chopped

1 tsp. dried basil, or ¼ cup fresh basil chopped

2 cups fresh or canned tomatoes, chopped

Salt and pepper

4 Italian rolls

1 cup Parmesan cheese, grated

Serves 4–6
Prep time: 20 minutes
Cook time: 20 minutes

1. In a large sauté pan, sauté the sausage in olive oil over high heat until cooked thoroughly and browned. Pour off excess grease as necessary.

2. Add onions, garlic, and peppers, reduce heat to medium, and sauté until onions are golden brown and peppers are tender. Add oregano, basil, and tomatoes, and cook another 5 minutes. Season with salt and pepper. Serve with Italian rolls topped with Parmesan cheese.

Roasted Pork Loin

Pork has less total fat than a skinless chicken breast. Because it's the fat that makes meat moist and flavorful, most pork loin recipes have added fat and fruit for moisture and flavor.

Serves 4–6	
Prep time: 15 minutes	
Cook time: 45 minutes	

1 (2–3-lb.) pork loin

4 strips uncooked bacon

1 yellow onion, sliced

2 TB. butter

1 TB. dried rosemary, or 1 fresh rosemary sprig

2 apples, peeled, cored, and sliced

½ cup golden raisins

½ cup prunes, chopped

1 cup white wine

1 cup apple juice

2 TB. cider vinegar

¼ cup cognac or brandy

Chefspeak

Dry rub is a method of flavoring meat for barbecue. A blend of spices is rubbed into raw meat and allowed to penetrate for several hours before the meat is cooked. Spice blends vary, but most contain salt, sugar, dried ground chiles, garlic, onion, and a variety of dried herbs and spices.

1. Preheat oven to 350°F. Place tenderloin in roasting pan and cover evenly with bacon strips. Bake for 30 to 45 minutes, until internal temperature is 160°F.

2. Meanwhile, sauté onion in butter over high heat until translucent. Add rosemary, apples, raisins, and prunes and sauté for 5 minutes until apples are golden brown. Add wine, apple juice, vinegar, and cognac, reduce heat, and simmer until the liquid is reduced to less than 1 cup.

3. Slice roasted loin into 1-inch medallions, and serve on a platter, coated in sauce.

Barbecue Pulled Pork: Use a 4- to 5-pound pork shoulder or butt roast. Rub it with your favorite *dry-rub* seasoning mix, and marinate overnight. Transfer to a baking dish, add 2 cups water, cover, and bake at 300°F for 2 hours. Cool roast and use two forks to pull meat apart into shreds. Return meat to a baking dish and combine with 2 cups barbecue sauce, three cloves chopped garlic, and one chopped onion. Cover and bake another hour until onions are tender. Serve on a bun.

Pork Chops and Applesauce

Meat and fruit is an ancient pairing, and apples especially offset the richness of pork with their tart, sharp flavor. If you grew up in the 1970s, this recipe will forever be associated with TV's *The Brady Bunch*.

4 (½-inch) pork chops

2 cloves garlic, minced

2 eggs

2 TB. plus 1 cup milk

2 cups seasoned bread crumbs

3 TB. canola oil

For Gravy:

2 TB. all-purpose flour

1 cup milk

Salt and pepper

½ tsp. grated nutmeg

Serves 4	
Prep time: 15 minutes	
Cook time: 45 minutes	

1. Rub the pork chops with minced garlic. In a small bowl combine eggs and 2 tablespoons milk and mix well. Dredge pork chops in egg mixture, then coat well with bread crumbs. Set aside for 10 minutes.

2. Heat sauté pan and add oil. Fry chops over high heat to brown both sides, then reduce heat and cook until firm and the juices run clear, about 20 minutes.

3. Remove chops from pan and discard all but 2 tablespoons of pan drippings. Return pan to heat and add flour. Whisk until all the fat is absorbed, then slowly add the 1 cup milk, whisking in all the crusty bits from the bottom of the pan. Season with salt, pepper, and nutmeg. Serve pork chops with potato pancakes (see Chapter 9) and a choice of the gravy, applesauce, or sour cream.

Dress It Up: Stuffed Pork Chops

Split to the bone is also known as butterflied, in which the chop is cut in half horizontally until the knife hits the bone, then opened up like a butterfly's wings.

Serves 6
Prep time: 30 minutes
Cook time: 45 minutes

1 small yellow onion, chopped

2 stalks celery, chopped

1 small fennel bulb, diced

2 TB. butter

2 apples, diced

½ cup raisins

1 tsp. dried sage

Salt and pepper

3 cups bread crumbs

6 (2-inch) pork chops, split to the bone

2 TB. olive oil

1. In a large sauté pan, cook the onion, celery, and fennel in butter over high heat until translucent. Reduce the heat and add apples, raisins, sage, and salt and pepper to taste. Sauté 10 minutes until all ingredients are tender and golden. Remove from heat and cool to room temperature.

2. Preheat oven to 350°F. Add bread crumbs to vegetables and stir to combine. Evenly distribute the stuffing between each chop, and using a spoon, fill each butterflied pocket. Close the pocket and secure with toothpicks.

3. In a sauté pan, sear the chops in olive oil until golden brown on each side. Transfer to a baking dish, cover, and bake for 30 to 45 minutes, until juices run clear.

Listen to Mom!

Which apple should you use in this recipe? Whichever kind you like the best. While it is generally thought in the United States that green apples stand up to cooking better than red, they are all grown for lunchbox eating, and will all remain intact for the mild cooking in this recipe. I prefer the in-between apples, such as the Fuji and Gala. They have variegated green and red skins, and are not too firm, too soft, too tart, or too sweet. They're just right.

Liver and Onions

The best liver comes from younger animals. They have a sweeter, milder flavor. The older the animal, the darker the liver becomes, so look for a lighter pink color.

2 lb. beef or calf liver, cleaned and sliced

2 cups milk

2 cups all-purpose flour

1 tsp. each salt and pepper

6 slices uncooked bacon, diced

2 large yellow onions, sliced

2 TB. butter

Serves 6
Prep time: 1–2 hours (includes soaking time)
Cook time: 45 minutes

1. Soak liver slices in milk for 1 to 2 hours. In a small bowl combine flour, salt, and pepper, and set aside.

2. In a large sauté pan, cook the bacon over high heat until crispy, and the fat is rendered. Remove the bacon and reserve. Add onions to bacon fat and cook over medium-low heat until golden brown, about 30 minutes. Remove onions and set aside.

3. Dredge the soaked liver in the seasoned flour to coat evenly. Shake off excess. Fry in butter over medium heat until browned, about 5 minutes per side. Serve topped with onions and bacon.

Braised Lamb Shank

The shank is the front leg muscle of an animal. This tough, stringy meat is perfect for slow, moist cooking. The gentle heat loosens the stringy fibers, tenderizing and flavoring the meat so that it melts in your mouth.

Serves 4
Prep time: 30 minutes
Cook time: 2 hours

4 lamb shanks

¼ cup olive oil

1 large onion, chopped

2 carrots, chopped

2 stalks celery, chopped

3 cloves garlic, chopped

3 TB. all-purpose flour

1 cup red wine

2 cups chopped fresh or canned tomatoes

2 cups beef stock

1 sprig fresh rosemary

1 bay leaf

Salt and pepper

1. In a large sauté pan, cook the shanks in olive oil over high heat until browned on all sides. Transfer to roasting pan.

2. In the same sauté pan, brown the onions, carrots, celery, and garlic. Add the flour and stir until all the fat is absorbed. Slowly whisk in the wine, tomatoes, and stock. Pour over the shanks, and top with rosemary and bay leaf. Cover and bake at 300°F for 2 hours, until meat falls off the bone. Remove rosemary and bay leaf, and season with salt and pepper. Reduce sauce if necessary by boiling until the desired texture is reached.

Osso Bucco: For this classic Italian favorite, substitute veal shank pieces for the lamb shanks and white wine for the red. Before serving, top the dish with *Gremolada*, a mixture of 2 TB. finely chopped garlic, grated zest of 1 lemon, 2 TB. finely chopped flat-leaf parsley, and 2 minced anchovies.

Chapter 8

Catch of the Day

In This Chapter

- ◆ Fabulously fried
- ◆ Fish cakes and croquettes
- ◆ Sautéed seafood
- ◆ Super summer shellfish

Seafood is the most varied, abundant source of protein there is. Consider all the varieties, all the market forms, and all the recipes in all the countries in the world. It's an immense, often overwhelming category of food. But if you narrow it down to its basic parts, it's actually not that hard to understand.

Seafood 101

There are two basic types of fish: *fin fish* (fish with fins) and *shellfish* (fish with shells). Of the fin fish, there are flatfish and round fish. The flatfish, which include flounder, halibut, and sole, really are flat, skimming along the bottom of the sea. Round fish only look round if you see them swimming straight toward you. Every fish that is not flat is considered round, including salmon, trout, tuna, catfish, and bluefish. Some reside in freshwater, others in saltwater. The freshwater fish have much smaller bones than their larger, ocean–going cousins.

Shellfish are separated into two categories, *mollusks* and *crustaceans.* Mollusks are further divided into three categories. The gastropod is a mollusk with one shell, and includes snails, limpets, and abalone. Bivalves are mollusks with two shells and a hinge, like mussels, oysters, and clams. Cephalopods, which include cuttlefish, squid, and octopus, don't really have shells at all, but they do have suction cups and tentacles. The crustaceans all carry their bones on their back, in the form of an exoskeleton. They count among their ranks crabs, lobsters, crayfish, and shrimp.

Frying Fish

There are many good fish recipes, but the ones that end up on the comfort food list almost always involve frying in oil. The quick heat of hot oil really seals in the delicate flavor of fish, and if cooked properly (not too long) keeps fish moist and tender. Batter dipped or dredged in seasoned flour or cornmeal, fried fish is as down-home as it gets.

Tidbits

In decades past, British fried-fish vendors would cool their oil by dropping in buckets of cool sliced potatoes. Then they'd give away these "chips" to hungry passersby.

Whenever you are deep-fat frying, it is important to regulate the oil's temperature. That does not necessarily mean you must continually check a thermometer. It does mean, however, that you must watch how fast the food is cooking. Browning should be gradual. If the food begins to darken too quickly, turn down the flame and let the oil cool a bit. If the oil is not hot enough, the food will soak it up, making your dish greasy rather than crispy. Test the oil by dropping in a small bit of food. Oil at 350°F to 375°F will cause the food to immediately begin sizzling, which is what you're looking for.

Fried food should be properly drained before serving. Let the food drain on a stack of paper towels for 3 to 5 minutes before salting and serving.

Cooking fish in an oven or frying pan is a little easier than deep-frying because there is an easy rule of thumb regarding cooking time. For moist, tender filets or steaks, use 10 minutes of moderate heat for every inch the fish is thick. Of course, doneness is a matter of taste, but for the most part, people opt for moist and tender over dry and rubbery. So remember, 10 minutes per inch and you'll get along swimmingly!

Fried Catfish

Catfish is a Southern institution, mild in flavor, with a tough, inedible skin. The *channel* and *blue* catfish are the main varieties found throughout the waters of the Southeast, and this recipe is the most common preparation. (Yes, they have whiskers, and no, they are not afraid of dogfish.)

2 eggs	1 tsp. each salt and pepper
2 cups milk	1 TB. Lawry's seasoning salt
1 tsp. Cajun seasoning	8 medium catfish filets
1 cup white or yellow cornmeal	2 cups vegetable shortening or canola oil for frying
⅓ cup all-purpose flour	

Serves 4

Prep time: 20 minutes

Cook time: 15 minutes

1. In a medium bowl, whisk together the eggs, milk, and Cajun seasoning. In a separate bowl combine the cornmeal, flour, salt, pepper, and seasoning salt. Rinse the filets, pat them dry, dredge them in the egg mixture, then coat them well with the cornmeal mixture. After dredging, let them rest at room temperature for 10 minutes.

2. Heat the shortening over high heat until it reaches 375°F. Fry the fish filets until golden brown, about 5 minutes on each side. Drain on paper towels and sprinkle with salt. Serve with collard greens (see Chapter 9), mac and cheese (see Chapter 10), and sliced tomatoes.

Pan-Fried Trout

Don't be put off by the appearance of a head with eyes on your dinner plate. Removing the head would cause the dish to lose moisture, drying it out into a most unpleasant affair.

Serves 4
Prep time: 60 minutes
Cook time: 20 minutes

4 whole trout, gutted, with heads

4 cups milk

3 cups all-purpose flour

1 tsp. each salt and pepper

¼ cup *clarified* butter

1 yellow onion, chopped

½ cup white wine

4 TB. butter

Salt and pepper

1 TB. chopped fresh parsley

1. Soak the trout in milk for 30 to 60 minutes. Drain and discard milk. In a medium bowl combine flour, salt, and pepper. Dredge fish in flour and shake off excess. Set aside at room temperature for 10 minutes.

2. Heat skillet, add clarified butter, and fry fish until very dark, about 5 minutes per side. Transfer to a serving dish and cover with foil to keep warm. Return pan to the heat and add onion, sautéing until golden brown. Add wine, stirring to scrape up crusty bits from the bottom of the pan. Reduce liquid to 1 tablespoon and remove from heat. Add butter, salt and pepper to taste, and parsley. Pour sauce over fish and serve immediately.

Trout Amandine: Before adding wine to the pan sauce, add ½ cup sliced almonds. Sauté until they begin to toast, then continue with the recipe.

Chefspeak

Clarified butter is pure butter fat minus the salts and solids that burn easily at high temperatures. You can buy it in gourmet markets, but it's just as easy to make. Simmer butter gently until melted. Never stir it. Gentle bubbles force the solids to the surface, where they can be easily skimmed off. Pour the pure fat off gently for use in recipes. In the bottom of the pan you'll discover more solids that should also be discarded. Clarified butter will keep for weeks in the fridge or freezer.

Calamari Fritto

Calamari means squid, and *Fritto* means *fried* in Italian. Calamari are tender and sweet, but easily overcooked to a rubber band texture, so beware. They are available fresh (look for clear eyes and a sweet ocean smell) or frozen. The smaller the squid, the more tender and sweet the meat will be.

2–3 lb. calamari slices (rings and tentacles)

2 cups all-purpose flour

1 tsp. each salt and pepper

½ tsp. cayenne pepper

2 cups shortening or canola oil for frying

Salt

Serves 4
Prep time: 10 minutes
Cook time: 10 minutes

1. Rinse and pat dry calamari. In a large bowl combine the flour, salt, and peppers. Add the calamari, stir to coat, and shake off excess.

2. Heat the shortening over high heat until it reaches 375°F. Drop the calamari into the hot oil piece by piece, and fry until golden brown, 1 to 2 minutes. Drain on a paper towel, sprinkle with salt to taste, and serve with lemon wedges or marinara sauce.

Fried Oysters

You can buy oysters already shucked in cans and jars, and sometimes a specialty seafood purveyor will shuck them for you while you wait.

Serves 4
Prep time: 75 minutes
Cook time: 10 minutes

2 cups shortening or canola oil for frying

½ cup all-purpose flour

½ tsp. each salt and pepper

2 eggs

3 cups cracker crumbs

2 dozen large shucked oysters

1. Heat the shortening over high heat until it reaches 375°F.

2. In a small bowl, mix the flour, salt, and pepper. In a separate bowl, whisk the eggs. Fill a third bowl with the cracker crumbs.

3. Coat the oysters evenly with the flour, shaking off the excess. Next, dip them in the eggs, and finally, roll them in the cracker crumbs.

4. Drop the coated oysters into the hot oil piece by piece, and fry until golden brown, 1 to 2 minutes. Drain on a paper towel, sprinkle with salt, and serve with lemon wedges, tartar sauce, or blue-cheese dressing.

Tidbits

My favorite fried oysters in the world are served up at the very nostalgic, very touristy Durgin Park at Faneuil Hall Marketplace in Boston. Yes, there is a line, but the wait is worth it. The sign on the wall is right on the money. It reads "Your grandfather probably ate here." Mine did, and he took me in 1976. I had fried oysters, a lobster, and Indian pudding. I took my own kids a few years back, and it looked just the way I remembered. Unfortunately, I could not get them to eat the good stuff. (They had hot dogs!)

Dress It Up: Oysters on the Half-Shell with Mignonette Sauce

An oyster is generally named for its place of origin, like the Olympia (from Washington), the Malpeque (from Malpeque Bay and Prince Edward Island), the Cape Cod (from Massachusetts), and the Marennes (from the central Atlantic coast of France).

½ cup white wine vinegar

1 TB. sherry vinegar

¼ tsp. salt

½ tsp. pepper

1 shallot, minced

12–16 fresh oysters in their shells

Serves 4
Prep time: 10 minutes
Cook time: 45 minutes

1. For the mignonette sauce, combine vinegars, salt, and pepper in a small saucepan. Place it over high heat, bring to a boil, and reduce by half. Add shallot, remove from heat, pour into ramekins, and set aside.

2. Scrub the outer shell of the oysters to remove grit and sand. Place the oyster on the counter wrapped in a towel, with the hinge exposed. Hold the oyster tightly on the counter. Wiggle an *oyster knife* straight into the hinge between the top and bottom shell. Put some muscle into it. When you get it in, run the knife all the way around the shell. The oyster will still be clinging onto the top shell, so carefully scrape it free. Discard the top shell, and place the bottom shell, with the oyster inside onto a pan of crushed ice. Be careful not to spill the delicious juice inside, which is called the oyster liquor. Repeat with the remaining oysters. Serve immediately on chilled oyster plates or on a plate of crushed ice with mignonette sauce and lemon wedges on the side.

Chefspeak

An **oyster knife** is not at all sharp, but it is very strong. And because there is so much force behind it when shucking, take care not to hurt yourself. Oyster knives range in length from 2 to 7 inches, and are available with or without a metal guard between the blade and the handle. Oyster gloves made out of chain mail also are available and will keep the knife from penetrating your skin.

Fish 'n' Chips

Fish 'n' chips became a popular working-class food in the 1800s, when fishermen began trawling and making good, inexpensive fish accessible to all. Traditionally served in grease-absorbing newspaper, today you sometimes find them wrapped in butcher paper printed with fake news, which is considered more sanitary.

Serves 4
Prep time: 30 minutes
Cook time: 30 minutes

2 cups all-purpose flour

1 TB. baking powder

1 tsp. each salt and pepper

1 cup beer

1 cup cornstarch

1 TB. Old Bay seasoning

3 large russet potatoes

2 cups shortening or canola oil for frying

1½ lb. *cod, pollock,* or *haddock* filets, sliced into strips

1. In a large bowl, combine the flour, baking powder, salt, and pepper. Add the beer, whisk until smooth, then refrigerate for 20 minutes. In a separate bowl, stir together the cornstarch and Old Bay, and set aside.

2. Using a mandoline or a chef knife, slice the potatoes into ½-inch thick sticks and set them aside submerged in a bowl of water.

3. Heat the shortening over high heat until it reaches 325°F. Drain and dry potatoes and fry until they are limp. Remove from oil, and drain on paper towels. Increase heat and bring the oil to 375°F. Rinse and pat dry the fish strips. Dredge them well in the cornstarch, shake off the excess, then dip each piece into the batter to coat thoroughly. Drop the fish carefully into the hot oil and cook until golden brown, about 3 to 4 minutes. Drain on paper towels and sprinkle with salt. Return the limp potatoes to the hotter oil and fry until brown and crisp, about 2 to 3 minutes. Drain on paper towels and sprinkle with salt. Serve fish and chips with malt vinegar, lemon wedges, or tartar sauce.

Chefspeak

Cod is the classic white-meat, all-purpose fish. It has a delicate, mild flavor, firm flesh when raw, but tender when cooked. You may know cod by its Spanish name, *bacalao.* **Pollock** and **haddock** are closely related, and can be used interchangeably. Scrod is a young, smaller cod, haddock, or pollock.

Dress It Up: Fish Tacos

Guacamole is the must-have accompaniment to this dish. To whip up a batch, mash up two ripe avocados, add 2 tablespoons of lime juice and ½ teaspoon salt, and add a little cumin, hot pepper sauce, and minced onion to taste.

3 large ripe tomatoes, chopped

3 scallions, chopped

3 cloves garlic, chopped

1 bunch cilantro, chopped

2 jalapeño peppers, chopped

Juice of 5 limes (about ¾ cup), divided

1 TB. ground cumin

1 tsp. pepper sauce

1 tsp. salt

1–2 lbs. firm white fish, sliced into 1-inch strips

2 eggs

1 cup all-purpose flour

1 tsp. salt

½ tsp. pepper

12 corn tortillas

2 cups shortening or canola oil

2 cups cabbage, shredded

1 cup sour cream

Serves 4		
Prep time: 35 minutes		
Cook time: 20 minutes		

1. In a large bowl, combine the tomatoes, scallions, garlic, cilantro, jalapeños, half the lime juice, cumin, pepper sauce, and salt. Mix well and set aside. Rinse fish, pat dry, drizzle with the remaining lime juice and set aside.

2. In a separate bowl, whisk the eggs well, and add flour, salt, and pepper, whisking until smooth. Refrigerate 20 minutes. Wrap the tortillas in tin foil and warm in a 200°F oven.

3. Heat the shortening over high heat until it reaches 375°F. Add the fish to the batter and stir to coat. Drop the fish into the hot oil piece by piece, and fry until golden brown, 2 to 3 minutes. Drain on a paper towel and sprinkle with salt. To serve, fill tortillas with fried fish, tomato mixture, shredded cabbage, and a dollop of sour cream.

Baked Salmon

This cooking method retains the steam, which in turn holds in all the moisture, flavor, and nutrients. But watch out! Steam is hot and it can burn you. Open the foil pouches carefully!

Serves 4
Prep time: 30 minutes
Cook time: 10 minutes

4 (½-lb.) salmon filets or steaks

4 TB. butter

1 tsp. each salt and pepper

1 bunch chopped fresh dill (or 2 TB. dry)

1 lemon, sliced

1. Preheat oven to 400°F. Wash salmon and pat dry. Place each filet in the center of a large piece of foil. Rub each piece with butter, sprinkle with salt and pepper, top with dill and three or four lemon slices.

2. Fold foil up and seal fish tightly inside like an envelope. Place foil packets on a baking sheet and bake 10 minutes for every inch of thickness. When done, the salmon flesh turns opaque. Unwrap carefully and transfer to serving plate. Serve with steamed rice and vegetables.

Listen to Mom!

Much of the salmon available in the markets today is farmed, or aquacultured. While salmon is high in the heart-healthy omega-3 fatty acids, recent studies indicate that toxin levels in aquacultured salmon are 10 times higher than that of wild salmon. Toxins are thought to originate in the feed, which is made from fish caught in polluted waters. So look for wild salmon, like the Pacific Chinook, King, Coho, Pink, and Sockeye. Limit your intake of farmed species, mainly the Atlantic Salmon, to once or twice a month.

Poached Salmon: Combine 4 quarts water, one bottle dry white wine, one sliced lemon, 1 teaspoon peppercorns, 1 stalk chopped celery, and 1 large chopped onion. Bring to a boil and add fish. Decrease heat to a bare simmer and cook 10 minutes for every inch of thickness. Drain and serve.

Grilled Salmon: Marinate the salmon in olive oil, lemon juice, and dill for 1 hour before cooking on a grill over high heat, 10 minutes for every inch of thickness. To prevent meat from falling through the rack, use a two-sided grilling basket, or line the rack with foil.

Salmon Croquettes

A croquette is any mixture of food that is bound together; formed into patties, balls, or little football-shaped torpedoes; and fried. It's a charming way to serve seafood.

1 (15-oz.) can pink salmon

2 scallions, chopped

1 stalk celery, chopped

½ tsp. each salt and pepper

2 cups all-purpose flour, divided

1 tsp. baking powder

1 egg

1 cup white wine

¼ cup olive oil

Serves 4
Prep time: 30 minutes (plus 1 hour for refrigeration)
Cook time: 10 minutes

1. In a large bowl, combine salmon, scallions, celery, salt, and pepper. Mix well, and add ½ cup flour and baking powder. In a separate bowl combine the egg and wine, then add to the salmon mixture. Form into 2- to 3-inch discs and refrigerate for 1 hour.

2. Heat oil in a large sauté pan over high heat. Use the remaining flour to coat each croquette lightly and shake off the excess. Fry until golden brown, about 3 to 5 minutes on each side. Serve immediately with lemon wedges, a dollop of sour cream, and a green salad.

Fish Patties: Combine 1½ cup of cooked, flaked fish with 1½ cup mashed potatoes, an egg, a minced onion, and the herbs or spices of your choice (such as Old Bay seasoning, curry powder, or herbes de Provençe). Form into patties and fry as above.

Garlic Shrimp

Shrimp are sold by size, and labeled by numbers that indicate how many shrimp of that size are in a pound. For instance, 16/20 means there are between 16 and 20 pieces per pound.

Serves 4
Prep time: 15 minutes (plus 1 hour for marinating)
Cook time: 10 minutes

2 lb. medium, large, or jumbo shrimp, peeled and deveined, with tails intact

2 TB. lemon juice

¼ cup olive oil

1 small yellow onion, chopped

1 TB. Old Bay seasoning or red pepper flakes

½ tsp salt

2 TB. olive oil

8 cloves garlic, chopped

¼ cup chopped flat-leaf Italian parsley

1. Rinse and pat dry shrimp. Place them in a large bowl with the lemon juice, olive oil, onion, Old Bay seasoning, and salt. Mix well and marinate for 1 hour.

2. Heat a large sauté pan over high heat and add enough olive oil to coat the pan. Add the garlic and cook until golden brown. Add the shrimp and cook for 2 to 3 minutes, stirring, until the shrimp turn pink. Serve immediately with a sprinkle of the fresh parsley and some fresh lemon wedges.

Dress It Up: Coconut Shrimp

Coconut comes shredded or desiccated (ground fine), toasted or untoasted, sweetened or unsweetened. For this recipe I prefer unsweetened, untoasted shredded coconut. But that's just me. You can also shell and grate a fresh coconut.

2 lb. medium, large, or jumbo shrimp, peeled and deveined, with tails intact

Juice of 1 lemon (about 2 TB.)

¼ cup orange marmalade

¼ cup Dijon mustard

¼ cup honey

1 TB. hot pepper sauce

1 cup all-purpose flour

1 tsp. salt

½ tsp. cayenne pepper

3 eggs

4 cups shredded coconut

2 cups shortening or canola oil

Serves 4	
Prep time: 20 minutes	
Cook time: 10 minutes	

1. Rinse and pat dry shrimp. Place them in a large bowl with the lemon juice and set aside in the refrigerator. In a small bowl, combine the marmalade, mustard, honey, and hot pepper sauce. Set aside.

2. In another small bowl, combine the flour, salt, and cayenne pepper. In a separate bowl, whisk together the eggs. Fill a third bowl with coconut. Dredge the shrimp first in flour, then in the eggs, then press into the coconut. Set aside to rest at room temperature for 10 minutes.

3. Heat the shortening over high heat until it reaches 375°F. Drop the shrimp into the hot oil piece by piece, and fry until golden brown, 1 to 2 minutes. Drain on a paper towel, sprinkle with salt, and serve with marmalade dipping sauce.

Clambake

Clambakes are supposed to take place on the beach, but here is a recipe you can make anytime in the comfort of your own kitchen. To get that beachy flavor, add some seaweed to your pot.

Serves 6–8
Prep time: 60 minutes
Cook time: 30 minutes

8 red new potatoes

4 ears corn, cut in half

2 (1–2-lbs.) live lobsters

2 lb. whole linguica, chorizo, andouille, or Polish sausage

1 dozen live littleneck or cherrystone clams

1 dozen live oysters

1. Light the coals inside a barbecue and let them burn until white hot. Place potatoes into a large stockpot and fill with water halfway. Place over high heat and bring to a boil for 15 minutes. Add corn and lobsters, return to boil for another 10 to 15 minutes, until lobsters are red. Drain and set vegetables and lobsters aside.

2. Spread out white-hot coals and cover evenly with soaked wood chips. On the barbecue rack make an even layer of sausage, lobsters, and vegetables. Layer the clams and oysters on top of the first layer. Close the lid of the barbecue, open a vent, and cook for 30 minutes, until shells open. Serve with bread and lots of melted butter.

Oven Clambake: Preheat the oven to 400°F. Slice the sausage in 2-inch pieces and sauté in butter until brown. Layer a roasting pan with the vegetables, lobster, sausage, clams, and oysters. Cover tightly with foil and bake 30 minutes, until the shells open.

Crab or Shrimp Boil: In an 8-quart stockpot, boil sausage and corn. Cut two onions into wedges, add a packet of crab boil seasoning, and one crab or ½ pound of shrimp per person. Cook until shellfish is pink. Drain, and serve with crusty bread and melted butter.

Boiled Lobster: Drop live lobster into a large pot of boiling water, which will stop the boil. When the boil resumes, cover and cook for 12 to 15 minutes, until lobster is red.

Kitchen Tips

To hold a real clambake on the beach, dig a pit in the sand and line the bottom with rocks. Gather driftwood and build a fire on the rocks. Keep it going for several hours, so the rocks get really hot. Spread out coals, and using a few more rocks, place a rack or metal plate just above the coals. Spread seaweed on the rack and line it with the potatoes and corn. Pile on more seaweed and drop in the live lobsters and sausage. Add more seaweed and then add the oysters and clams. Add more seaweed, then top it off with a water-soaked tarp and let it steam for a couple of hours. When the shellfish opens, it's time to eat! Oh, c'mon … doesn't that sound like fun?

Crab Cakes

You can buy crabmeat in cans, frozen in tubs, cooked and in the shell, or uncooked in the shell of a crab that's alive and kicking (or pinching).

Serves 4

Prep time: 30 minutes (plus 1–2 hours for refrigeration)

Cook time: 10 minutes

---

2 scallions, chopped

2 cloves garlic, minced

2 TB. butter

1 (4-oz.) can chopped pimentos, drained

1 tsp. dry dill or ¼ cup chopped fresh dill

1 tsp. Old Bay seasoning

1 TB. Dijon mustard

¼ cup heavy cream

1 egg

1 cup bread crumbs, divided

½ tsp. each salt and pepper

1 lb. crabmeat

½ cup Parmesan cheese

1 TB. butter

2 TB. olive oil

1. In a large sauté pan over high heat, sauté the scallions and garlic in butter until golden brown. Remove from the heat and add the pimentos, dill, Old Bay, and mustard. In a medium bowl, whisk together the cream and egg, and add it to the pan. Add ½ cup bread crumbs, salt, pepper, and crabmeat, and mix well to thoroughly combine. Form the mixture into patties 2 to 3 inches in diameter. In a separate bowl combine the remaining bread crumbs and the Parmesan cheese. Coat the crab cakes in the crumbs, the set aside to chill for 1 to 2 hours.

2. In a large sauté pan over high heat, melt the butter and olive oil. Add the crab cakes and cook until golden brown, about 3 to 4 minutes per side. Serve immediately with lemon wedges, tartar sauce, or sour cream.

Kitchen Tips

Making your own tartar sauce is easy as pie. Combine 1 cup of mayonnaise with 1 tablespoon each of pickle relish, minced onion, Dijon mustard, white wine vinegar, prepared horseradish, one clove of minced garlic, 1 teaspoon chopped capers, salt, and pepper.

Chapter 9

On the Side

In This Chapter

- ◆ Savory vegetable casseroles
- ◆ Great greens, wilted, fried, and creamed
- ◆ Roots, roasted and glazed
- ◆ Classic spuds

Never underestimate the value of a good side dish. It can turn a good meal into a great one or, heaven forbid, a mediocre meal into a dud. Often, it's the side dishes we remember with the most fondness. The special way Mom had of preparing the brussels sprouts, or the particular texture of the creamed spinach at your favorite restaurant. And oh, the soothing qualities of a well-made potato dish! Sometimes, the side dish is all I want.

Vegetables: Nutritional Powerhouses

Without a doubt, veggies are the most misunderstood members of the dinner plate. They are feared by some, loathed by others, and avoided by much of America's youth. The USDA goes so far as to fund special educational programs designed to get kids to eat their veggies. But despite all their efforts, we still don't get enough. It's a shame, because there is no better, cheaper, tastier way to get your vitamins and minerals than from veggies.

Their color is key. Bright-colored veggies carry more vitamins and minerals, and each color is a clue to the goodness inside:

◆ Orange and yellow veggies contain beta carotene, a precursor to vitamin A, and a powerful antioxidant known to prevent heart disease and some cancers. It assists in bone growth, tissue repair, and helps the body fight infection.

◆ Vegetables with the red and purple pigment anthocyanine, also high in antioxidants, can block some cancer-causing chemicals, suppress tumor growth, and improve wound healing.

◆ Blue pigments are thought to help slow aging.

◆ Chlorophyll, the green pigment, is a major source of iron, and is used to prevent and treat liver, skin, and colon cancers; it also improves your breath. The cabbage family in particular is thought to fight against breast and prostate cancers.

Knowing that the nutritional value of vegetables is directly related to the vegetable's color, it makes sense to cook them in such a way as to retain as much of the color as possible. Nutritionally, raw is best. But most comfort food meals don't include a plate of raw vegetables. It's the cheese sauce, the butter, and the cream that warms our hearts.

Listen to Mom!

To maximize the nutritional value of vegetables, try not to overcook them. Many of these recipes include a quick precooking step before all the rich fatty goodness is piled on. This step is not meant to completely cook the vegetable, especially if there is more cooking ahead in a casserole or sauce. The longer a veggie boils in water, the more nutrients are lost into the water. Remove them from the water while they are still brightly colored, and you can rest assured they will still be good for you.

Washing

Most of the food-borne illness in this country comes from cross-contamination onto vegetables that are not properly washed. Even if you plan on peeling the vegetable, contaminants can still be transferred from the skin to you, cooking surfaces, and other recipe ingredients.

There is no need for a special food cleanser. Just a good wash with water is adequate. Thicker vegetables that can withstand the pressure, like potatoes, should be scrubbed. More delicate vegetables, like greens, should be soaked in clean water for 2 to 3 minutes, and rinsed. If you feel the need to be extra safe, use distilled or filtered water.

Some veggies need extra care just to remove the dirt and grit. Vegetables grown in sandy soil, like spinach, need to be soaked and drained several times before they are completely clean.

Potatoes

In Chapter 4 I suggested using waxy potatoes for making potato salads, because they hold their shape well. Now, I want you to use the other, mealy potatoes. Russet, Burbank, and Idaho potatoes, with mature, thick brown skins, disintegrate with heat into the soft, crumbly, fluffy potato you expect in a mashed or baked side dish. French fries, too, are better when made from these potatoes. Crispy on the outside, tender on the inside can only be accomplished with these mealy spuds.

Potatoes should never be stored in the refrigerator. Potatoes are loaded with starch, and low temperatures cause that starch to convert to sugar. Sugar caramelizes and quickly burns when applied to high temperature. So for example, French fries made from a potato with excess sugar will burn quickly and be bitter. To avoid this, buy potatoes as you need them, and store them on your counter, at room temperature.

Succotash

Succotash is a corruption of the Algonquin word *msickquatash*, meaning boiled corn or kernels. It seems clear that the colonists received a similar dish from the Narragansett Indians, but it probably didn't include lima beans until much later, when trade routes opened up to Central America, where the lima bean was first cultivated.

Serves 4
Prep time: 15 minutes
Cook time: 15 minutes

6 slices uncooked bacon, or ¼ lb. salt pork, diced

1 small yellow onion, chopped

2 cups corn, fresh off the cob, canned, or frozen

2 cups lima beans, fresh shelled, canned, or frozen

2 TB. butter

2 TB. chopped fresh parsley

1. Sauté bacon in a saucepan over high heat to render fat.

2. Add onion and cook until both bacon and onion are browned. Add corn and beans and cook to warm through. Remove from heat. Add butter, parsley, and serve.

Ratatouille

Ratatouille is easy to make in large batches, keeps well for several days, and only improves with age. Try it as a topping for canapés or baked potatoes, a layer of lasagna, a cold salad, a sauce for fish, a stuffing for peppers, or in vegetable ravioli.

3 cups diced eggplant

3 TB. salt

½ cup olive oil

1 large onion, diced

4 cloves garlic, minced

¼ cup fresh oregano, minced

2 cups red bell peppers, seeded and diced

3 cups zucchini, diced

2 cups roma tomatoes, peeled, seeded, and diced

2 TB. fresh basil, minced

Salt and pepper

Serves 4	
Prep time: 30 minutes	
Cook time: 60 minutes	

1. Combine eggplant and salt in a large bowl, mix to coat well, and set aside for 30 minutes. (This step keeps the eggplant from absorbing too much oil. The salt draws out the moisture, causing cells of air to collapse, making it harder for them to absorb oil.)

2. Heat oil in large sauté pan and add onion, garlic, and oregano, and cook until golden. Add peppers, zucchini, and tomatoes. Rinse off excess salt and add eggplant. Cover and simmer 45 minutes. Remove lid and cook to reduce liquid. Add basil, salt, and pepper. Serve hot or cold.

Kitchen Tips

To peel and seed tomatoes, cut an X in the end, drop it in boiling water for 30 seconds, and then directly into ice water. The temperature shock loosens the skin, and it peels right off. To remove the seeds and juice, cut the peeled tomato in half, not from end to end, but through the middle. Squeeze out the seeds and juice as if it were an orange you were juicing. Then dice it up. Voilà! *Tomato Concassé!*

Broccoli and Cheese

I like to use cheddar for this dish. I encourage you to try out some other cheeses, but stay away from stringy cheeses like mozzarella, which make the dish hard to eat.

Serves 4
Prep time: 5 minutes
Cook time: 10 minutes

2 lb. fresh broccoli flowerettes and trimmed stems

2 TB. butter

2 TB. all-purpose flour

1 cup milk

1 TB. Dijon mustard

½ tsp. salt

1 tsp. fresh grated nutmeg

1 cup cheddar cheese

1½ tsp. paprika

1. Cook broccoli in 3 cups boiling water until barely tender, about 5 minutes. Drain and set aside.

2. Melt butter and add flour, stirring until all the fat is absorbed. Slowly add milk, and stir until thickened. Add mustard, salt, nutmeg, and cheese, and stir to melt. Add broccoli and mix well to evenly coat. Transfer to serving dish and sprinkle with paprika.

Broccoli Au Gratin: Transfer cheesy broccoli to a buttered casserole dish. Top with bread crumbs and Parmesan cheese, dot with butter, and bake at 350°F until brown and bubbly.

Cheesy Cauliflower: Replace broccoli with an equal amount of cauliflower. Try this variation au gratin, too.

Creamed Spinach

Try this terrific dish with other greens, too, like Swiss chard, arugula, mustard, or beet greens.

1 small onion, chopped

3 TB. butter

2 TB. all-purpose flour

1 cup heavy cream

1½ tsp. fresh grated nutmeg

½ tsp. sugar

4 cups cooked spinach, freshly boiled or frozen, thawed and drained

Salt and pepper

Serves 4	
Prep time: 10 minutes	
Cook time: 15 minutes	

1. In a large sauté pan, cook onion in butter until golden brown.

2. Add flour and cook, stirring, until the fat is absorbed. Add the cream slowly while whisking. Add nutmeg and sugar and stir to combine. Add the spinach and stir to coat evenly. Season to taste with salt and pepper.

Tangy Creamed Spinach: Replace the flour and cream with 1 cup of softened cream cheese or sour cream.

Spinach and Bacon: Replace the butter with six slices of diced uncooked bacon. Fry it until crispy, then add the onions and resume the recipe.

Creamed Onions: Omit the small chopped onion and replace the spinach with 2 pints peeled pearl onions that have been simmered in chicken stock until tender, about 20 minutes. You can serve in the sauce, or transfer it all to a buttered casserole dish, top with bread crumbs and Parmesan cheese, dot with butter, and bake at 400°F until brown and bubbly.

Kitchen Tips

It's easy to skin a pearl onion. Drop it in boiling water for 30 seconds, then immediately transfer it to ice water. The shock in temperature loosens the skin. With a paring knife, trim off the root end, and the skin will slide off with it.

Collard Greens

Collards are a prehistoric member of the cabbage family. There is evidence that they were eaten by the ancient Greeks, Romans, and Celts.

Serves 4
Prep time: 15 minutes
Cook time: 2 hours

1 ham hock

3 lb. collard greens, washed well, stemmed, and chopped

Salt and pepper

Hot pepper sauce

1. Place ham hock into stockpot, cover with water, and bring to a boil over high heat. Reduce heat and simmer until meat falls off the bone, about 1 hour.

2. Add greens in batches into simmering ham hock, letting each batch wilt down to make room for the next. Cook for 45 to 60 minutes, until tender. Transfer greens to a serving platter. Top with chopped ham hock meat and cooking broth, and season to taste with salt, pepper, and hot pepper sauce.

Tidbits

In the United States, collard greens were slave food, tossed aside with leftover meat and bones as the dregs of the kitchen. Unlike most greens, the collards benefit from prolonged cooking. As they cook, the water becomes infused with vitamins, and this "pot likker" was an important part of the slave diet. When combined with the protein from the boiled bones and sopped up with a wedge of cornbread, boiled greens provided a nutritious meal.

Mixed Greens: Try the same recipe using kale, turnip, or mustard greens.

Dress It Up: Wilted Mixed Greens

Wilted greens are meant to be just that. Not cooked and soggy, and not fresh and crisp. Just slightly limp. Watch the cooking time carefully, and don't overdo it.

Serves 8
Prep time: 30 minutes
Cook time: 10 minutes

1 TB. olive oil

1 TB. sesame oil

3 cloves garlic, minced

1 TB. freshly grated ginger

2 cups spinach, cleaned and chopped

2 cups Swiss chard, cleaned and chopped

2 cups beet greens, cleaned and chopped

2 cups Napa cabbage, cleaned and chopped

Zest and juice of 1 lemon

3 TB. soy sauce

2 TB. toasted sesame seeds

1. Heat oils in sauté pan over high heat.

2. Add garlic and ginger, stirring until golden brown. Add greens, stir and cover for 1 minute, until wilted, but still bright green. Add lemon zest and juice, soy sauce, and stir to coat evenly. Serve immediately sprinkled with sesame seeds.

Fried Okra

It seems that the ancient Egyptians were the first to cultivate okra, which grew wild along the Nile.

Serves 4
Prep time: 60 minutes (includes soaking time)
Cook time: 10 minutes

1 lb. okra, fresh or frozen, rinsed and sliced

1 quart white vinegar

2 eggs

1 tsp. salt

2 cups all-purpose flour

2 cups cornmeal

1 TB. cayenne pepper

2 cups vegetable shortening or canola oil for frying

Salt and pepper

1. Soak sliced okra in vinegar for 30 to 60 minutes. Drain and rinse thoroughly. In a small bowl, whisk together eggs and salt. In a separate bowl combine flour, cornmeal, and cayenne pepper.

2. Heat the shortening over high heat until it reaches 375°F. Working in batches, dredge okra in egg, then cornmeal. Shake off excess and fry until golden brown, about 3 minutes. Drain on paper towels and sprinkle with salt and pepper.

Kitchen Tips

It's the slime that turns many people off of okra. The vinegar soak is a great way to combat this. Slicing the okra in small rounds releases more of the slime in the vinegar rinse. If you like the slime, then by all means, omit the vinegar and leave the okra whole.

Fried Green Tomatoes

Most of America became familiar with this recipe from the book *Fried Green Tomatoes at the Whistle Stop Café* by Fanny Flagg, and the subsequent movie. But the recipe is a Depression-era staple of rural America, as was green tomato pie, soup, and pickles.

2 eggs

½ tsp. salt

2 cups all-purpose flour

2 cups cornmeal

1 tsp. cayenne pepper

4 green tomatoes, sliced in ½-inch-thick rounds

¼ cup canola oil

Salt and pepper

Serves 4
Prep time: 15 minutes
Cook time: 10 minutes

1. In a small bowl, whisk together eggs and salt. In a separate bowl combine flour, cornmeal, and cayenne pepper.

2. Dip tomato slices in egg, then cornmeal. Shake off excess and fry in oil over high heat until golden brown, about 3 minutes on each side. Drain on paper towels, sprinkle with salt and pepper, and serve immediately.

Brussels Sprouts

First popularized in Belgium, brussels sprouts look like baby cabbages and are in fact a member of the cabbage family. Fresh is best, because they develop a stronger flavor the longer they are stored. Really fresh brussels sprouts are sold still attached to their long stalk.

1 lb. brussels sprouts, washed

½ cup vegetable stock, chicken stock, or water

2 cups bread crumbs

¼ cup grated Parmesan cheese

4 TB. butter

Serves 4
Prep time: 15 minutes
Cook time: 25 minutes

1. Preheat oven to 350°F. Trim off end of each sprout and cut an *X* in the stem end. Boil in 2 quarts of water until barely tender, about 10 minutes.

2. Drain and transfer to buttered casserole dish. Add stock, cover with bread crumbs and Parmesan cheese, and dot with butter. Bake uncovered until golden brown, about 15 minutes.

Roasted Root Vegetables

The more color you have on your plate, the more vitamins and minerals you'll have in your diet. Choose a variety of colorful root vegetables for this dish. There are dozens of varieties available, especially in the fall.

Serves 8
Prep time: 15 minutes
Cook time: 60 minutes

1 small butternut squash, peeled and diced

3 parsnips, peeled and diced

1 turnip, peeled and diced

2 beets, peeled and diced

2 fennel bulbs, sliced

8 new potatoes, halved

4 carrots, peeled and diced

2 large yellow onions, sliced

8 cloves garlic, peeled and left whole

1 cup olive oil

¼ cup fresh rosemary needles, minced

1 tsp. each salt and pepper

1. Preheat oven to 400°F. In a large bowl, combine the squash, parsnips, turnip, beets, fennel, potatoes, carrots, onions, and garlic. Add the oil, rosemary, salt, and pepper, and toss well to thoroughly coat all vegetables.

2. Spread the vegetables out onto a cookie sheet in one single layer. Bake, stirring occasionally, until tender and golden brown, about 1 hour.

Spaghetti Squash: This is a great option for those who can't eat wheat. Roast the squash whole for 1 hour, until tender to the touch. Allow to cool 10 minutes before cutting in half. Use a large spoon to scrape out the center stringy squash. Serve with butter or your favorite pasta sauce.

Glazed Carrots

Glazed carrots are known in France as *carrot à la Vichy* (carrots in the style of Vichy). Vichy is the city in central France where a well-known sparkling mineral water is bottled. To be truly authentic, Vichy carrots must be made with real Vichy water.

4 cups carrots, peeled and thinly sliced

3 TB. butter

1½ TB. sugar

½ tsp. salt

1 TB. white wine vinegar

1 cup water

Serves 4	
Prep time: 10 minutes	
Cook time: 20 minutes	

1. In a large sauté pan, combine carrots, butter, sugar, salt, vinegar, and water.

2. Set over medium heat, cover tightly, and simmer 10 to 15 minutes, until carrots are tender. Remove lid and cook until liquid is evaporated.

 Tidbits

Carrots are available in other colors, too. In fact, they were originally purple. All orange vegetables are high in vitamin A, which, among other things, promotes good vision. Carrots are also high in antioxidants, which protect against cardiovascular disease and some cancers.

Mashed Potatoes

Is there anyone out there who doesn't love mash? Smooth or lumpy, creamy or buttery, garlicky or *au naturel*, it's comfort food at its best!

Serves 4
Prep time: 45 minutes
Cook time: 10 minutes

4 medium russet potatoes, peeled and quartered

4 TB. butter

½ cup cream

Salt and pepper

1. Boil potatoes in 3 quarts of water until tender, about 30 minutes. Drain thoroughly and spread out on a baking sheet to dry for 15 minutes.

2. Combine butter and cream in a saucepan and set over low heat until melted and warm. Put cooled potatoes through a ricer or mash by hand and add to the cream. Beat with a whisk until smooth. Season with salt and pepper and serve immediately. Potatoes may also be transferred to a casserole, covered with a little more cream, and baked at 350°F until golden brown.

Kitchen Tips

Although the best potato to use in a mash is a mature, mealy potato, it's fun to try something different from time to time. Yukon gold are thin skinned with a buttery flavor, and they have a lovely yellow color. And if you want to delight the young people in your life, try the purple Peruvian potato. It's Barney's favorite!

Roasted Garlic Mash: Wrap two whole heads of garlic in aluminum foil and bake for 30 minutes at 400°F, until soft. Cut in half horizontally and squeeze out the soft roasted garlic. Add it to the butter and cream and simmer 5 minutes before adding the potatoes.

Parsnip Potatoes: Boil three peeled and chopped parsnips along with the potatoes. Parsnips have more sugar, which makes the finished dish sweeter.

Celery Root Potatoes: Boil one bulb of celery root (also called celeriac) along with the potatoes.

Dress It Up: Pommes Duchess

These potatoes are perfect to make when you want to impress. Pipe them directly onto individual plates and brown them just before serving.

2 egg yolks

1 recipe mashed potatoes (see previous recipe)

1 whole egg

¼ tsp. salt

Serves 4
Prep time: 60 minutes
Cook time: 10 minutes

1. Mix the egg yolks into the warm (but not hot) mashed potatoes. Transfer to a piping bag and pipe decorative rosettes and curlicues directly onto dinner plates.

2. In a small bowl, combine the whole egg and salt and whisk thoroughly. Brush the potatoes lightly with the egg wash. Just before serving, brown potatoes under a broiler, or in a 450°F oven.

Tidbits

Pommes duchess is a classic accompaniment to planked steak. A good porterhouse or T-bone is grilled and served on a seasoned oak plank. The potatoes are piped around the meat and the whole thing is browned briefly under a broiler. Both meat and potatoes take on a terrific oaky-smoke flavor.

Candied Yams

Yams and sweet potatoes are similar, but come from two different plant species. Markets often get the two confused but, for this recipe, the two are interchangeable. I prefer the prettier red yam, with a little more sugar and moisture.

Serves 4
Prep time: 60 minutes
Cook time: 20 minutes

3 large yams or sweet potatoes

Juice and zest of 1 lemon

¼ cup maple syrup

½ tsp. salt

¼ tsp. pepper

¼ tsp. nutmeg

¼ tsp. ground ginger

¼ tsp. cinnamon

1 cup brown sugar

4 TB. butter

1. Boil yams whole, in their skins until tender, about 45 minutes. Cool, then peel and slice into ½-inch-thick coins. Layer evenly in a buttered casserole, and drizzle with lemon juice (reserving zest) and maple syrup.

2. Preheat oven to 350°F. In a small bowl combine the lemon zest, salt, pepper, nutmeg, ginger, cinnamon, and brown sugar. Mix well, and distribute evenly over the top of the yams. Dot with butter and bake until golden brown and bubbly, about 20 minutes.

Kitchen Tips

While it's true that vegetables cook faster when they are cut smaller, they also tend to disintegrate. In addition, more exposed surface area means more vital nutrients are lost in the water. Cooking them whole, with the skin on, holds them together and holds in all the good stuff.

Roasted Yams: If you want to bake the yams instead of boiling them, place them in a 450°F oven until tender, about 30 minutes.

Au Gratin Potatoes

Au gratin is the melting and browning of the top of a dish. It can be done in the oven, under a broiler, or even in a toaster oven.

4 medium potatoes, peeled and halved

2 TB. butter

2 TB. all-purpose flour

1 cup milk

1 TB. Dijon mustard

½ tsp. salt

1 tsp. fresh grated nutmeg

1 cup cheddar cheese

2 cups bread crumbs

¼ cup grated Parmesan cheese

4 TB. butter

Serves 4
Prep time: 30 minutes
Cook time: 30 minutes

1. Boil potatoes in 3 quarts of water until just tender, about 30 minutes. Drain, cool, and slice into ½-inch rounds. Spread evenly in buttered casserole and set aside.

2. Preheat oven to 400°F. Melt butter and add flour, stirring until all the fat is absorbed. Slowly add milk, and stir until thickened. Add mustard, salt, nutmeg, and cheese, and stir to melt. Pour over potatoes. Top with bread crumbs and Parmesan cheese, and dot with butter. Bake until brown and bubbly, about 20 minutes.

Potatoes O'Brien: Add to the potatoes one diced onion and one diced green or red bell pepper, sautéed briefly in butter.

Kitchen Tips

Both au gratin and O'Brien potatoes are a great use for leftover boiled potatoes.

Baked Potatoes

For years I wrapped my spuds in aluminum foil. But I discovered that the foil holds in the moisture and steams the interior of the potato. If you prefer your potatoes flaky, leave off the foil. The steam can escape, and the interior will be soft and dry.

Serves 4
Prep time: 10 minutes
Cook time: 75 minutes

4 medium russet potatoes, scrubbed, skin on

1 TB. butter

1. Preheat oven to 400°F. Rub the skins of the potatoes with butter, place them on a baking sheet and roast for 1 hour. After 1 hour, carefully puncture the skins and return to the oven for another 15 minutes.

2. Carefully slice baked potatoes open lengthwise along one edge. Pinch the end toward the center to open the potato. Serve immediately with an assortment of condiments, including butter, sour cream, crumbled crispy bacon, and chopped chives.

Potato Skins: Cool the baked potatoes, slice in half and scoop out the centers (save it for mash or hash). Slice the skins into strips and arrange on a baking sheet, skin side down. Brush with melted butter, and top with grated cheese and bacon bits. Bake at 350°F until the cheese is brown and bubbly, about 10 minutes. Serve with sour cream or ranch dressing.

Listen to Mom!

Be careful when pinching open the hot spuds. The steam is hotter than the potato itself and can give you a nasty burn.

French Fries

Potatoes for French fries can be held in water as long as 12 hours before frying to prevent oxidation. But be sure to dry them completely before dropping them into the hot fat. Water spatters dangerously if dripped into hot oil.

3 large russet potatoes   **Salt**

2 cups shortening or
canola oil

Serves 4	
Prep time: 30 minutes	
Cook time: 20 minutes	

1. Using a mandoline or a chef knife, slice the potatoes into ½-inch-thick sticks and set them aside submerged in a bowl of water.

2. Heat the shortening over high heat until it reaches 325°F. Drain and dry potatoes and fry until they are limp. Remove from oil, and drain on paper towels. Increase heat and bring the oil to 375°F. Return the limp potatoes to the hotter oil and fry until brown and crisp, about 2 to 3 minutes. Drain on paper towels and sprinkle with salt.

Oven Fries: Coat sliced potatoes in one egg white that has been whipped lightly and mixed with 1 tablespoon Cajun seasoning and ½ teaspoon salt. Spread in one even layer on a nonstick cookie sheet that has been coated with pan spray. Bake at 450°F, stirring every 10 minutes, until they are golden brown on all sides.

Shoestring Root Vegetables: Make traditional French fries or oven fries using butternut squash, carrots, parsnips, turnips, beets, or yams instead of potatoes.

Kitchen Tips

Why fry potatoes twice? This technique is called *blanching*, and it is the secret to crispy fries. The first dip in the oil is to cook the potato through. The second is at a hotter temperature to brown them crisp. If you cooked them start to finish in the higher temperature, they would be underdone in the center.

Potato Pancakes

Latkes are potato pancakes made during Hanukah. Food is fried in oil to celebrate the Miracle of the Oil, in which a menorah with only enough oil for one day miraculously burned for eight. There are as many recipes for potato pancakes and latkes as there are potato lovers. Here's my favorite.

Serves 4
Prep time: 10 minutes
Cook time: 15 minutes

3 eggs

2 TB. all-purpose flour

½ tsp. salt

¼ tsp. pepper

2 large russet potatoes, peeled and grated

1 medium yellow onion, grated

2 TB. vegetable oil

2 TB. butter

1. In a large bowl, combine the eggs, flour, salt, and pepper, and mix well. Stir in the potatoes and onion, and mix to coat thoroughly.

2. Heat oil and butter in a large skillet, and drop in ½-cup-size patties of the potato mixture. Do not crowd patties in the pan. Fry until browned, about 3 minutes per side. Drain on paper towels, and repeat with remaining potatoes. Serve immediately, or keep warm in a 150°F oven. Top with sour cream and applesauce.

Straight Potatoes: Many potato pancakes are nothing but fried potatoes. No flour, no egg. Just a little salt. The key to frying straight potatoes is to make sure the oil and butter are very hot, and to grate the potatoes just before frying to retain all the starch.

Listen to Mom!

Potatoes oxidize, or turn gray, when exposed to air. The color does not affect the flavor, but it certainly affects the appeal. To prevent discoloration, many chefs soak potatoes in cold water. For potato pancakes, however, this is a bad idea. Soaking leaches out starch, which the grated potato needs if it's going to stick together. Your pancakes will be better if you grate the potatoes right before frying.

Dress It Up: Pommes Anna

In French, *pommes* are apples, but *pommes du terre* (apples of the ground) are potatoes. Confusing? Many chefs avoid the whole *pomme-pomme* issue by calling this dish potatoes Anna.

6 TB. butter, melted

3 large russet potatoes, peeled and sliced paper thin

Salt and pepper

Serves 6
Prep time: 30 minutes
Cook time: 60 minutes

1. Preheat oven to 375°F. Coat bottom of pan with 2 tablespoons melted butter. Arrange one layer of potatoes on the bottom of the pan in an overlapping spiral, covering the entire bottom of the pan. Brush with more melted butter, sprinkle lightly with salt and pepper, then arrange another layer. Repeat using all the potatoes, brushing melted butter and sprinkling salt and pepper between each layer.

2. Cover with foil and bake for 30 minutes. Uncover and continue baking until tender and golden, another 15 to 20 minutes. Cool for 5 minutes before inverting pan onto a serving platter. To serve, cut into wedges.

Anna and Onions: Alternate layers of potatoes with layers of thinly sliced yellow onions.

Pumpkin Anna: Replace the potatoes with thinly sliced pumpkin or butternut squash. These vegetables can also be layered alternately with potatoes. Add a sprinkle of nutmeg with the salt and pepper between the layers.

 Tidbits _____

You can spend lots of money on a nifty copper pan made exclusively for this dish. Both the fitted lid and the deeper pan itself have two handles. The finished potatoes are inverted into the lid, and can be served right from it.

Chapter 10

Oodles of Noodles

In This Chapter

- ◆ Using your noodle
- ◆ Cooking pasta to perfection
- ◆ Baked, creamy, and cheesy
- ◆ Delicious dumplings
- ◆ Timeless classics

We love everything that's starchy, gooey, warm, and filling. No wonder noodles are right up there near the top of everyone's comfort food list! Noodles are also inexpensive and easy to prepare. Noodles are the base of many other wonderful flavors, from the bland cheese and cream sauces we had as a kid, to spicy Thai noodle soups. What's not to love?

Ancient Noodles

Every culture has its own form of noodles. Speculation circulates around Marco Polo, Italy, Arabia, China, and who exactly had the first noodles. But recently 4,000-year-old noodles were unearthed at an archeological site in northwestern China, which places sophisticated noodle production in the Bronze Age. Let's give it up for the Xia Dynasty!

It's more likely that noodle making spontaneously evolved everywhere that people had grain and wanted to preserve it. By creating a gruel or paste, rolling it thin, cutting, and drying it, grain could be successfully stored for months. It was a perfect food for long trips (including those by ship, which would explain the Marco Polo connection).

Noodles are made of all kinds of grain, not simply the wheat variety we and our Italian brethren are accustomed to. The ancient Chinese noodles were made out of the high-protein über-grain *millet*. (In our infinite wisdom, we Americans use millet mainly as bird seed.) Noodles are made from rice flour, soy flour, buckwheat flour, potato flour, chickpea flour, mung bean flour, and even yams.

Cooking Pasta

Pasta, the Italian word for *paste*, is made from protein-rich *durham wheat*, which is too tough for regular bread, but perfect for making strong noodles. It is ground into a flour called semolina, which resembles a fine yellow cornmeal. (You can find it in fancy supermarkets and specialty gourmet stores.)

Much has been written about the proper way to cook pasta. It really isn't difficult. The key is to use plenty of boiling water. Choose a large pot that holds at least 5 quarts. Look for clever pasta pots with built-in colander inserts, which make draining the noodles a breeze.

To cook noodles, add them to the water when it hits a full, rolling boil. Stir them to get them moving independently of one another, then stir occasionally to be sure they aren't sticking together. Oil added to the pot of water does nothing to keep the pasta from sticking. It just floats on the surface of the water. But tossing in some oil or butter after the pasta is drained will keep them loose while the rest of the dish is prepared. Rinsing the pasta with cold water will stop the cooking process immediately. This is useful if you need to hold the pasta for a while. But if you are serving it right away, don't bother. It will only cool your pasta down.

All pasta and noodles should be cooked *al dente*. This Italian term means *to the tooth*, but it is often misinterpreted as meaning *crunchy*. Crunchy is not what we are looking for. The noodles should be cooked, but not mushy. They should offer just a little resistance to the bite, but not so much that they seem raw.

Italian or American?

Pasta has a long history in Italy, with more variations than you can count. Throughout Italy pasta dishes take many forms, showcasing local ingredients. But here in America, many of the dishes that we think of as Italian (spaghetti, pasta, and lasagna), are as American as apple pie. On our shores these foods look and taste drastically different than what you'd find in Italy. That's not to say one is better than the other. But we're talking comfort food here. Warm, gooey, cheesy comfort food. So if it is authentic Italian pasta recipes you're looking for, keep moving.

Baked pasta dishes were traditionally designed to use leftovers and less appealing cuts of meat. The meat would be cooked slowly to tenderize it, then shredded and chopped for incorporation into sauce Bolognese. Today, ground beef is the norm because it is more readily available.

No matter where they originate, we can all agree that pasta, noodles, and dumplings from all ends of the earth warm our hearts and tummies.

Mac and Cheese

Just because this classic kid favorite is most often made from elbow macaroni doesn't mean it has to be that way. Try using pasta shells (conchigli), bow ties (farfalle), curlicues (fusilli), or tubes (rigatoni or ziti).

Serves 4
Prep time: 30 minutes
Cook time: 30 minutes

1 lb. elbow macaroni

2 TB. olive oil

3 TB. butter

½ small yellow onion, diced

3 TB. all-purpose flour

2 cups milk

2 cups grated cheddar cheese

½ tsp. nutmeg

1 tsp. salt

½ tsp. pepper

1 cup bread or cracker crumbs

2 TB. butter

½ cup grated Parmesan cheese

1. Preheat oven to 350°F. Bring 2 quarts water and 1 teaspoon salt to a full rolling boil. Add macaroni, stir, and cook until half done, about 8 minutes. Drain and rinse with cold water. Add olive oil, stir to coat, and set aside.

2. Melt butter in a medium saucepan, add onion, and cook until golden brown. Add flour and stir until all the fat is absorbed. Slowly whisk in milk. Remove from heat and add cheddar cheese, stirring until melted. Mix in nutmeg, salt, pepper, and macaroni. Transfer to 9×13 casserole dish, top with bread-crumbs, dot with butter, and sprinkle with Parmesan cheese. Bake until golden brown and bubbly, about 30 minutes.

Mac and Sausage: Satisfy the hungriest members of the family by adding some meat to this dish. Dice 2 cups of precooked Polish sausage, Italian sausage, or ham, and fold it into the cheese sauce with the macaroni.

Cheeseburger Macaroni: Brown 1 pound of ground beef, drain excess fat, and fold it into the cheese sauce with the macaroni.

Kitchen Tips

Not everyone likes their macaroni baked, especially if they grew up eating the blue-box variety. If that's you, simply boil the macaroni until it's fully cooked, stir it into the cheese sauce, and serve.

Dress It Up: Truffle Mac

Truffles are an expensive delicacy. If you're in the mood to splurge, you can find them online at www.trufflefrance.com, or at gourmet grocery stores. Truffle oil is relatively inexpensive and easy to find at specialty grocers and some farmers' markets.

1 tsp. salt

1 lb. radiatori pasta

4 TB. truffle oil, divided

3 TB. butter

3 TB. all-purpose flour

2 cups milk

1 small yellow onion, quartered

1 bay leaf

1 whole clove

2 cups grated fontina cheese

1 tsp. salt

½ tsp. pepper

½ tsp. nutmeg

6 thin slices of black or white truffles (optional)

1 cup panko bread crumbs (coarse Japanese bread crumbs)

2 TB. truffle oil

1 tsp. dried thyme

Serves 6
Prep time: 30 minutes
Cook time: 30 minutes

1. Preheat oven to 350°F. Bring 2 quarts water and 1 teaspoon salt to a full rolling boil. Add pasta, stir, and cook until half done, about 8 minutes. Drain and rinse with cold water. Add 2 TB. truffle oil, stir to coat, and set aside.

2. Melt butter in a medium saucepan. Add flour and stir until all the fat is absorbed. Slowly whisk in milk. Add onion, bay leaf, and clove and cook, stirring, for 5 minutes until thickened. Remove from heat, and remove bay leaf, clove, and onion. Add fontina cheese, and stir until melted. Add pasta, salt, pepper, and nutmeg, stirring to combine.

3. Place a slice of truffle at the bottom of 6 individual ceramic, oven-proof bowls. Fill each bowl with cheesy pasta. In a small bowl combine bread crumbs, 2 TB. truffle oil, and thyme. Sprinkle mixture on top of each pasta bowl. Bake until golden brown and bubbly, about 30 minutes. Place each hot bowl on a napkin-lined plate and serve immediately.

 Tidbits

The clove in this recipe is not a garlic clove, but the dried spice clove. It is a classic ingredient in French béchamel sauce, which we have used here, enriched with cheese. The unique flavor combination of clove, bay leaf, and onion in this cream sauce is fantastic.

Fettuccini Alfredo

This recipe was created in the early twentieth century at Alfredo's Restaurant in Rome but was made famous by actors Douglas Fairbanks and Mary Pickford, who ate it on their honeymoon and raved about it back home in Hollywood.

Serves 4
Prep time: 30 minutes
Cook time: 30 minutes

1 tsp. salt

1 lb. fettuccini

4 TB. butter

2 cloves garlic, minced

3 cups heavy cream

1 cup grated Romano cheese

1 cup grated Parmesan cheese

1 egg yolk

1 TB. cold milk

1 tsp. salt

½ tsp. pepper

½ tsp. nutmeg

1. Bring 2 quarts water and 1 teaspoon salt to a full rolling boil. Add fettuccini, stir, and cook until al dente, 8 to 10 minutes. Drain and rinse with cold water.

2. Melt the butter in a large saucepan over high heat. Add garlic and cook until golden brown. Add cream and reduce by half. Add Romano and Parmesan cheeses and stir until melted.

3. In a separate bowl, whisk together egg yolk and milk, then add to the sauce. Reduce heat and cook, stirring continuously 3 to 5 minutes to warm and thicken. Add salt, pepper, and nutmeg. Add fettuccini and toss to coat. Serve pasta in large flat bowls, topped with more grated Parmesan cheese.

Dress It Up: Fettuccini Carbonara

Carbon is the Italian word for coal, and this dish is thought to have been named for Italian coal miners. Then again, some think the black pepper added at the end looks like charcoal ash. The recipe calls for pancetta, which is sweet, unsmoked bacon. It is often sold prepackaged in paper-thin slices, but if you can, ask the deli to slice it thick. Thicker slices are easier to dice and tastier to chew.

8 oz. pancetta, diced

1 lb. fettuccini

2 cups heavy cream

1 cup grated Parmesan cheese

4 eggs

1 tsp. each salt and freshly ground pepper

Serves 4
Prep time: 10 minutes
Cook time: 15 minutes

1. Cook the pancetta in a large saucepan until crisp, then remove from the heat and set aside.

2. Bring 2 quarts water and 1 teaspoon salt to a full rolling boil. Add fettuccini, stir, and cook until al dente, about 12 minutes. Drain.

3. Combine the cream, Parmesan cheese, and eggs in small bowl, whisk well, and add to pancetta. Add hot pasta and stir well to coat. Season with salt and pepper and serve immediately.

Listen to Mom!

Don't heat the sauce once the eggs go in, or you'll have fettuccini à la scrambled eggs!

Kugel

Historically, kugel was a baked pudding made from bread, potatoes, rice, or other grains. But in the United States, if someone says kugel, they mean noodle kugel by default.

Serves 4
Prep time: 30 minutes
Cook time: 50 minutes

1 (12-oz.) package wide egg noodles

2 cups cottage cheese

2 cups sour cream

1 cup sugar

5 eggs

4 oz. (1 stick) butter, melted

2 tsp. vanilla extract

½ tsp. nutmeg

¼ cup sugar

1 TB. cinnamon

1. Preheat oven to 350°F. Bring 2 quarts water and 1 teaspoon salt to a full rolling boil. Add noodles, stir, and cook until half done, about 5 minutes. Drain and rinse with cold water.

2. In a large bowl stir together the cottage cheese, sour cream, sugar, eggs, butter, vanilla, and nutmeg. Add the cooked noodles and mix well. Transfer to baking dish. In a small bowl, combine sugar and cinnamon, then sprinkle over the top of the kugel. Bake until the center is firm, about 45 minutes. Cool for 10 minutes before serving.

Spaetzle

The word literally means *little sparrow*, although it is more likely that the name of these little noodles is a Bavarian corruption of the Italian *spezzare*, which means *cut into pieces*.

1 cup all-purpose flour	¼ cup milk
1 tsp. salt	6 TB. butter
2 eggs	½ tsp. nutmeg
1 tsp. canola oil	Salt and pepper

<table>
<tr><td>Serves 4</td></tr>
<tr><td>Prep time: 60 minutes</td></tr>
<tr><td>Cook time: 30 minutes</td></tr>
</table>

1. In a large bowl combine flour and salt. In a separate bowl combine eggs, oil, and milk and gradually stir them into the dry ingredients. Beat until the dough is smooth and elastic, adding a little water if necessary. The consistency should be like a sticky paste. Cover and rest the dough for 30 to 60 minutes.

2. Melt butter in a large sauté pan, and let it cook 2 to 3 minutes, until it begins to brown. Remove from heat and set aside.

3. Bring 4 quarts water and 1 teaspoon salt to a full rolling boil. Press the spaetzle dough through a colander into the boiling water. Work in small batches. Boil until the spaetzle floats, 2 to 3 minutes, then transfer with slotted spoon to browned butter pan. Repeat with remaining dough. Warm spaetzle in brown butter, season with nutmeg, salt, and pepper, and serve.

Kitchen Tips

Spaetzle can be a bit tricky, but help is available. Visit www.aaltonet.com and order your very own Spätzle Hex spaetzle machine.

Lasagna

There is enough moisture and heat in the center of the lasagna to cook the noodles in the oven. So try this no-boil method and give yourself a break.

Serves 8
Prep time: 45 minutes
Cook time: 60 minutes

1 large yellow onion, diced

2–4 TB. olive oil

6 large cloves of garlic, minced

1 lb. ground beef

1 lb. Italian sausage (removed from casing if necessary)

3 TB. dried oregano

2 TB. dried basil

1 TB. dried crushed fennel seed

1 TB. dried sage

1 (29-oz.) can tomato sauce

1 (1-oz.) package lasagna noodles

1 lb. grated mozzarella cheese, divided into 4 portions

1 (15-oz.) package ricotta cheese (optional)

½ cup grated Parmesan cheese

1. Preheat oven to 350°F. In a large saucepan, sauté the onion in olive oil over high heat, stirring continuously until translucent. Add garlic and continue to stir until golden brown.

2. Add the ground beef and Italian sausage and cook until browned, about 15 minutes. Drain off excess fat. Add oregano, basil, fennel, sage, and tomato sauce, and stir to incorporate. Cook over low heat until the sauce is warmed through, about 5 minutes.

3. Cover the bottom of the lasagna pan with a thin layer of sauce to prevent the noodles from burning. Lay 3 uncooked lasagna noodles in the bottom of the pan, being careful not to overlap them too much. Break them into pieces if necessary to cover the bottom of the pan. Cover with ¼-inch of sauce. Add a generous handful of mozzarella cheese and 4 or 5 dollops of ricotta cheese. Cover the cheese with another layer of noodles as before. Repeat until you have several layers. Finish the layering with sauce, mozzarella cheese, and top with Parmesan cheese.

4. Cover and bake until the sauce is bubbly and the cheese is melted, about 45 minutes. Uncover the dish and cook another 10 minutes to brown the top. Serve immediately with a fresh green salad and some crusty Italian bread.

Tidbits

The tomato-based sauce in this recipe is based on the traditional Italian red sauce, *sauce Bolognese*, from the Bologna region of northern Italy. In Italy it is known as a *ragu*, and it is full of rich meats and vegetables.

Lasagna Florentine: Add a center layer of spinach sautéed in chopped garlic and olive oil. Use fresh spinach leaves or well-drained frozen chopped spinach.

Vegetarian Lasagna: The sauce can be made without the meat, or it can be beefed up (so to speak) with more vegetables, including chopped mushrooms, zucchini, eggplant, or artichokes, to name just a few. There are also several vegetable-based meat substitutes available that can be used in place of the meat in this recipe. Check the frozen foods aisle.

Cheesy Lasagna: Add up to 2 extra cups of mixed grated cheese with the mozzarella. Some of my favorites include Italian fontina, buffalo mozzarella, provolone, Muenster, or plain-old jack. Anything that melts well is welcome between the noodles.

Homemade Cheese Ravioli

This stuffed pasta can be dressed with any sauce you like, including marinara, pesto, alfredo, or, as I have here, simple browned butter.

Serves 8
Prep time: 60 minutes
Cook time: 30 minutes

1¾ cup semolina flour

3 eggs, divided

¼–½ cup water, as needed

1 cup ricotta cheese

½ cup grated mozzarella cheese

2 TB. grated Parmesan cheese

½ tsp. each salt and pepper

½ tsp. nutmeg

4 TB. butter

1. In a medium bowl, mix together semolina flour and 2 eggs. Add water slowly, and continue to stir until a firm dough is formed. Move dough to counter and knead for 3 to 5 minutes until smooth. Wrap and chill 30 minutes.

2. In a medium bowl, combine the ricotta, mozzarella, and Parmesan cheeses; 1 egg; salt; pepper; and nutmeg. Mix well and refrigerate. Divide dough into three portions, and run it through a pasta machine at the widest setting five to six times, until it holds together and is smooth. Continue to roll the dough through each consecutively smaller setting, one time each, until the dough is as thin as possible.

3. Lay each strip of dough out on a work surface dusted with semolina flour. Drop a teaspoon of cheese filling along the strip every 2 inches. Lightly moisten the dough around the strip with water, lay another strip of dough on top, and press the doughs together to seal in the filling. Use a cookie cutter or a fluted pastry wheel to trim the raviolis into circles or squares. Repeat with the remaining dough and filling. Dough scraps can be rerolled as necessary.

4. Melt the butter in a large sauté pan, and cook 2 to 3 minutes, until it begins to brown. Turn off the heat and set aside. Bring 2 quarts water and 1 teaspoon salt to a full rolling boil. Add ravioli in small batches and cook until they float, about 2 to 3 minutes. Transfer with a slotted spoon to the butter pan, and repeat with remaining ravioli. Warm in browned butter before serving.

Spaghetti and Meatballs

This dish has very little in common with traditional Italian food. Golf ball-size meatballs and thin tomato sauce is definitely an American original. We love it so much, we even sing camp songs about it.

1 egg

1 cup bread crumbs

1 lb. ground beef

1 lb. Italian sausage

1 TB. olive oil

1 small yellow onion, diced

3 cloves garlic, minced

1 TB. dried oregano

1 tsp. fennel seed

1 (15-oz.) can tomato sauce

1 tsp. salt

½ tsp. pepper

½ tsp. red pepper flakes, crushed

1 lb. spaghetti

2 TB. olive oil

1 cup grated Parmesan cheese

Serves 4

Prep time: 15 minutes

Cook time: 45 minutes

---

1. Preheat oven to 350°F. In a large bowl, place egg and bread crumbs and stir to combine. Add the beef and sausage, and mix well. Form into golf ball-size balls. Fry in a large skillet over medium heat, turning the meatballs periodically until they are browned on all sides. Transfer to 9×13 casserole dish.

2. In the same skillet heat olive oil, add onion, and cook over medium heat until translucent. Add garlic, oregano, and fennel, and cook until golden brown. Reduce heat, stir in tomato sauce, and cook for 5 minutes to warm through. Season with salt, pepper, and red pepper flakes, pour over meatballs, cover and bake until bubbly, about 30 minutes.

3. Bring 2 quarts water and 1 teaspoon salt to a full rolling boil. Add spaghetti, stir, and cook until al dente, about 12 minutes. Drain, add olive oil, stir to coat, and transfer to serving platter. Top with meatballs, red sauce, and Parmesan cheese. Serve immediately with a green salad and some crusty Italian bread.

Listen to Mom!

To keep them a uniform shape and to ensure even browning, don't crowd the meatballs in the skillet. And don't worry if your meatballs aren't perfectly round—no one's are!

Linguini and Clams

When buying live clams be sure that their shells are closed tightly. When you get them home, never cover them in ice or submerge them in tap water. They'll live quietly and happily in your fridge for a day or two wrapped loosely in paper. You can make this dish with canned clams, but it's not as much fun.

Serves 4
Prep time: 15 minutes
Cook time: 20 minutes

1 lb. linguini

3 TB. butter

4 cloves garlic, minced

1 (8-oz.) bottle clam juice

2 cups dry white wine

2 TB. lemon juice

24 littleneck clams, in closed shells, scrubbed

¼ cup fresh Italian flat leaf parsley, minced

1 cup Parmesan cheese

1 tsp. salt

½ tsp. pepper

½ tsp. red pepper flakes, crushed

1. Bring 2 quarts water and 1 teaspoon salt to a full rolling boil. Add linguini, stir, and cook until al dente, about 12 minutes. Drain and rinse with cold water.

2. Melt butter in a large saucepan. Add garlic and cook until golden brown. Add clam juice, white wine, lemon juice, and reduce by half. Add clams, cover and steam for 5 minutes, or until the shells open. Remove opened clams (discard unopened clams), cover and keep warm. Add linguini, parsley, Parmesan cheese, salt, and peppers to wine and clam liquid, and toss to coat. Serve pasta in large flat bowls, topped with opened clams.

Kitchen Tips

If you are unfamiliar with wine, look for a chablis, chenin blanc, sauvignon blanc, pinot grigio, or anything labeled white table wine. If you'd like to omit the wine completely, you can replace it with ½ cup of white wine vinegar and 1½ cups water.

11

Pot-Lucky: Casseroles with Heart

In This Chapter

- ◆ The appeal of the casserole
- ◆ Casserole bakeware
- ◆ One-dish tuna meals
- ◆ Green beans and baked beans
- ◆ Savory pies

Why is it that you rarely find a casserole on a restaurant menu? What are the chefs afraid of? Are casseroles too pedestrian? Too bourgeois? Oh, please! The fact is, casseroles have a long and illustrious history.

Classy Casseroles

The word *casserole* is French, and it means *stew pan*. The word has been a part of the English language for 400 years, referring to a recipe of meat, vegetables, and broth, cooked slowly in a covered dish. This method preserves and mingles the flavors of all the ingredients in a way that no quick-cooking method can. Casseroles are common all over the world, and dishes such as the Moroccan *tagine* have been satisfying hunger for centuries.

The popularity of the casserole is no mystery. These dishes provide a means to make the cheap, tough cuts of meat and poultry tender and flavorful, and they offer a disguise for leftovers. Throughout history's hard times these recipes provided an economical way to feed the family by stretching and making palatable what was on hand.

Chefspeak

The **tagine,** or tajine, is not only the name of the recipe, but also the cooking vessel. Stews of meat, vegetable, olives, preserved lemons, and spices are slow-cooked in these terra-cotta pots with the distinctive conical lid. The pot doubles as a serving dish, and is presented to the table, always accompanied by a dish of couscous.

Bakeware

The casserole, as we understand it today, sprang up in the United States in the 1950s popularized by women's magazines as a way to free up time, stretch a dollar, and use new oven-proof baking materials, like Corning Ware and Pyrex.

The names of these recipes vary from region to region, and in fact, in the northern regions of our country these recipes are known as *hotdish*. This region also refers to cream of mushroom soup as the Lutheran binder, don't ya know.

The recipes in this chapter call for the use of a 9×13 baking dish, which is the size of a standard casserole dish. The size is by no means mandatory, and whatever size and shape casserole dish you have is fine. If you don't have a casserole dish, any oven-proof container will do, covered with foil if necessary. It should hold 2 to 3 quarts, but if it's bigger or smaller, simply fill the dish accordingly. For easy serving and cleanup, I coat the dish lightly with nonstick spray before filling it.

Don't wait for the church potluck to try these comforting recipes. They are easy and fun, and guaranteed to bring a smile to the table.

Tuna Noodle Casserole

There are hundreds of variations to this classic casserole. You can use different soups, different vegetables, or different crunchy elements on top, like potato chips, cornflakes, or breadcrumbs. Use what you've got. If casseroles represent anything, it's how to make do.

1 (12-oz.) package egg noodles

1 (12-oz.) can of tuna, undrained

1 (10¾-oz.) can cream of mushroom soup

1 cup milk

2 cups frozen peas

1 cup grated cheddar cheese

1 cup crushed saltine crackers

¼ cup grated Parmesan cheese

Serves 4	
Prep time: 20 minutes	
Cook time: 30 minutes	

1. Preheat oven to 350°F. Bring 2 quarts water and ½ teaspoon salt to a boil over high heat. Add the noodles, stir, and cook until tender. Drain and rinse with cold water to stop the cooking.

2. In a casserole dish, combine tuna, soup, milk, frozen peas, cheddar cheese, and cooked noodles. Stir to combine, cover with crushed crackers and Parmesan cheese. Bake until bubbly and golden brown, about 30 minutes.

Noodle Switch: Replace the noodles with elbow macaroni, shells, bow ties, a box of macaroni and cheese (made as directed), or cooked rice.

Make It Moist: Replace half the milk with sour cream or mayonnaise.

Dress It Up: Mediterranean Baked Tuna

Tuna is plentiful in the Mediterranean Sea. This dish highlights other common foods of the region, too, which are abundant and commonly used together in the cuisines of Provençe, Spain, Portugal, and Italy.

Serves 4
Prep time: 45 minutes
Cook time: 30 minutes

1 (12-oz.) package whole-wheat penne pasta

½ cup olive oil, divided

4 shallots, chopped

4 cloves garlic, chopped

1 TB. herbes de Provençe

2 cups dry white wine

8 oz. fresh ahi or yellow fin tuna

2 large tomatoes, chopped

½ cup oil-packed sun-dried tomatoes, chopped

1 (9-oz.) package frozen artichoke hearts, thawed and sliced

2 red bell peppers, roasted and chopped

¼ cup Spanish olives

½ cup freshly grated Parmesan or Romano cheese

4–6 (½-inch) slices of good, crusty French or Italian bread

2 cups Gruyere cheese, grated

1. Preheat oven to 350°F. Bring 2 quarts water and ½ teaspoon salt to a boil over high heat. Add the pasta, stir, and cook until tender. Drain and rinse with cold water to stop the cooking. Transfer the pasta to a large bowl, add 2 tablespoons of olive oil, stir to coat, and set aside.

2. Sauté shallots in 2 tablespoons olive oil over high heat until translucent. Add the garlic and herbes de Provençe and sauté until lightly brown. Deglaze with white wine, add tuna, reduce heat, cover and simmer until the tuna is slightly firm, about 10 minutes. Cool, flake tuna apart, and set aside.

3. To the tuna cooking liquid, add the tomatoes, sun-dried tomatoes, artichokes, roasted red peppers, and olives and simmer for 5 minutes. Remove from heat and combine with pasta and tuna. Stir in the Parmesan or Romano cheese and transfer the mixture to a 9×13 baking dish. Brush bread slices with olive oil, place on top of casserole, and top with grated Gruyere cheese. Bake until golden brown and bubbly, about 30 minutes.

Green Bean Casserole

There's a reason this dish sits on every Thanksgiving church pot-luck table in America. It's easy and delicious. And to top it off, it's a surprisingly successful way to get your kids to eat their veggies.

1 (10¾-oz.) can cream of mushroom soup

½ cup milk

4 cups green beans, fresh, frozen, or canned

1⅓ cups french-fried onions

Serves 4
Prep time: 10 minutes
Cook time: 35 minutes

1. Preheat oven to 350°F. In a 9×13 casserole dish, whisk together soup and milk until smooth. Add beans and half the onions and mix to combine.

2. Bake for 25 minutes until bubbly. Sprinkle remaining onions on top and return to the oven for 10 more minutes to brown the top. Serve immediately.

Dress It Up: Haricot Vert with Bacon and Pecans

Haricot vert are tender, thin French green beans. They are available seasonally, but can be replaced with any green bean—or for that matter, asparagus, broccoli, and even zucchini. The trick is not to overcook the vegetables. They easily turn mushy and lose their flavor if overcooked.

Serves 6
Prep time: 10 minutes
Cook time: 10 minutes

3 lb. haricot vert	2 TB. fresh thyme, minced
6 slices bacon, diced	Salt and pepper
2 TB. butter	¼ cup red wine vinegar
2 shallots, minced	1 cup pecans, toasted and chopped

1. Bring 2 quarts water and ½ teaspoon salt to a boil. Add beans and cook for 5 minutes, stirring occasionally. At the 5-minute mark they should be bright green and still a little crunchy (al dente). Immediately drain and drop into a quart of ice water to stop the cooking.

2. Brown the diced bacon and pour off excess fat. Add the butter, shallots, and thyme and cook until golden. Season with salt and pepper. Deglaze with vinegar and reduce by half. Drain the green beans and add to pan, stirring to combine. Top with pecans and serve immediately.

Boston Baked Beans

Baked beans have a long history in New England. Native Iroquois, Penobscot, and Narraganset tribes ate similar dishes of slow-cooked beans flavored with maple syrup and bear fat. Since bear fat is hard to come by these days, use bacon.

½ lb. bacon, diced

1 large yellow onion, diced

2 (15-oz.) cans great north-ern beans

2 (15-oz.) cans pork and beans

2 TB. molasses

1 cup ketchup

1 cup hickory barbecue sauce

Serves 8	
Prep time: 15 minutes	
Cook time: 45 minutes	

1. Preheat oven to 350°F. Sauté the bacon and onion together until crispy.

2. Remove from heat and drain off excess fat. Stir in beans, molasses, ketchup, and barbecue sauce. Transfer to a 9×13 casserole dish and bake, covered with a lid or foil, for 45 minutes. Uncover for the last 10 minutes to brown the top.

Dress It Up: Cassoulet Toulousain

The great-grandmother of all baked beans, the name refers to the individual ceramic baking dish used for both baking and serving. Recipes vary from region to region in France, but it is thought to have originated in the southern Languedoc region, where it combines white beans with aromatic vegetables and a variety of slow-cooked meats.

Serves 6
Prep time: 2 hours, plus a 12-hour bean soak
Cook time: 3 hours

1 lb. dried white beans, soaked overnight in cold water and then rinsed

1 bouquet garni (bay leaf, parsley, thyme, peppercorn, clove)

1 large yellow onion, diced

4 large tomatoes, diced

1 leek, chopped

6 cloves garlic, minced

Salt and pepper

1 lb. bacon, diced

1 lb. garlic sausage (preferably spicy sausage from Toulouse)

1 lb. lamb shoulder or breast, diced for stew

2 cups white wine

2 lb. duck or goose confit

2 cups bread crumbs

2 TB. butter

1. Combine soaked beans, bouquet garni, onion, tomatoes, leek, and garlic in a large pot. Cover with water and bring to a boil. At the boil, reduce heat to a simmer, cover partially, and cook until beans are tender, about 2 hours. Check periodically to be sure that there is plenty of water. When beans are tender remove from heat and drain, reserving 2 cups cooking liquid. Season the beans with salt and pepper and set aside.

2. Preheat oven to 300°F. Sauté the bacon, sausage, and lamb. Pour off any excess fat, and deglaze with 2 cups white wine. Cook, stirring, until reduced to ½ cup. Remove from heat.

3. Spread a layer of beans 1 inch thick in the bottom of a 9×13 casserole dish. Top with a layer of browned meat, and a few pieces of confit. Repeat the layering, finishing with a layer of beans on the top. Cover with a lid or foil and bake for 3 hours. Check the cassoulet periodically. If it looks dry, pour a little reserved bean liquid on top. During the last 30 minutes of baking, remove the lid or foil, top the cassoulet with bread crumbs, dot with butter, and cook uncovered until golden brown.

Tamale Pie

As with all home-cooked meals, there is more than one right way to make this dish. The cornmeal crust can be pressed around the dish like an actual pie shell, spread on top like a cobbler, or both, completely encasing the filling. I have also seen corn chips as a bottom crust, or crushed on top, like the crackers of a tuna casserole.

2 TB. vegetable oil

1 medium yellow onion, diced

1 lb. ground beef

1 TB. ground cumin

1 TB. red chili powder

1 TB. dried oregano

1 (15-oz.) can of corn, drained

1 (2¼-oz.) can sliced black olives

1 (14½-oz.) can diced tomatoes

1 (10-oz.) can enchilada or taco sauce

3 cups boiling water

½ tsp. each salt and pepper

1 cup cornmeal

1 cup cold water

Salt and pepper

2 cups grated cheddar cheese

4 TB. butter

Serves 6–8
Prep time: 30 minutes
Cook time: 30 minutes

1. Preheat oven to 350°F. Sauté onions in oil over high heat until translucent. Add ground beef, cumin, chili powder, and oregano and cook until browned. Remove from heat, pour off excess fat, and transfer to 9×13 casserole dish. Stir in corn, olives, tomatoes, and enchilada sauce, and set aside while you make the crust.

2. Bring 3 cups of water to a boil and add salt and pepper. In a small bowl combine the cornmeal and cold water, stirring to combine. When the water is at a full rolling boil, add the cornmeal paste. Stir continuously until thickened, 5-10 minutes. Remove from heat, season with salt and pepper, stir in cheese, and immediately spread evenly over casserole. Dot with butter and bake until golden and bubbly, about 30 minutes. Serve with a dollop of sour cream on top.

Meaty Pie: Add shredded pork, lamb, chicken, or turkey in place of the ground beef.

Spicy Pie: Add a can of green chilies, jalapeños, or a pinch or two of cayenne pepper. You can also search out spicier taco or enchilada sauces.

 Tidbits

Do not confuse this dish with Frito Pie, which is a vastly different recipe, consisting of Velveeta cheese, Rotel diced tomatoes, canned chili con carne, and corn chips, all baked together like nachos. Yee haw!

Chicken Pot Pie

Like all good casseroles, this one began as a way to use leftovers. The entire dish can be made with canned ingredients, but there is nothing like the real thing, made with last night's bird and a good pie dough. For special occasions, try cooking your pot pies in individual dishes.

Serves 6
Prep time: 30 minutes
Cook time: 30 minutes

4 TB. unsalted butter

1 medium yellow onion, diced

2 stalks celery, chopped

1 large carrot, chopped

1 tsp. dried thyme

1 tsp. dried sage

1 tsp. dried oregano

4 TB. all-purpose flour

2 cups milk

1–2 cups chicken broth

2 cups cooked chicken meat, chopped or shredded

1 large baking potato, peeled and diced

1 cup green peas, fresh or frozen

1 cup corn, fresh or frozen

Salt and pepper

2 cups grated cheddar cheese

Pie dough or biscuit dough (see following variations)

1 egg yolk

2 TB. cream

Pinch salt

1 cup Parmesan cheese

1. Preheat oven to 375°F. Sauté onion, celery, carrot, thyme, sage, and oregano in butter until translucent, about 5 minutes. Add flour and stir until it absorbs all the butter and begins to brown. Slowly add milk, ¼ cup at a time, stirring constantly. As each addition is absorbed by the roux, add more. When the milk is all in, add broth in the same manner, until a thick-soup consistency is reached. Remove from heat.

2. Off the heat, add the chicken, potato, peas, and corn. Stir well to combine, season with salt and pepper, and transfer to a 9×13 casserole dish. Sprinkle with cheddar cheese and top with pastry dough. Combine yolk, cream, and salt and brush lightly on the top of the dough. Sprinkle with the Parmesan cheese and bake until brown and bubbly, about 30 minutes.

Biscuit Pot Pie: Use prepared biscuit dough biscuit mix, or follow my Basic Pie Dough recipe in Chapter 14. You can also make it a little more interesting by adding some cheese or herbs to the dough.

Pie Dough: For a pot pie that lives up to its name, buy frozen pie dough in flat rounds or in shells, or make it from scratch (see Chapter 14 for a basic pie dough recipe). Jazz it up by adding savory herbs, spices, or cheese.

Puff Pastry: For an elegant alternative to the standard pot pie, use puff pastry as the crust. There are several quality frozen brands on the market. Be sure to defrost it completely before unwrapping it or the butter-rich dough will crack into pieces.

Listen to Mom!

The amount of liquid a roux will hold varies tremendously, especially if there are vegetables added. The moisture in the vegetables depends on the size they are chopped, the degree they are cooked, and how much water is retained after washing. The flour and butter play a role, too. Different brands and styles of flour absorb differently, and all butter brands retain a different percentage of water. So use your eye, and don't be afraid to add more or less liquid than a recipe calls for.

Shepherd's Pie

This is British peasant food, designed to utilize tough old mutton. Technically, this casserole can only be called shepherd's pie if it is made from mutton. But in the United States, we usually make it with ground beef because we are not big lamb eaters or big lamb farmers. (We're cowboys.) The Brits make a beef version across the pond, known fondly as cottage pie.

Serves 6–8
Prep time: 45 minutes
Cook time: 30 minutes

5 large potatoes, peeled

½ cup cream

2 large eggs

4 oz. (one stick) butter, divided

1 large yellow onion, diced

1 stalk celery, chopped

2 large carrots, chopped

1 lb. ground lamb or beef

1 tsp. Worcestershire sauce

1 cup frozen peas

1 (14½-oz.) can diced tomatoes, drained

Salt and pepper

1. Preheat oven to 350°F. Boil potatoes in a large saucepan until tender. Drain and spread out on a cookie sheet to dry and cool. Mash the cooled potatoes and combine them in a bowl with cream, eggs, and 4 tablespoons butter. Mix well and set aside.

2. Sauté onion, celery, and carrots in 2 tablespoons butter over high heat until tender. Add meat and brown. Drain off any excess fat. Remove from heat and add Worcestershire, peas, and tomatoes, and season with salt and pepper.

3. Pour the meat mixture into a 9×13 casserole dish and spread evenly. Top with an even layer of mashed potatoes. Dot the potatoes with remaining butter and bake until brown and bubbly, about 30 minutes.

Listen to Mom!

Mashing potatoes is not hard, but it can be done wrong. The potato is full of starch, and the more it is beaten, the more starch is released. When this happens, the mash becomes gluey. The best method is to force them through a ricer or sieve first, then gently stir in the butter and cream. A hand masher or fork is the next best tool. Anything electric, especially a food processor, is much too rough, and will turn your mash into impeccably seasoned wallpaper paste.

12

Fire Up the 'Q

In This Chapter

- ◆ Barbecue and grill basics
- ◆ Grilling beef and chicken
- ◆ Mouthwatering marinades and rubs
- ◆ Old and new favorites cooked on the grill
- ◆ Vegetable accompaniments

All over the world people cook meat over open flames. Fast or slow, in or out of sauces or marinades, it's a tradition everyone loves. *Satay*, *tandoor*, *teriyaki*, *jerk*, and *bulgogi* are all forms of BBQ. And across America we are very particular about our barbecue. Your state of origin has much to do with your opinion of the barbecue, and the meat you eat off it. Throughout the Deep South, pork is king. In Alabama, it's hickory smoked. In Memphis, it's pulled. In Texas, beef brisket rules. Sauces can be chili based, tomato based, sweet, spicy, thick, or thin. Everyone has a favorite.

Barbecue or Grill?

The term *barbecue* most likely originated from the West Indian *barbacoa*, a method in which meat was preserved by drying over smoky fires to keep the bugs off.

The term *barbecue* today is used and misused to mean anything cooked over a fire, on a grill. But barbecue is traditionally a very slow, smoky cooking method, designed to tenderize lesser cuts of meat. In colonial America the wild boar was barbecued to make its tough stringy meat edible. In the Southern states hog farming became widespread because the animal required relatively little care. Wild hogs gave way to well-fed, plumped-up pigs, which is still the barbecued meat of choice in the South. Farther west, cowboys on cattle drives slow-cooked tough cuts of beef. In Texas the term *barbecue* still means beef by default, usually brisket.

The common thread, regardless of meat, is the slow smoking heat. A hamburger or steak cooked on a barbecue is not, by definition, barbecuing. Just because you cook outdoors does not mean it's a barbecue. Cooking meat and other foods over an open flame is defined as grilling. The grilling method is designed for tender meats that do not contain fibrous connective tissue and stringy muscle.

Choose Your Meat Wisely

Certain kinds and cuts of meat do better when cooked long and slow. In general, older animals such as hens, roosters, and mutton have tougher meat, and require slow cooking to break down tough connective tissues and melt marbled fat. All animals have tough meat in the muscle groups that get a lot of movement, like legs, shoulders, and breast.

Young animals and meat with little fat do better cooked quickly at high temperature. Chicken, veal, fish, and beef steaks from the animal's back (rib and loin cuts) are a few examples. There are no strings of cartilage, no tough connective tissue, no fat that needs to melt and soften. The high heat of a grill, like that of a frying pan, can cook the meat quickly, searing in the juices while adding a distinctive carbonized flavor.

Grilling Beef

There is nothing like a great grilled steak. Every person has his or her preference, and many a steak house has flourished catering to each and every one of them. I like mine very rare, with just a little salt. Other members of my family (who shall remain nameless) cook it to death. Death! Some like a good steak sauce. Others concoct their own blend of barbecue sauce, horseradish, and other never-to-be-revealed secret ingredients. The French are fond of melting a nice pat of herb-infused butter over their steaks. What's better than that?

Beef is readily available in American supermarkets, and for the most part, quality is high. The United States Department of Agriculture (USDA) grades the meat for consumption based on muscle-to-bone and fat-to-muscle ratios. The grades, from best to worse, are *Prime*, *Choice* and *Select*. Lesser grades, used mainly for processed meat products, include *Standard*, *Commercial*, and *Utility*. Grades are stamped in purple on the outer carcass of the animal, and are usually prominently advertised by retailers, especially if the grade is high.

Beef cows are taken to market between 18 and 24 months of age. Before that time, it is either veal or baby beef. These tender meats do well prepared quickly over a hot flame. As the beef matures past 2 years, it must be cooked in slow moist heat (like braising and stewing) to render it palatable. The age of beef is easily determined by the color of the muscle. Young beef is pink, and it gets darker with age, maturing to a dark purple-red.

The most popular grilled beef, by far, is hamburger. Known in bygone eras as hamburger steak, or Hamburg beefsteak, the preparation was probably brought to the United States by German immigrants. It was a common practice to utilize lesser cuts of beef by grinding, shredding, and salting it before cooking. Often the meat was stretched with the addition of onions and bread crumbs.

Tidbits

The Hamburger Hall of Fame in Seymour, Wisconsin, claims to have created the first hamburger at the Outagamie County Fair in 1885. Similar claims have been made by Tulsa, Oklahoma; Akron, Ohio; Newhaven, Connecticut; and the St. Louis World's Fair of 1904. (That fair, incidentally, is the apocryphal origin of many foods, including the ice cream cone, iced tea, hot dogs, cotton candy, and Dr. Pepper. While these claims are mostly myth, these foods certainly gained wide popularity after their appearance at the fair.)

Grilling Chicken

Chicken is the trickiest food to cook on a grill because there is no such thing as rare, medium, or well done. The bird is either cooked or raw—and unlike eating rare beef, eating undercooked chicken presents a significant health hazard (see the following sidebar). If your grill experience revolves mainly around hamburger, you'll find that chicken requires more time and attention.

While grilling is by definition a high-heat method, the heat should be substantially lower when cooking chicken. Lower heat will prevent the skin and outer flesh from charring. Gas grills should be turned down to low, and charcoal briquettes should be pushed to one side, creating clearly defined hot and cool spots on the grill.

To help ensure that the chicken cooks evenly, cut the pieces into uniform sizes. A bird will yield eight pieces: two wings, two thighs, two legs, and two breasts. But for grilling, I find the breasts (and sometimes the thighs) take longer to cook than everything else. For that reason, I cut these larger pieces in half crosswise using a large chef knife. Focus the pressure on the rear of the blade to cut through the bone.

Listen to Mom!

Raw chicken is the perfect home for bacteria. Rinse your bird well, and thoroughly clean and sanitize all surfaces that came into contact with the raw meat before they are used for anything else. Chicken should be cooked until the meat is no longer pink. An instant-read thermometer inserted into the largest piece (usually the thigh) must read at least 180°F.

Flavorings

Marinades were historically used as a method of tenderizing tough meat, but modern cookery uses them mainly as a means of adding flavor. All marinades contain spice for interest and acid for tenderizing, which vary from region to region. In general, the longer you can marinade your meat, the better it will be. The same is true for dry spice rubs. However, take care with marinades that contain a high proportion of acid. Acid will cook meat thoroughly if left on too long. Pure vinegar and juices such as lemon, lime, or pineapple should not be left more than an hour on chicken or fish. Beef can take it a little longer, and tough cuts will benefit from the tenderizing acids.

The same cut of meat becomes culturally representative when saturated with indigenous flavors. Asian marinades contain rice vinegar, sesame oil or seeds, and soy sauce. Indian mixes include curries and yogurt. Europeans utilize wine and herbs, while those from the Caribbean and Central and South America slather on the chiles, lime juice, and tropical fruits.

The Hamburger

The hamburger as we know it today is quintessentially American. The hamburger bun is said to have originated at White Castle, the first fast-food restaurant chain.

2 lbs. ground beef (85–90 percent lean)

Salt and pepper

6 large hamburger buns, toasted

Assorted toppings:

Cheese slices

1 medium purple onion, sliced and soaked in cold water for 15–30 minutes

1 ripe beefsteak tomato, sliced

6–8 large leaves iceberg lettuce, washed and dried

Pickles

Ketchup, mustard, mayonnaise, Thousand Island dressing

Serves 6
Prep time: 30 minutes
Cook time: 15 minutes

1. Divide hamburger into six equal portions. Work the meat in your hand, patting out the air and compacting the meat. Form into ½-inch thick discs and make a hole in the center of each disc with your finger. This hole will keep the patty from puffing up into a ball on the grill.

2. Preheat the grill for 5 to 10 minutes with the lid on. Place the burgers on the hot grill and cook 2 to 3 minutes with the lid on. Open the lid, flip burgers, and cook another 2 to 3 minutes, or to desired doneness. If the burgers do not come off the grill easily for the first flip, close the lid and cook another minute. For a cheeseburger add a slice of cheese to the top of the burger during the last minute of cooking and close the lid. Season with salt and pepper, and serve on toasted buns, and let your guests top them any way they like!

Kitchen Tips

Never press the burger onto the grill with your spatula. It pushes all the yummy burger juice out. Shutting the lid on your barbecue cooks the meat more evenly.

Barbecued Chicken

There are two tricks to good barbecued chicken. The first is to leave the sauce off until the last minute. If it goes on too soon it will burn. The second is to take your time. Don't rush it. An hour or more at low temperature yields better chicken than 30 minutes of rearranging and fussing.

Serves 4
Prep time: 10 minutes
Cook time: 60 minutes

1 (3–4-lb.) chicken, skin on, cut into serving pieces

¼ cup olive oil

1 tsp. salt

1 tsp. red pepper flakes

2 tsp. pepper

2 TB. dried thyme

2 cups barbecue sauce, divided

1. Preheat grill on high heat. Rub chicken with oil. Combine salt, red pepper flakes, pepper, and thyme and rub onto chicken.

2. Grill skin side down over direct high heat for 5 minutes with the lid down. Reduce heat to low, flip chicken over, and move off direct heat. Close cover and cook for 40 to 45 minutes, basting with olive oil every 10 minutes as needed. During the last 10 minutes of cooking, brush with barbecue sauce. Serve hot with extra barbecue sauce.

Listen to Mom!

Throw out the basting oil and barbecue sauce when you're done cooking. It has likely been cross-contaminated with bacteria from raw chicken. Use new barbecue sauce to serve on the side.

Lemon-Herb Marinated Chicken

1 (3–4-lb.) chicken, skin on, cut into serving pieces

¼ cup plus ¼–½ cup olive oil

Zest and juice of 1 lemon

1 tsp. salt

½ tsp. pepper

½ tsp. paprika

2 TB. chopped fresh thyme (or 2 tsp. dried)

2 TB. chopped fresh rosemary (or 2 tsp. dried)

2 TB. chopped fresh tarragon (or 2 tsp. dried)

4 scallions, chopped

4 cloves garlic, chopped

Serves 4
Prep time: 30 minutes (plus 1 hour to overnight for refrigeration)
Cook time: 60 minutes

1. Rub chicken with ¼ cup oil. In a small bowl, combine the remaining ingredients. Place chicken in a large zipper bag and add marinade. Zip it tight and massage marinade into the chicken. Refrigerate for 1 hour or overnight.

2. Preheat grill on high heat. Grill skin side down over direct high heat for 5 minutes with the lid down. Reduce heat to low, flip chicken over, and move off direct heat. Close cover and cook for 45 to 60 minutes, basting with marinade every 10 minutes as needed.

Southwestern Marinade: Combine zest and juice of one lime, ¼ cup tequila, one diced jalapeño, one bunch chopped cilantro, four cloves chopped garlic, 1 tablespoon of cumin, and salt and pepper. Marinade and cook as above.

Jerk Chicken: Combine ¼ cup soy sauce; ¾ cup rice vinegar; ½ cup each orange juice and lime juice; 1 tablespoon each brown sugar, allspice, thyme, cayenne, and black pepper; 1 teaspoon each of sage, nutmeg, cinnamon, cumin, and garlic powder; and 1 chopped scotch bonnet or jalapeño chile pepper. Marinade and cook as above.

Baby-Back Ribs

The best ribs are cooked long and slow. If you have time, slow it down. It'll be worth the wait. Don't forget extra napkins!

Serves 4

Prep time: 15 minutes
(plus 1 hour to overnight
for refrigeration)

Cook time: 60 minutes

½ cup brown sugar

2 TB. salt

½ tsp. pepper

1 TB. chili powder

1 tsp. dried thyme

½ tsp. cayenne pepper

½ tsp. garlic salt

½ tsp. onion powder

2 racks baby-back ribs

2–4 cups of your favorite
barbecue sauce

1. In a small bowl, combine brown sugar, salt, pepper, chili powder, thyme, cayenne pepper, garlic salt, and onion powder. Mix
   well, and rub evenly onto rib slabs. Cover and refrigerate for 1
   hour or overnight.

2. Preheat grill on high heat. Grill over indirect low heat for 30
   minutes with the lid down. Flip ribs over and cook another
   30 minutes. Turn ribs, baste with barbecue sauce, and cook
   another 30 minutes with the lid open until tender. To serve,
   transfer rack to cutting board and separate ribs.

Braised Ribs: After marinating ribs in dry rub, set in a covered baking dish with 1 inch of water. Cover and braise in a 250°F oven for
2 to 3 hours until tender. Finish on a hot grill, for 8 to 10 minutes
per side, basted with barbecue sauce.

Dress It Up: Homemade Barbecue Sauce

This is just one of thousands of barbecue sauce recipes out there. Play around with it and adjust it to your personal taste. See the variations for some additional ideas.

1½ cup ketchup	1 TB. Worcestershire sauce
1½ cup coffee	1 TB. chili powder
1 cup red wine vinegar	1 TB. pepper
½ cup brown sugar	1 TB. garlic salt
½ cup molasses	

Makes 5 cups of sauce
Prep time: 10 minutes
Cook time: 30 minutes

1. Combine all ingredients in a medium saucepan and bring to a boil over high heat. Reduce and simmer for 30 minutes on low, stirring.

2. Cool and store in the refrigerator.

Smoky Sauce: Add 2 to 3 teaspoons of liquid smoke.

Spicy Sauce: Add 1 to 4 tablespoons hot pepper sauce and 1 tablespoon cayenne pepper.

Honey-Mustard Sauce: Replace the brown sugar with 2¼ cup honey and add ½ cup mustard.

Carne Asada

The name means *roasted meat*, and it refers to lime-marinated steak, grilled over an open fire. While Mexican carne asada traditionally uses tougher cuts of flank or skirt steak, the dish works really well with well-marbled chuck and round steaks.

Serves 4–6
Prep time: 30 minutes (plus 4 hours to overnight for refrigeration)
Cook time: 30 minutes

1 bunch cilantro, chopped

5 cloves garlic, chopped

1 bunch green onions, chopped

1–3 jalapeño chilies, chopped

1 TB. ground cumin

1 tsp. pepper

¼ cup white wine vinegar

2 cups olive oil

Zest and juice of 6 limes

Zest and juice of 1 orange

1 can or bottle of beer

2–3-lb. beef skirt, flank, or chuck steaks

1. In a large bowl, combine cilantro, garlic, onions, jalapeños, cumin, and pepper. Stir well and add white wine vinegar, oil, zest and juice of limes and orange, and beer. Submerge the steaks in marinade. Cover and refrigerate 4 hours or overnight.

2. Preheat grill on high heat. Grill over direct high heat for 5 minutes with the lid down. Reduce heat to low, flip meat over, and move off direct heat. Close cover and cook for 10 minutes. Flip the meat and cook with the lid open to desired doneness, 5 to 10 minutes. Remove from grill. Cover with foil and let rest 5 minutes. Slice thin strips against the grain and serve with warm tortillas, salsa fresca, guacamole, and sour cream.

Kitchen Tips

There is nothing like homemade salsa fresca. In a large bowl, combine four chopped ripe tomatoes, one bunch chopped cilantro, one small diced red onion, three chopped scallions, three cloves minced garlic, one to three minced fresh chile peppers (try, from hottest to mildest, serrano, jalapeño, Poblano, Anaheim), 2 tablespoons ground cumin, salt and pepper to taste, ¼ cup olive oil, and the juice of three to five limes. Mix and marinate for 1 to 4 hours. Other additions include diced cucumber, jicama, avocado, oranges, melon, and papaya.

A Juicy T-Bone Steak

The T-bone is a supersize cut that combines the filet and strip steaks. You can use these same instructions for other steaks, too. To get it just the way you want, use an instant-read thermometer to test internal temperatures. Cook the meat to 102°F for rare, 125°F for medium rare, and 130°F for medium.

2 T-bone steaks   **Salt and pepper**

1. Remove the steaks from refrigeration 1 hour before grilling. Preheat grill on high heat. Sprinkle both sides of the meat with salt and pepper.

2. Grill over direct high heat for 5 minutes with the lid open. Flip meat over and cook for another 3 minutes for rare, 5 minutes for medium. Remove the meat from grill, cover with foil, and let rest 5 minutes. Serve with green salad and a warm baked potato with all the fixin's.

Serves 2
Prep time: 5 minutes
Cook time: 15 minutes

Shish Kebab

The name means *skewer of roasted meat*, and similar dishes are found throughout eastern Europe, the Middle East, and Asia. Both metal and wooden skewers work fine, but be sure to soak wooden ones in warm water for at least 30 minutes to prevent them from burning.

Serves 4
Prep time: 10 minutes (plus 1 hour to overnight for refrigeration)
Cook time: 30 minutes

1 bottle red wine

2 TB. plus ½ cup olive oil

1 TB. Worcestershire sauce

1 TB. red wine vinegar

1 TB. dried thyme

1 tsp. salt

2 lbs. beef top round, top sirloin, or lamb shoulder, cut into 2-inch cubes

12 skewers

1 pint cherry tomatoes

8 oz. small button mushrooms

2 small zucchini, sliced into 2-inch wheels

2 small Chinese eggplant, sliced into 2-inch wheels

1 large yellow onion, quartered

1. Mix together wine, 2 TB. olive oil, Worcestershire, red wine vinegar, thyme, and salt. Place cubed meat in a large zipper bag and add marinade. Zip it tight and massage marinade into the beef. Refrigerate for 1 hour or overnight.

2. Preheat grill on high heat. Skewer the meat together, separately from the vegetables, to ensure even cooking. Skewer the vegetables and brush with olive oil. Grill kebabs over direct high heat for 5 to 10 minutes, turning frequently to brown evenly. Grill vegetables off direct heat, turning frequently until they are golden brown, about 10 minutes. Remove meat and vegetables from skewers onto platters. Serve with rice.

Grilled Pizza

What could be better than two of America's favorites combined into one? If you've never grilled a pizza before, you're in for a treat. The high, smoky heat makes a lovely, crisp crust.

2 pkg. rapid-rise yeast

2 cups warm water

¼ cup olive oil

2 TB. honey

5–6 cups all-purpose flour

½ cup olive oil

Optional toppings:

3 cups tomato sauce

Shredded mozzarella cheese

Sliced pepperoni

Cooked sausage

Sliced mushrooms

Sliced olives

Sliced onions

Anchovies

Serves 4
Prep time: 90 minutes
Cook time: 15 minutes

1. In a large bowl combine yeast, water, oil, and honey. Mix well, then add flour slowly, until a firm dough is formed. Knead on a floured countertop for 5 to 8 minutes until smooth and elastic. Return to bowl, cover, and set aside to double in volume, about 1 hour. Meanwhile, prepare toppings.

2. Preheat grill on high heat. Divide dough into four pieces, and stretch or roll each one out into a thin flat disc. Brush dough with olive oil and lay it directly on the grill. Cook over high heat for 2 to 3 minutes, flip it over and reduce heat to low. Top each pizza with desired toppings. Close the lid and grill another 2 to 3 minutes to melt cheese. Remove pizzas carefully onto a cutting board, slice, and serve.

Hobo Packs

This is an old camping tradition. If you're cooking in a campsite fire pit, wait until the coals are white before throwing the hobo packs in. Let each camper customize their own packs, then take turns telling spooky camp stories until the food is ready.

Serves 4
Prep time: 15 minutes
Cook time: 30 minutes

1 large yellow onion, sliced

4 hamburger patties, minute steaks, pork chops, or boneless chicken breasts

12 new potatoes, halved

1 large carrot, sliced

Salt and pepper

Salsa, barbecue sauce, steak sauce, or ketchup

1. Preheat grill on high heat. Give each person a large piece of heavy-duty aluminum foil. In the center of the foil, layer one-quarter of the onion, meat, potatoes, and carrot. Sprinkle with salt and pepper, then fold the foil over the food like an envelope and seal tightly.

2. Place on the grill and cook over medium heat with the lid down for 20 to 30 minutes. Hobo packs are ready when the carrots and potatoes are tender. Remove from foil onto serving plates and top with condiments of your choice.

Herby Hobos: Add your choice of fresh or dried herbs to the packs before sealing and grilling.

Veggie Hobos: Any number of vegetables can be added to the packs, or you can cook a mess of veggies separately from the meat. Try corn, green beans, zucchini, eggplant, brussels sprouts, cauliflower, or broccoli.

Corn on the Cob

You'll find grilled corn at every street fair and parking-lot festival across America. Why? Because it's easy to make and tastes great! Soaking the corn in water keeps the husks intact and creates steam to cook the corn. If you like your corn with a smokier flavor, omit the soaking and let the husks burn.

4 large ears of corn, husks intact

4 oz. (1 stick) butter, melted

Salt and pepper

Serves 4
Prep time: 10 minutes (plus 1 hour soaking time)
Cook time: 15 minutes

1. Peel back husks but do not detach. Remove corn silk and fold husks back into place. Soak in cold water for 1 hour.

2. Preheat grill on high heat. Drain corn and put on the grill, turning frequently for 10 to 15 minutes, until husks begin to char. To serve, peel back husks, brush with melted butter, and sprinkle with salt and pepper.

Chili-Salt: In a small bowl combine 1 tablespoon each chili powder, dried cumin, garlic salt, and onion powder. Sprinkle over buttered corn.

Mixed-Herb Rub: In a small bowl combine 1 tablespoon each dried sage, thyme, parsley, and basil. Add 1 teaspoon each of salt and pepper, mix well, and sprinkle over buttered corn.

Tomato-Basil Butter: In a medium bowl combine one softened stick of butter, one chopped roasted red pepper, ¼ cup chopped sun-dried tomatoes (oil packed), 1 tablespoon chopped fresh basil, and salt and pepper. Mix into a paste and spread on warm grilled corn.

Marinated Grilled Vegetables

This is an easy and delicious way to get your veggies. They're great the next day, too. Dice leftover grilled vegetables and toss with your favorite vinaigrette.

Serves 4
Prep time: 20 minutes (plus 2 hours to overnight for refrigeration)
Cook time: 15 minutes

1 cup olive oil

¼ cup red wine vinegar

2 TB. chopped fresh rosemary (or 1 tsp. dried)

2 TB. chopped fresh basil (or 1 tsp. dried)

2 TB. chopped fresh thyme (or 1 tsp. dried)

2 TB. chopped fresh oregano (or 1 tsp. dried)

2 TB. chopped fresh sage (or 1 tsp. dried)

1 tsp. salt

½ tsp. pepper

4 cloves garlic, minced

1 purple onion, sliced in ½-inch rings

1 eggplant, sliced in 1-inch wheels

1 zucchini, sliced in 1-inch wheels

1 bunch asparagus, stems trimmed

8–10 large mushrooms

1. Mix together oil, red wine vinegar, rosemary, basil, thyme, oregano, sage, salt, pepper, and garlic. Mix well. Place vegetables in a large zipper bag and add marinade. Zip it tight and massage the marinade into the vegetables. Refrigerate for 2 hours or overnight.

2. Preheat grill on high heat. Spread out marinated vegetables over direct heat and grill 2 to 3 minutes per side until marked. Reduce heat, close cover and cook another 5 minutes until vegetables are tender. Serve warm or cold.

Part 4

Sweet Stuff and Snacks

Salt and sugar are my most frequent cravings. Regardless of the inevitable tummy ache, I always have room for at least a dish of ice cream. The day is incomplete without it. But late at night, from time to time, a desire for salty snacks hits hard.

We spend a lot of time snacking. In fact, there is a corresponding snack for almost everything we do. At the ballpark we chomp on peanuts. At the movies it's popcorn. We eat cotton candy at the circus, nachos at the race-track, snow cones on the boardwalk, and corn dogs at the amusement park.

You'll find each sweet and snack genre represented in this chapter. Some are simple, others definitely require forethought, but all of them are worth the effort. You deserve a reward!

Chapter 13

Old-Fashioned Cakes

In This Chapter

- ◆ Mixing wet and dry ingredients
- ◆ Secrets for better baking
- ◆ Tips for working with chocolate
- ◆ Meringue 101
- ◆ Holiday and special occasion cakes
- ◆ Childhood and old-world favorites

Cakes are fun. Cakes are special. Cakes tell someone that you care. They're fun to bake, fun to decorate, and fun to eat. And the homemade cakes always win-out over the grocery store variety. No matter what the occasion, you'll find a cake here to fit it.

Mixing Ingredients

Many recipes in this chapter require that you add dry and wet ingredients alternately. This means that you add a little bit of the sifted flour mixture, work it in completely, then add a little bit of the wet ingredients. The ingredients are added in three or four segments, and each is worked in completely before the next is added. This method ensures that the ingredients blend thoroughly, and easily. If you tried to add all the dry ingredients at once, you'd have trouble mixing it well, and it would make a real mess.

Folding is a common instruction, and it typically appears when a foam, like whipped eggs, yolks, or whites, are added into a batter. The intention is to incorporate the foam without deflating any of the air that has been whipped in. To accomplish this as efficiently as possible, I fold with a big whisk. The 30 or 40 wires of the whisk drag through the batter, pulling the foam along with it. The ingredients combine much faster, and with fewer strokes, than the same task done with a rubber spatula.

When folding, I always use the same motion. I envision the bowl of batter as a clock, and I drag my whisk from 12 o'clock to 6 o'clock, turn the bowl counter-clockwise for ¼ turn, and bring the whisk around to 9 o'clock. I repeat this motion five or six times, bringing the whisk through a different patch of batter each time. The goal is to mix as thoroughly as possible in as few strokes as possible. If, as you are folding, the batter loses its peak and becomes thin and runny, you have probably folded too much. Try to keep the volume full and thick.

Better Baking

All pans must be prepared properly, which means greasing them and lining them with parchment paper. To grease a pan, I prefer butter, melted and applied lightly but evenly with a pastry brush. My second choice would be pan spray, which applies easily and evenly, but doesn't taste as good.

Parchment paper, carefully cut to fit snugly in the bottom of a cake pan, helps the finished cake release cleanly. The paper should also be greased lightly after it goes into the pan. Flour can be used in pans that are impossible to paper, like bundt pans. But generally, the flour sticks to the outside of the cake, and is not pleasant to eat. I have indicated flouring in some recipes, when necessary, but usually I avoid it.

Most recipes call for a 10×2 round cake pan. This is a standard size, but it is only a suggestion. You can bake cakes in any size pan, from cupcake size to sheet cake size and beyond. Smaller pans will bake faster, and should be baked at a higher temperature for the best structure, usually 25° hotter than indicated. Large cakes benefit from a cooler oven, at least toward the end of baking.

Kitchen Tips

Monitor the cooking process carefully. If your supersize cake is browning faster than the batter is setting, reduce the oven temperature and be patient. It takes the heat longer to enter the center of a large cake than a small one.

Larger pans will, of course, need more batter. The recipes can simply be multiplied as much as is necessary. Keep the size of your mixers and bowls in mind when increasing recipes. Large recipes are sometimes hard to mix thoroughly, it is often better to make a batter twice than to wrestle with an overflowing mixer bowl.

To ensure even cooking I always take the time to rotate my pans during baking. Halfway through the allotted time I rotate the pans from front to back. If I have more than one pan in the oven I rotate their positions, switching left to right, top to bottom, or back to front. But beware! It is important to move quickly and to keep the cakes in the oven. Removing the pans from the oven, even briefly, will cause a drop in temperature that can collapse a cake. It's better to reach into the oven and carefully slide things around as best you can.

The timing indicated on each recipe includes a cooling time. Cakes cannot be frosted when hot, especially if the frosting includes butter or shortening. The heat of the cake will melt the fat and you'll have a runny mess on your hands. To speed up the cooling process, you can place the cake in the refrigerator or freezer for 15 to 20 minutes. This method, however, only cools the outside of the cake. The center will still be warm. The cake can then be sliced into layers and returned to refrigeration in sections to complete the cooling. There is a downside to rushing a cake this way. The crumb will dry out from uncovered refrigeration. To avoid this problem, plan ahead and allow for adequate cooling time!

Finishing a cake, or filling, icing, and decorating it, takes time. I have allotted time for this process when necessary, but keep in mind your experience level. If you're a novice, you may want to give yourself a little longer.

Mmmm, Chocolate!

The chocolate recipes in this book call for chocolate chips. I like using chips because they are easy to find and they melt quickly and easily. The flavor of most chocolate chips, however, is unremarkable. If you long for a more refined chocolate, feel free to make the substitution. Just be sure to use the type of chocolate called for in the recipe (bittersweet in most cases). Milk and white chocolates have more fat, and do not work properly unless adjustments to the recipe are made. Be sure to chop your chocolate into pieces roughly the same size as a chocolate chip for even melting.

Melting chocolate is not hard, but it can be temperamental. It can burn easily, which is why it is usually done over a water bath or double boiler. You can rig up your own water bath by placing a bowl over a simmering pot of water. Stir the chocolate frequently, and when it is nearly melted turn off the heat and let it sit and finish melting. Try not to get any water in the bowl of chocolate, as even a small drop will cause the chocolate to clump or seize.

Listen to Mom! _____

Chocolate can be melted in the microwave, but it takes careful monitoring. Never cook chocolate in a microwave for more than 15 seconds, or it will burn in patches. Put the chocolate in a glass or ceramic bowl, and heat it in 5- to 15-second intervals, stirring between each. The meltier it gets, the less time it needs to be zapped.

Whipped Egg White Meringue

Some of these recipes incorporate a meringue into the batter for lightness and leavening. When whipping egg whites, there are a couple of rules to follow. The bowl and the whip must be clean. Any speck of fat in the mix will inhibit the whites from taking in air. Egg yolks are full of fat and are a common culprit. When separating the eggs, don't let any yolk into the white bowl. The smallest amount can drastically reduce the amount of air an egg white can hold.

Some recipes call for a simple or common meringue, with raw egg whites whipped until they are stiff, and granulated sugar sprinkled in at the medium- or stiff-peak stage. This is an unstable method, so it is important to stop the whipping at the appropriate time. To judge the peak stage, spoon a bit of meringue out of the bowl and hold it upright. If it makes a peak that stands erect at the tip of the spoon, it is a stiff peak. If the peak bends over a bit at the tip, it is a medium peak. If the peak flops all the way over, it is a soft peak.

Some of the recipes call for sugar syrup to be poured into the whipping whites. This method is also known as Italian meringue, 7-minute icing, white mountain icing, and boiled icing. It is important to cook the sugar to the proper stage. Use a candy thermometer, or the traditional ice test, for best results. (See Chapter 16 for a thorough discussion of cooking sugar.) Once the syrup is ready, pour it slowly into the whites as you whip. The movement is important to prevent the heat of the sugar from overcooking the eggs. If you don't have an electric mixer, get a friend to drizzle in the sugar while you whip. If you don't have a mixer or an extra set of hands nearby, place the bowl of egg whites on a damp towel. The wet cloth will hold the bowl in place for you as you whip and pour.

The cake recipes in this chapter are paired with traditional frostings, but these are merely suggestions. Feel free to switch them up and pair cakes and icings as you see fit. That's what makes baking fun!

Chocolate Birthday Cake with Chocolate Fudge Frosting

This is the world's best chocolate cake. Even those with a preference for vanilla will love it!

1¾ cups cake flour

½ cup cocoa powder

2 tsp. baking soda

½ tsp. salt

⅔ cup vegetable oil

¾ cup buttermilk

¾ cup cold black coffee

½ tsp. vanilla extract

1⅓ cups sugar

2 eggs

For the frosting:

½ cup brown sugar

¼ cup water

2 TB. corn syrup

1 cup chocolate chips

3 TB. butter, softened

1 TB. vanilla extract

1 lb. box powdered sugar, sifted

2 TB. hot water

Makes 1 10-inch layer cake
Prep time: 30 minutes
Cook time: 60 minutes, plus 60 minutes cooling
Finishing time: 30 minutes

---

1. Preheat oven to 350°F. Butter two 10-inch round cake pans and line with parchment paper. Sift together flour, cocoa, baking soda, and salt and set aside. In a medium bowl combine the oil, buttermilk, coffee, and vanilla and set aside. In a large bowl, use a whisk or electric mixer to whip sugar and eggs until light and fluffy, about 5 minutes. Fold dry ingredients into eggs alternately with the wet ingredients. Divide batter between two pans and bake for 30 to 45 minutes, until a pick inserted at the center of the cake comes out clean. Cool 10 minutes before inverting onto a rack. Cool completely before frosting.

2. For frosting, combine the brown sugar, water, and corn syrup in a large saucepan and bring to a boil. When sugar is dissolved, remove from heat and add chocolate chips, butter, and vanilla, stirring to melt. Add powdered sugar alternately with hot water. Adjust frosting consistency with more hot water or powdered sugar as needed. Frost cake immediately.

Fruit Filling: Add fresh raspberries, strawberries, or orange sections between the two cake layers for a pleasant, tart counterpoint to the sweet chocolate icing.

Cupcakes: Bake the batter in muffin pans lined with paper cups. Bake time will be much shorter, about 10 to 15 minutes.

Listen to Mom!

Don't make this frosting until the cake is cool. If it sits around it will firm up and be very hard to spread. If this happens, place the bowl of frosting over a pan of simmering water and stir until it softens.

Devil's Food Cake with Chocolate-Sour Cream Frosting

This cake is baked, frosted, and served in a rectangular pan. It's a great way to go when time is tight. You can, however, bake, invert, and decorate it in layers if you prefer. In that case, remember to paper your pans and cool the layers on a rack.

Makes 1 9×13 rectangular cake

Prep time: 30 minutes

Cook time: 45 minutes, plus 60 minutes cooling

Finishing time: 30 minutes

---

1 cup chocolate chips

¾ cup water

8 oz. (2 sticks) butter

1 cup plus 2 TB. brown sugar

1 tsp. vanilla extract

3 eggs

3½ cups cake flour

1½ tsp. baking soda

½ tsp. baking powder

½ tsp. salt

⅔ cup sour cream

For the frosting:

1 cup chocolate chips

4 TB. (½ stick) butter, softened

½ cup sour cream

1 TB. vanilla extract

1 (1-lb.) box sifted powdered sugar

2–4 TB. hot water

1. Preheat oven to 350°F. Coat a 9×13 rectangular pan with melted butter or spray. Combine the chocolate and the water in a small saucepan and bring to a boil, stirring. At the boil, remove from the heat and set aside to cool. In a large bowl with a sturdy spoon or an electric mixer, cream the butter and brown sugar together until smooth. Add the vanilla and the eggs one by one. Add the cooled chocolate.

2. Sift together the flour, baking soda, baking powder, and salt. Add to the butter mixture alternately with the sour cream. Pour into cake pan and bake for 30 to 45 minutes, until a pick inserted at the center of the cake comes out clean. Cool completely before frosting.

3. For frosting, melt together chocolate and butter in a double boiler or a bowl and set over simmering water. Stir in sour cream and vanilla. Remove from heat and add powdered sugar alternately with water. Adjust frosting consistency with more hot water or powdered sugar as needed. Spread evenly over cooled cake.

 Tidbits

Devil's food cake is so named because the crumb has a slightly reddish-brown hue, caused by a reaction between baking soda, chocolate, and acid. It is also devilishly delicious.

Dress It Up: Individual Molten Chocolate Cakes

These popular cakes started out as undercooked flourless chocolate cakes. If you don't have a muffin pan, glass or ceramic custard cups work just as well. They turn out best when baked as individual cakes, as they are here, but the batter makes a terrific 10-inch flourless chocolate cake as well.

10 oz. (2½ sticks) butter	**¼ tsp. cream of tartar**
1 (12-oz.) bag chocolate chips	**1¼ cup sugar, divided**
7 eggs, separated	

> *Makes 12 muffin-sized cakes*
>
> **Prep time:** 30 minutes
> **Cook time:** 30 minutes

1. Preheat oven to 350°F. Butter and flour a muffin pan. Combine butter and all but ¼ cup chocolate chips and melt in a double boiler or bowl set over simmering water. Set aside.

2. In a medium bowl using a whisk or an electric mixer, whip egg whites with the cream of tartar until medium peaks form. Slowly add ¼ cup of sugar and continue whipping until stiff peaks form. Set aside. In another bowl, whip yolks and ½ cup sugar until thick and pale yellow. Add the chocolate to the yolks, then fold in the whites. Fill each muffin cup ¾ full with batter. Drop a few chocolate chips in each cup, and bake for 15 minutes until the tops look shiny and set. Cool for 10 minutes. To unmold, turn muffin pan upside down and give it a firm tap. Serve warm with a dollop of whipped cream and fresh berries.

Kitchen Tips

Flouring a pan helps keep the cake from sticking once it's baked and is used when lining with parchment paper is impractical. After brushing a thin coating of melted butter in each cup, fill the muffin cups with flour. Shake it around to coat every inch, then tap out the excess firmly. The end result should be only a light layer of flour.

Yellow Cake with Vanilla Frosting

I know—yellow is not a flavor. The color comes from the egg yolks, but no one wants to eat an egg yolk cake. You can pump up the flavor in this tender cake with more vanilla, lemon or orange zest, or your favorite spices.

Makes 1 10-inch layer cake

Prep time: 30 minutes

Cook time: 45 minutes, plus 60 minutes cooling

Finishing time: 30 minutes

---

3 cups cake flour

1 TB. baking powder

½ tsp. salt

½ cup sour cream

½ cup milk

8 oz. (2 sticks) butter

2 cups sugar

1 TB. vanilla extract

4 eggs

For the frosting:

12 oz. (2½ sticks) butter, softened

2 TB. vanilla extract

3½ cups powdered sugar, sifted

¼ cup heavy whipping cream

1. Preheat oven to 350°F. Butter two 10-inch round cake pans and line with parchment paper. Sift together flour, baking powder, and salt and set aside. Mix together sour cream and milk and set aside. In a large bowl with a sturdy spoon or electric mixer, cream together the butter and sugar until light and fluffy. Add the vanilla and the eggs one by one. Add the sifted ingredients alternately with the sour cream mixture. Divide batter evenly between two cake pans and bake for 30 to 45 minutes, until a pick inserted at the center of the cake comes out clean. Cool 10 minutes before inverting onto a rack. Cool completely before frosting.

2. For the frosting, cream butter in a large bowl with a sturdy spoon or electric mixer until smooth and lump free. Add vanilla. Slowly add half the powdered sugar, beating until light and fluffy. Add half the cream and mix well. Add the remaining sugar, then cream, beating until fluffy. Store at room temperature until cake is ready to be frosted, up to 8 hours.

Strawberry Shortcake: Frost cake with sweetened whipped cream and fill or top it with fresh, ripe strawberries.

Boston Cream Pie: Fill cake with vanilla custard and cover with chocolate glaze. To make glaze, boil 1 cup whipping cream and pour over 3 cups chocolate chips and 2 tablespoons butter. Let mixture sit for 3 minutes, then whisk until smooth. Pour over filled cake.

Dress It Up: Coffee Crunch Cake

As a child growing up in the San Francisco Bay area, trips into the city were full of traditions. One was a stop at Blum's Restaurant on Union Square for a slice of Coffee Crunch Cake, a delectable creation covered in crunchy, honeycomb candy. This restaurant was every child's fantasy destination, with its pink banquettes and cases full of pastries and candies. Sadly, it's gone now, but the recipe lives on.

1 recipe yellow cake
(see previous recipe)

1 TB. baking soda

¼ cup strong black coffee

1½ cup sugar

¼ cup corn syrup

2 cups whipping cream

2 TB. sugar

1 TB. vanilla extract

> *Makes enough topping for
> 1 10-inch layered cake*
>
> **Prep time:** 2 hours for yellow cake
>
> **Cook time:** 30 minutes, plus 60 minutes cooling
>
> **Finishing time:** 20 minutes

1. Generously butter a large baking-sheet-size piece of wax paper. Sift baking soda and set aside. Combine coffee, sugar, and corn syrup in a medium saucepan and bring to a boil. Cook over high heat until the mixture reaches the soft crack stage, 290°F on a candy thermometer. Remove from heat and stir in baking soda. The mixture will bubble up like lava. Stir to distribute the bubbles evenly and pour out quickly onto the prepared waxed paper. Let cool completely, about 1 hour.

2. Combine cream and sugar in a large bowl and, using a whisk or electric mixer, whip until medium peaks form. Stir in vanilla. Fill layers and frost yellow cake with whipped cream.

3. Cover cooled candy with another sheet of wax paper and a clean towel. Use a rolling pin or meat mallet to crush it into bits. Cover the entire surface of the cake with the coffee-crunch candy. Keep refrigerated until ready to serve.

Coffee Lover's Cake: Flavor the whipped cream frosting with coffee extract, coffee syrup, or a shot of cooled espresso.

Ice Cream Topping: Coffee crunch candy makes an incredible topper for your everyday hot fudge sundae. It's not bad folded into chocolate chip cookie dough, either!

Listen to Mom!

Cooking sugar is not hard, but it does bear careful attention. Read all about it in Chapter 16.

Pound Cake

This pound cake is vanilla, but it can be jazzed up with any number of flavors. I like to use rose water in place of the vanilla, which was a favorite flavoring of the Victorians. You can find rose water in Indian and Middle Eastern markets.

Makes 1 6×9 loaf
Prep time: 30 minutes
Cook time: 60 minutes, plus 45 minutes cooling

2¼ **cup cake flour**	**1 cup sugar**
1 tsp. baking powder	**1 TB. vanilla**
¼ **tsp salt**	**4 eggs**
8 oz. (2 sticks) butter	**2 TB. milk**

1. Preheat oven to 325°F. Butter a 6×9 loaf pan and line with parchment paper. Sift together flour, baking powder, and salt and set aside.

2. In a large bowl with a sturdy spoon or electric mixer, cream together the butter and sugar until light and fluffy. Add vanilla and eggs, one by one. Add milk, and slowly add the sifted ingredients.

3. Pour the batter into the loaf pan and bake for 45 to 60 minutes, until a pick inserted at the center of the cake comes out clean. Cool 10 minutes before inverting onto a rack. Cool completely before slicing.

Lemon Pound Cake: Add the grated zest of four lemons to the creaming butter and sugar. Make a glaze to pour over the finished cake by mixing 1 cup sifted powdered sugar with ¼ cup lemon juice. You can do the same with other citrus fruits like oranges, tangerines, or ruby grapefruits.

Tidbits

Pound cake is so named because the original recipe called for a pound of each ingredient: eggs, sugar, flour, and butter. The batter was beaten vigorously by hand to incorporate air, which was the sole leavening (this was before baking soda or powder). Baking the cake in the traditional manner yields a dense but delicious loaf. In the 1950s Sara Lee upped the ante by making delicious light and buttery pound cake available to the masses, and folks now expect a lighter texture from a pound cake than was traditional.

Dress It Up: Trifle

The custard that holds this dessert together is a classic English cream, or crème Anglaise. In addition to being the basis for this dessert, crème Anglaise can be made into a multitude of sauces, and it's the foundation for many desserts, including ice cream.

4 cups half-and-half

½ cup sugar

8 egg yolks

1 recipe pound cake (see previous recipe), cut into 1-inch cubes

3 cups assorted fresh fruit, including strawberries, raspberries, blackberries, peeled and sliced kiwi, sliced peaches or plums, and orange segments

2 cups whipping cream

2 TB. sugar

1 TB vanilla extract

Serves 8–10
Prep time: 45 minutes (plus 4 hours or overnight for refrigeration)

1. Fill a large bowl with ice, and set another large bowl on top of the ice. Have a fine strainer nearby, and set this all aside until custard is cooked. Over high heat, bring the half-and-half to a boil in a large saucepan. In a small bowl, whisk together the sugar and egg yolks. At the boil, ladle ½ cup of hot half-and-half into the yolks and whisk quickly to combine. Pour the warmed yolks back into the saucepan and, over high heat, whisk immediately and vigorously until the mixture begins to resemble thick cream, about 2 minutes. Strain immediately into the bowl sitting on ice, and stir until cool.

2. Layer the bottom of a large glass serving bowl with ⅓ of the diced cake. Arrange on top of the cake half of the fresh fruit. Take care to place attractive fruits against the glass. Add another ⅓ of the cake cubes, the remaining fruit, and finish with cake. Pour the cooled custard sauce over the cake, evenly distributing. Cover tightly with plastic wrap and refrigerate for 4 hours or overnight.

3. Just before serving, whip cream and sugar together in a large bowl using a whisk or an electric mixer. When medium peaks form, stir in vanilla. Spread whipped cream evenly over the top of the trifle. To serve, dig deep with a large serving spoon to scoop out cake and fruit.

Carrot Cake with Cream Cheese Frosting

I doubt this cake would have ever caught on if it weren't for the cream cheese frosting. Who in their right minds would make a cake from carrots? It sounds weird, but it's oh-so-good!

Makes 1 9×13 cake
Prep time: 20 minutes
Cook time: 45 minutes, plus 60 minutes cooling
Finishing time: 20 minutes

2 cups all-purpose flour

2 tsp. baking powder

1½ tsp. baking soda

1 tsp. salt

2 tsp. cinnamon

2 tsp. nutmeg

½ tsp. clove

2 cups sugar

1½ cup vegetable oil

4 eggs

2 cups grated carrots

1 (8-oz.) can crushed pineapple with juice

1 cup chopped walnuts, divided

For the frosting:

2 oz. (½ stick) butter, softened

1 (8-oz.) package cream cheese, softened

1 TB. vanilla

1 (1-lb.) box powdered sugar, sifted

1. Preheat oven to 350°F. Butter a 9×13 rectangular pan. Sift together flour, baking powder, baking soda, salt, cinnamon, nutmeg, and clove and set aside. In a large bowl, mix together sugar, oil, eggs, carrots, pineapple with juice, and nuts. Slowly add the sifted ingredients, combine thoroughly and fold in half the nuts. Pour into prepared pan and bake for 30 to 45 minutes, until a pick inserted at the center of the cake comes out clean. Cool completely before frosting.

2. For the frosting, cream together the butter, cream cheese, and vanilla with a sturdy spoon or electric mixer until lump-free. Slowly add powdered sugar and mix until smooth. Spread on top of cooled carrot cake and sprinkle with remaining nuts. To serve, slice into squares.

Coconut Cake

I am a firm believer that coconut cake should be white. For that reason, I always use this delicious white cake recipe, which uses white shortening instead of yellow butter.

3 cups cake flour

1 TB. baking powder

¼ tsp. salt

1 cup shortening

2 cups sugar

1 TB. coconut extract

1 TB. vanilla extract

4 eggs, separated

1 cup milk

2 cups shredded coconut, lightly toasted and divided

For the frosting:

1 cup sugar

½ cup light corn syrup

¼ cup water

½ tsp. salt

4 egg whites

1 tsp. vanilla extract

Makes 1 10-inch layer cake

Prep time: 30 minutes

Cook time: 45 minutes

Finishing time: 45 minutes

---

1. Preheat oven to 350°F. Butter two 10-inch round cake pans and line with parchment paper. Sift together flour, baking powder, and salt and set aside. In a large bowl, use a sturdy spoon or electric mixer to cream the shortening and sugar until light and fluffy. Add the extracts and the egg yolks one by one. Add the sifted ingredients alternately with the milk. Fold in 1 cup shredded coconut. In a medium bowl using a whisk or an electric mixer, whip egg whites to medium peaks, then fold into batter. Divide batter between 2 pans, and bake for 30 to 45 minutes, until a pick inserted at the center of the cake comes out clean. Cool 10 minutes before inverting onto a rack. Cool completely before frosting.

2. For the frosting, in a large saucepan, combine the sugar, corn syrup, water, and salt. Bring to a boil and cook over high heat until it reaches the firm ball stage, 245°F. In a large bowl, using a whisk or an electric mixer, whip the egg whites until stiff peaks form. Continue whipping while slowly drizzling in the sugar syrup. Add vanilla and whip until stiff peaks are formed. Fill and frost cooled coconut cake, and top with remaining coconut.

Kitchen Tips

Omit the coconut extract if you want. The white vanilla cake is a great base for all kinds of icings, like chocolate fudge, or strawberries and whipped cream.

Red Velvet Cake

This recipe came from an old-fashioned Southern belle. Real red-velvet cake should never be bright red. It's a deep, dark red, like Scarlet's dress. The color is achieved by adding cocoa powder along with red food coloring.

Makes 1 10-inch layer cake
Prep time: 20 minutes
Cook time: 45 minutes, plus 60 minutes cooling
Finishing time: 30 minutes

1 cup vegetable oil

1½ cup sugar

2 eggs

1 cup buttermilk

2 TB. cocoa powder

¼ cup red food coloring

2½ cups all-purpose flour, sifted

1 tsp. salt

1 tsp. baking soda

1 TB. cider vinegar

For the frosting:

2 oz. (½ stick) butter, softened

1 (8 oz.) package cream cheese, softened

1 TB. vanilla

1 (1-lb.) box powdered sugar, sifted

Tidbits

You can tell this recipe is old, because the cake is leavened by vinegar and baking soda. This is how all cakes and cookies were leavened before the advent of baking powder (a product that premixes the baking soda and acid for you). I like the flavor the vinegar imparts, and to me, that flavor makes this cake special.

1. Preheat oven to 350°F. Butter two 10-inch round cake pans and line with parchment paper. In a large bowl, use a sturdy spoon or electric mixer to combine the oil, sugar, eggs, and buttermilk. In a separate bowl combine the cocoa and food coloring, mix well, and add to the buttermilk mixture. Add the flour and salt and mix thoroughly. In a small bowl, combine baking soda and vinegar and mix until foamy. Add immediately to, and stir just to combine. Divide batter between two pans, and bake for 30 to 45 minutes, until a pick inserted at the center of the cake comes out clean. Cool 10 minutes before inverting onto a rack. Cool completely before frosting.

2. For the frosting, cream together the butter, cream cheese, and vanilla with a sturdy spoon or electric mixer until lump-free. Slowly add the powdered sugar and mix until smooth. Fill and frost the cake, and refrigerate 30 minutes before serving.

Gingerbread

Christmas doesn't come at our house unless the smell of this cake is wafting through the air. The lemon icing is the perfect accompaniment, setting off the rich spicy cake with a pleasant tartness.

2⅓ cup all-purpose flour

1½ tsp. baking soda

½ tsp. salt

1 tsp. ground ginger

1 tsp. cinnamon

1 tsp. nutmeg

½ tsp. clove

1 cup hot water

1 cup molasses

4 oz. (1 stick) butter

¼ cup brown sugar

1 egg

For the frosting:

2 oz. (½ stick) butter

2 (1-lb.) boxes powdered sugar, sifted

Grated zest of 1 lemon

¼ cup lemon juice

1 TB. milk

Makes 1 9×13 cake
Prep time: 20 minutes
Cook time: 40 minutes, plus 60 minutes cooling
Finishing time: 30 minutes

1. Preheat oven to 350°F. Coat a 9×13 rectangular pan with melted butter. Sift together the flour, baking soda, salt, ginger, cinnamon, nutmeg, and clove and set aside. Combine the hot water and molasses and set aside. In a large bowl, using a sturdy spoon or an electric mixer, cream together the butter and brown sugar. Add the egg and mix well. Add the sifted ingredients alternately with the molasses mixture and blend until smooth. Pour into prepared pan and bake for 30 to 40 minutes, until a pick inserted at the center of the cake comes out clean. Cool completely before frosting.

2. For the frosting, cream together the butter and half the powdered sugar using a sturdy spoon or an electric mixer. Add the lemon zest, lemon juice, and milk and blend until smooth. Add remaining powdered sugar and beat until fluffy. Adjust consistency with more sugar or milk as needed. Spread frosting evenly onto gingerbread. To serve, slice in squares.

Cheesecake

There are several styles of cheesecake, including New York style, Californian, and Italian (made with ricotta cheese). This recipe is based on the famous cheesecake found at Lindy's Restaurant in New York City. It has an egg-white foam folded in, which gives it a heavenly light texture.

Makes 1 10-inch cake
Prep time: 30 minutes
Cook time: 2 hours, plus 4 hours or overnight for refrigeration

For the crust:

2 cups graham cracker crumbs

2 TB. sugar

2 oz. (½ stick) butter, melted

For the filling:

3 (8-oz.) packages cream cheese, softened

1 cup sugar

½ cup cream

1 TB. vanilla

Zest of 1 lemon

5 eggs, separated

2 TB. sugar

1. Preheat oven to 350°F. Coat a 10-inch springform pan with melted butter and line with parchment paper. Mix together the graham cracker crumbs, sugar, and melted butter and press into prepared pan, covering the bottom and halfway up the sides. Bake until lightly toasted, about 10 minutes. Set aside to cool. Reduce oven temperature to 325°F.

2. In a large bowl with a sturdy spoon, cream together the cream cheese, sugar, cream, vanilla, and lemon zest until lump-free. Add five egg yolks one by one. Mix well and set aside. In a separate bowl, using a whisk or an electric mixer, whip three egg whites until medium peaks form. Slowly add 2 tablespoons of sugar and continue whipping until stiff peaks form. Fold carefully into batter. Pour batter into crust and bake at 325°F for 1 hour. Turn off oven, open door slightly, and let cake sit inside oven another hour. Chill completely in refrigerator 4 hours or overnight before unmolding and slicing.

Kitchen Tips

The key to a good cheesecake is in the baking. If you bake it in an oven that's too hot the top will expand and crack. But if it's not baked long enough the center will be runny. The trick is to bake it slowly, giving the heat plenty of time to penetrate the center of the batter.

Chapter 14

Sweetie Pies

In This Chapter

- ◆ Cutting-in fat, blind-baking, and other pie-making techniques
- ◆ The number-one rule for a great pie crust
- ◆ Sweet and flaky doughs and crusts
- ◆ Fruit pies
- ◆ Custard pies
- ◆ Other pie favorites

When people find out that I am a baker, the first thing they want to know is how to make a good pie crust. With most things, if you fail at it once, you usually try again. But one pie dough failure puts most people off of baking entirely. I suppose, without the proper arsenal of pie-dough knowledge, it can be a bit intimidating. Then again, it is only pie dough.

Cutting-In Fat

The cut-in technique is a method of incorporating fat and flour together by crumbling. The butter and flour do not actually combine, but remain separate. The mixture should never look like a paste. Little hunks of fat are the key to tender, flaky crust.

Use your fingertips, a pastry blender, or a couple of knives or forks to break down the butter into pea-size pieces. While they do not have to be round like a pea, they should be approximately that small.

Many bakers prefer to make pie crust with lard. It can be cut into the flour in smaller, thinner bits while still remaining separate. But lard is not as common as it used to be, and many people avoid it because it is a pork product. If you're a lard fan, simply replace the butter in the pie dough recipe with an equal amount of lard. Others prefer the flavor of butter in their pie dough. I like the best of both worlds, and use half lard and half butter. I do not recommend using vegetable shortening in pie dough. It works, but leaves a distinctive aftertaste that many find disagreeable.

Keep It Cool

To make a successful pie dough, there is one simple rule to follow: keep the dough cold. From the time you begin making the dough until it hits the oven, everything about it must remain cold. Cold butter, cold lard, cold flour, cold water, cold room, cold hands. The thing that sets pie dough apart from tart dough, cookie dough, or bread dough is its flakiness, and cold is what makes flakiness possible.

Flakiness is achieved through the tiny pieces of fat that are suspended within the flour. Butter and lard contain water. In the heat of the oven, that water turns into steam, which creates pockets of air within the crust. If the ingredients are not cold, or they are allowed to warm up, the tiny pieces of fat will cream together with the flour, rather than remain in separate chunks. That creates tough, hard crusts, not tender, flaky ones.

Remember that fat softens with heat. Think about the way butter feels directly out of the fridge, versus how it feels after it's been allowed to sit out for a while. Fat gets soft and sticky as it warms. If you keep the dough cold while you are working with it, it will be easy to roll out. The warmer it gets, through room temperature or over-handling, the harder it is to roll. It sticks to the counter, the pin, your hands, and it becomes the source of much frustration. To combat the problem, work quickly. As soon as the dough shows signs of warming, throw it in the fridge.

Once the dough is in the pan, and the pie is ready to bake, the fat is still there, and it can still melt. Keep it very cold before baking to ensure that your decorative crimping keeps its shape. Better yet, freeze it solid and bake it directly from the freezer. If the fat is frozen, the protein in the dough will solidify before the fat has a chance to melt.

Blind-Baking

There is nothing more disappointing to me than cutting into a beautiful pie only to find a raw bottom crust. Bakers often forget that it takes time for heat to penetrate a pie, and that unlike a cake, a baked top does not necessarily mean a baked bottom. How do you ensure your crust is baked on the bottom? Prebaking is the key. This is known in the business as blind-baking.

Blind-baking allows you to precook a pie shell, either fully or partially, so that once the filling goes in, it is only necessary to bake the pie as long as the filling requires. In some cases, like cream pies, the filling isn't baked at all, in which case blind-baking is essential.

To blind-bake a pie shell, place the rolled-out dough in the pan, decoratively flute the edges, and chill until firm. Line the shell with foil, parchment paper, or heavy-duty plastic wrap (the kind that shrinks, but doesn't melt), then fill it to the rim with dried beans or rice. The weight of this filling will keep the shell from melting, shrinking, and bubbling up. Bake at 350°F until the edges are golden brown. At this point the shell is half-cooked and can be used for several recipes in which the filling needs only to be cooked a short while. To cook it completely, carefully remove the weights and return to the oven until the bottom is browned.

Kitchen Tips

Blind-baking does not work for a double crust pie because the top crust must be pinched and crimped to the bottom crust, which can only be done if the dough is raw. So to help ensure the bottom of a double crust pie is cooked, be sure to bake it long enough. How long is that? It should be long enough to get the filling really bubbly and to turn the top crust a deep, dark golden brown. When you think your pie is at that point, leave it in another 5 minutes. Then, if your oven allows it, move the pie off the rack and cook it 5 more minutes directly on the floor of the oven. This final direct burst of heat is my perfect crust insurance.

The Crimped Edge

My favorite part of pie is the crimped crust edge. If it's formed and baked right, it's like a crisp, buttery cookie. If not, it's a sad lump of undercooked dough. Most problems arise because the dough is too thick, and not chilled adequately before baking.

To crimp the edge of a single crust pie shell, start by trimming the dough an inch from the edge of the pan. Scissors make this job a snap. Roll the edge of the dough under itself all the way around, then pinch it tightly, until it is the thickness of a single layer of dough. The fluted edge can be achieved by pinching with two fingers from the outer edge while simultaneously pressing in with one finger from the inner edge. The edge can also be pressed with a fork or spoon, or with decorative fluting tools.

Crimping a double crust is done the same way, but the two crusts must be trimmed, folded and crimped together. Care should be taken here to press the two doughs together as thin as possible. If the rim is more than ¼ inch thick, the center will be raw and doughy.

Working with Fruit

The success of fruit recipes depends entirely on the quality of the fruit itself. While the flavor of fruit remains fairly constant, the amount of sugar contained within its skin does not. A recipe may require more or less sugar as the sweetness of the fruit varies throughout the year. Additionally, different suppliers, farmers, and markets offer drastically different qualities of the same product.

To combat this variant, use your taste buds. Taste the fruit raw to determine if it needs a lot, or a little, sugar. Taste it again when sugar is added to be sure you've got enough.

Basic Pie Dough

All elements of this recipe should be kept as cold as possible. On really hot days, I will go so far as to freeze my flour. Every little bit helps.

½ cup ice water

1 TB. cider vinegar

3 cups all-purpose flour

1 tsp. salt

2 TB. sugar

8 oz. (2 sticks) butter, diced and chilled

Makes enough dough for 3 8-inch circles
Prep time: 20 minutes
Chilling time: 1 hour

1. Combine water and vinegar and set aside. In a medium bowl, sift together the flour, salt, and sugar and mix well. Add diced butter and cut in to pea-size pieces. Add half the water/vinegar mixture, stirring with a fork to moisten. Add enough additional water/vinegar to just hold the dough together. Press it into a disc, wrap in plastic, and refrigerate for 1 hour. The dough should look marbled, with visible patches of butter and flour. Dough can be refrigerated for 2 days or frozen for up to 1 month.

2. To roll out dough, divide into 3 even pieces. Work with only one piece of dough at a time, keeping the remaining dough refrigerated. Knead the dough briefly to soften, and form into a disc. Place on a floured surface and, with a rolling pin, roll over the center of the dough in one direction. Turn the dough 90° and roll in the center again. Turn again, and repeat this pattern until the dough is an 8-inch circle. Turning the dough in this manner keeps it round, and alerts you right away if it starts sticking to the counter. Spread flour under the dough as necessary to prevent sticking. Work quickly to prevent the dough from warming up.

3. Transfer dough to pie pan by rolling it up onto the pin, or folding it in half. Place the lined pie shells in the refrigerator while rolling out remaining dough and preparing filling.

Basic Graham Cracker Crust

You can buy graham cracker crumbs or make your own. Grind crackers in a food processor, blender, or place them in a zipper bag and crush them with a rolling pin.

---

*Makes crumbs for
1 9-inch pie shell*

Prep time: 20 minutes
Cook time: 10 minutes

1½ **cup graham cracker crumbs**

2 **TB. sugar**
2 **oz. (½ stick) butter, melted**

1. Preheat oven to 350°F. Lightly coat one 9-inch pie pan with butter or pan spray. In a medium bowl combine the graham cracker crumbs, sugar, and melted butter.

2. Mix well and press into prepared pan, covering the bottom and sides. Bake until lightly toasted, about 10 minutes. Cool completely before filling.

Nut Crust: Replace graham cracker crumbs with finely ground nuts.

Cookie Crust: Omit the sugar and replace graham cracker crumbs with finely ground cookie crumbs. If Oreos are used, you can omit the butter. The white filling holds it together.

Cherry Pie

I cannot tell a lie, this would be perfect for your President's Day party.

1 recipe basic pie dough

4 cups cherries, pitted and stemmed, or frozen without sugar

1 cup sugar, plus more as needed

1 TB. cornstarch

1 tsp. salt

Grated zest and juice of 1 lemon

2 egg yolk

2 TB. cream

¼ cup sugar

<table>
<tr><td>Makes 1 9-inch pie</td></tr>
<tr><td>Prep time: 20 minutes</td></tr>
<tr><td>Cook time: 60 minutes</td></tr>
</table>

1. Preheat oven to 350°F. Line pie pan with a circle of pie dough, and roll out an additional circle for a top crust. Refrigerate both.

2. In a large bowl, toss together cherries, sugar, cornstarch, salt, lemon zest, and juice. Mix well to thoroughly coat cherries. Taste a cherry to be sure it is sweet enough. If the coating of sugar is not enough, add 2 to 3 tablespoons more as needed. Pile cherries into pie pan lined with dough. Lay top circle of dough over fruit, and let dough warm up a bit, 3-5 minutes, until it bends easily without cracking. With scissors, trim bottom and top crust together, ½ inch from edge of pan. Squeeze top and bottom crusts together around the rim, and crimp with fingers or score with a fork. Chill dough until firm.

3. In a small bowl, make an egg wash by combining egg yolk and cream, and brush over the surface of the pie crust. Sprinkle with sugar, and bake at 350°F for 45 to 60 minutes, until golden brown and bubbly. Pies can be assembled and frozen raw for up to 2 weeks. Bake directly from the freezer for 60 to 90 minutes.

Other Fruits: This same method can be used for any number of fruits that do not require precooking. Try it with blueberries, peaches, nectarines, boysenberries, or rhubarb. Strawberries tend to be too watery, but work well when mixed with other fruits, the classic being rhubarb. Spices can be added to taste. Try nutmeg and cinnamon with peaches, or ginger with blueberries.

Apple Pie

To guarantee your apples are cooked to perfection, precook them on the stove until they are caramelized and tender. This prevents the filling from shrinking in the oven, which creates a gap of air between the apples and the top crust. Precooked apples produce a beautiful, full slice of pie, with an intact top crust and a generous amount of apple filling.

Makes 1 9-inch pie
Prep time: 40 minutes
Cook time: 60 minutes

1 recipe basic pie dough

8–12 Fuji apples, peeled, cored, and sliced (or use your favorite apple)

1 cup brown sugar

1 tsp. salt

1 TB. cinnamon

1 TB. nutmeg

4 TB. (½ stick) butter, divided, and more as needed

2 egg yolks

2 TB. cream

¼ cup sugar

1. Line pie pan with a circle of pie dough. Roll out an additional circle for a top crust, and refrigerate both.

2. In a large bowl, toss together apples, brown sugar, salt, cinnamon, and nutmeg. Mix well to thoroughly coat apples. In a large sauté pan over high heat melt 2 tablespoons butter. Add one layer of apples and cook, stirring often, until tender and caramelized. Transfer apples to a baking sheet to cool, and repeat with remaining apples. Do not crowd apples in pan, or they will cook too slowly and won't caramelize. Cool apples completely.

3. Preheat oven to 350°. Pile cooled apples into pie pan lined with dough. Be sure to add all the cooking juices. Lay top circle of dough over apples, and let dough warm up a bit for 3 to 5 minutes, until it bends easily without cracking. With scissors, trim bottom and top crust together, ½ inch from edge of pan. Squeeze top and bottom crusts together around the rim, and crimp with fingers or score with a fork. In a small bowl make an egg wash by combining egg yolks and cream and brush over the surface of the pie crust. Sprinkle with sugar and bake for 45 to 60 minutes, until golden brown and bubbly. Pies can be assembled and frozen raw for up to 2 weeks. Bake directly from the freezer for 60 to 90 minutes.

Dutch Apple Pie: Crimp the bottom crust alone and replace top crust with streusel (see streusel recipe in Chapter 2).

Apple Pie and Cheddar: "An apple pie without some cheese is like a kiss without a squeeze," or so the napkins read at Marie Calendar's when I was a kid. If you've never tried it, you haven't lived. Top a slice of apple pie with a big hunk of sharp cheddar and melt it in the oven.

Apple Turnovers: Roll out pie dough and cut into 6-inch squares. Moisten edges, fill with 2 tablespoons sautéed apples, fold over into triangles, seal, brush with an egg wash, sprinkle with sugar, and bake at 350° until golden and bubbly, about 15 minutes.

Tidbits _____

All apples are not created equal, but they're close. Most are grown for the lunch box and will generally hold up to heat just fine. So pick the apple you like the best. Fuji is my favorite.

Pumpkin Pie

While squash and gourds are familiar and ancient foods, pumpkins are definitely from the New World. They were quickly embraced by colonists and people back home in Europe because they were similar to the familiar gourds, easy to cultivate, and superior in flavor.

Makes 1 9-inch pie	
Prep time: 60 minutes	
Cook time: 60 minutes	

½ **recipe basic pie dough**   1 tsp. **cinnamon**

1 cup **brown sugar**   1 tsp. **nutmeg**

3 TB. **cream**   1 tsp. **cardamom**

2 **eggs**   ½ tsp. **clove**

2 oz. (½ stick) **butter, melted** ½ tsp. **ginger**

1 TB. **vanilla extract**   6 cups **pumpkin purée**

½ tsp. **salt**

Kitchen Tips

It is easier to open a can of pumpkin purée, but I find it more satisfying to bake and purée my own. Buy a sugar pie pumpkin, cut it in half, remove the seeds, and bake it cut side down until tender. Cool, scoop out the pumpkin, and purée it in a food processor or blender with the eggs in the recipe.

1. Preheat oven to 350°F. Line pie pan with a circle of pie dough, crimp edges, and blind-bake for 20 to 30 minutes, until edges just begin to set. (See "Blind-Baking" earlier in this chapter.) Cool completely and remove pie weights.

2. In a large bowl combine brown sugar, cream, eggs, butter, vanilla, salt, cinnamon, nutmeg, cardamom, clove, and ginger, and mix well. Add pumpkin, combine thoroughly, and pour into pie crust. Bake for 30 to 45 minutes, until lightly golden and just set. Chill for 2 to 4 hours before serving, topped with whipped cream.

Acorn or Butternut Squash Pie: Cut the squash in half, remove the seeds and roast until tender. Scoop out tender squash and use in place of pumpkin purée.

Pumpkin and Candied Ginger: Add an extra teaspoon of ground ginger and fold in ½ cup of diced candied ginger.

Pumpkin-Pecan Pie: Cut pumpkin and pecan pie recipes in half. Fill a half-baked pie shell half full with pumpkin pie filling. Top with pecans, and pour pecan custard on top (see the following recipe). Bake at 350°F until golden brown and set, about 45 minutes.

Pecan Pie

Because this holiday favorite is supersweet, I think it does well with a dollop of not-too-sweet whipped cream on the top. In fact, I like to tart it up a bit by mixing whipped cream with sour cream.

½ **recipe basic pie dough**	½ **tsp. salt**
2 cups pecan halves or pieces	**1 tsp. cinnamon**
1 cup sugar	**1 tsp. nutmeg**
1 cup corn syrup	**1 tsp. cardamom**
5 eggs	½ **tsp. clove**
2 oz. (½ stick) butter, melted	½ **tsp. ginger**
1 TB. vanilla extract	

> *Makes 1 9-inch pie*
> **Prep time:** 60 minutes
> **Cook time:** 60 minutes

1. Preheat oven to 350°F. Line pie pan with a circle of pie dough, crimp edges, and blind-bake for 20 to 30 minutes, until edges just begin to set. (See "Blind-Baking" earlier in this chapter.) Cool completely and remove pie weights.

2. Fill the half-baked crust with pecans. In a large bowl combine sugar, corn syrup, and eggs and mix well. Add butter, vanilla, salt, cinnamon, nutmeg, cardamom, clove, and ginger, mix well, and pour over nuts. Bake for 30 to 45 minutes, until golden brown and just set. Chill completely before serving.

Whole Pecans: Arrange whole pecans, rounded side up, in concentric or spiral circles before pouring in custard.

Assorted Nuts: This custard will work over any nut. Try a mixture, or just one, like macadamia or Brazil.

Lemon Meringue Pie

There are many tips and tricks to prevent the meringue on this pie from weeping. The best method I have found is this precooked Italian meringue. Sadly, all meringues break down after several hours, and weeping is inevitable. My advice: eat it fast!

Makes 1 9-inch pie
Prep time: 45 minutes
Cook time: 20 minutes
Chilling time: 3 hours to overnight
Finishing time (for meringue): 45 minutes

½ recipe basic pie dough

6 whole eggs

5 egg yolks (reserve whites)

1¾ cup sugar

Zest of 4 lemons

1 ⅓ cup lemon juice

½ tsp. salt

8 oz. (2 sticks) butter

For the meringue:

1 cup sugar

½ cup light corn syrup

¼ cup water

½ tsp. salt

4 egg whites

1 tsp. vanilla extract

1. Preheat oven to 350°F. Line pie pan with a circle of pie dough, crimp edges, and blind-bake for 30 to 45 minutes, until edges and bottom are golden brown. (See "Blind-Baking" earlier in this chapter.) Toward the end of baking, remove pie weights and return to oven to completely cook bottom of shell. Cool completely and remove pie weights.

2. In a large saucepan combine whole eggs, yolks, sugar, lemon zest, lemon juice, salt, and butter. Mix well and set over high heat. Stir continuously until mixture thickens to sour cream consistency. Pour immediately into precooked pie shell and refrigerate until set, 3 hours or overnight.

3. For the meringue, combine sugar, corn syrup, water, and salt in a large saucepan. Bring to a boil and cook over high heat until it reaches the firm ball stage, 245°F. Meanwhile, in a large bowl, using a whisk or an electric mixer, whip the egg whites until stiff peaks form. Continue whipping while slowly drizzling in the sugar syrup. Add vanilla and whip until stiff peaks are formed. Spread evenly, and mound high over the top of the chilled pie. Before serving set pie under a broiler briefly to brown meringue, about 2 to 3 minutes. Keep chilled.

Chocolate Cream Pie

The best chocolate cream pies are made with the best chocolate. It's worth the effort to shop around for something special. But be sure to stick with bittersweet chocolate. Milk or white chocolate is too pale and will turn this custard into an unappealing grayish-brown.

1 recipe basic graham cracker crust

4 egg yolks

1 cup sugar

⅓ cup cornstarch

4 cups half-and-half

1 TB. vanilla extract

2 oz. bittersweet chocolate, chopped

2 TB. butter

1 cup whipping cream

1 TB. sugar

1 tsp. vanilla extract

Makes 1 9-inch pie
Prep time: 10 minutes
Cook time: 60 minutes
Chilling time: 4 hours to overnight

1. In a small bowl whisk together egg yolks, sugar, and cornstarch and set aside. In a large saucepan combine half-and-half and vanilla and bring to a boil over high heat. At the boil, ladle ½ cup of hot half-and-half into the yolks and whisk quickly to combine. Pour the warmed yolks into saucepan and, over high heat, whisk immediately and vigorously until mixture begins to resemble thick sour cream, about 2 minutes. Remove from heat and add chocolate and butter, stirring to combine. Pour immediately into prepared graham cracker crust and chill until set, 4 hours to overnight.

2. Before serving, combine cream, sugar, and vanilla in a large bowl, and using a whisk or an electric mixer, whip until firm peaks form. Spread evenly over the top of the pie and garnish with grated or shaved chocolate.

Coconut Cream Pie: Omit the chocolate and replace 2 cups of half-and-half with 2 cups canned coconut milk. Add 1 teaspoon of coconut extract and sprinkle the top of the pie with toasted, shredded coconut.

Vanilla Cream Pie: Omit the chocolate and add 1 vanilla bean. Split the bean down the center, scrape the seeds out with a paring knife, and add them to the half-and-half. Save the pods for steeping in another recipe, or use them to scent a jar of sugar.

Banana Cream Pie: Line the bottom of the crust with two perfectly ripe bananas sliced into wheels. Pour vanilla cream pie custard over the bananas and chill. Top with whipped cream and toasted coconut, shaved chocolate, and macadamia nuts.

Chess Pie

Some say that this pie is so simple that when asked what kind of pie is baking, the cook's response was "It's just pie," which when slurred, sounded like "jess pie" or "chess pie." Others insist the pie's curdy texture is similar to cheese, which was misspelled "chess."

Makes 1 9-inch pie
Prep time: 30 minutes
Cook time: 45 minutes
Chilling time: 3 hours to overnight

½ **recipe basic pie dough**

3 **eggs**

⅔ **cup sugar**

2 **TB. cornmeal**

½ **cup cream**

Zest and juice of 1 lemon

1 **TB. vanilla extract**

4 **oz. (1 stick) butter, melted**

1. Preheat oven to 325°F. Line pie pan with a circle of pie dough, crimp edges, and blind-bake for 20 to 30 minutes, until edges just begin to set. (See "Blind-Baking" earlier in this chapter.) Cool completely and remove pie weights.

2. In a large bowl combine eggs, sugar, cornmeal, cream, lemon zest and juice, and vanilla. Mix well, then stir in butter. Pour into prebaked pie shell and bake for 30 to 45 minutes, until lightly golden and just set. Chill completely before serving.

Shoo-Fly Pie

This Pennsylvania Dutch classic is so sweet that you can't keep the flies away.

½ recipe basic pie dough

1 cup all-purpose flour

⅔ cup brown sugar

1 TB. butter, chilled and diced

1 egg

1 cup molasses

1 cup hot water

1 tsp. baking soda

Makes 1 9-inch pie
Prep time: 30 minutes
Cook time: 45 minutes

1. Preheat oven to 325°F. Line pie pan with a circle of pie dough, crimp edges, and blind-bake for 20 to 30 minutes, until edges just begin to set. (See "Blind-Baking" earlier in this chapter.) Cool completely and remove pie weights.

2. In a large bowl combine flour and brown sugar. Add chilled butter and cut in until the mixture resembles crumbs. Set aside ¼ cup of this mixture. To the remaining crumbs add egg and molasses. In a separate bowl combine hot water and soda, and add. The mixture will be lumpy. Pour into prebaked pie shell, top with reserved crumb mixture, and bake for 30 to 45 minutes, until lightly golden and just set. Chill completely before serving.

Grasshopper Pie

The grasshopper cocktail seems to have fallen out of favor, but its namesake dessert remains a family favorite.

Makes 1 9-inch pie
Prep time: 20 minutes
Chilling time: 2 hours to overnight

1 recipe basic graham cracker crust, Oreo variation (see earlier recipe)

1 (8-oz.) package cream cheese, softened

1 (14-oz.) can sweetened condensed milk

2 TB. lemon juice

¼ cup green crème de menthe

¼ cup clear crème de cacao

2–3 drops green food coloring

1 (4-oz.) container whipped topping

1. In a large bowl with a sturdy spoon beat cream cheese until smooth. Add condensed milk, lemon juice, liqueurs, and food coloring and stir to combine. Fold in whipped topping and pour into prepared cookie crust.

2. Chill until set, about 2 hours. Serve topped with whipped cream and shaved chocolate.

Chapter 15

Cookies, Brownies, and Bars, Oh My

In This Chapter

- ◆ Tips for great cookies
- ◆ Freezing cookie dough
- ◆ Chocolate chunks and chips
- ◆ Fruit and nut bars
- ◆ Cookie-jar staples
- ◆ Holiday favorites

After school with a big glass of milk, after dinner with a hot cup of coffee, or after a long hard week, cookies and bars have always satisfied my craving for comfort. They are, by far, my favorite food. Dressed up or plain and simple, it's hard to say no to such a treat!

Creaming

I find it fascinating that one cookie recipe from the back of a package of chocolate chips will turn out different with each person who makes it. Some cookies are thick and chewy, some dry and crisp, others thin and gooey. What causes this, besides user error? It's the butter.

Many cookie recipes begin with a method known as creaming, in which the butter and sugar are blended together until smooth. This step softens the butter and removes the lumps so that the remaining ingredients will blend evenly and thoroughly. But this step can be taken too far. Butter is fat, and fat melts when heated.

In the oven the fat melts. But if it's cool, the other protein-rich ingredients, like eggs and flour, solidify and hold it all together. If, however, the fat goes into the oven already warm, it will melt and spread before the proteins have a chance to set.

Overcreaming is the main culprit, and this is easily done when using a standing or hand-held machine. The very act of creaming heats up the batter through friction. Friction softens the fat so that the remaining ingredients can be absorbed. If you're not paying attention, friction can build up to a point that liquefies the fat. If the fat goes into the oven in a liquid state, the cookies will spread, ending up chewy and wet. The phenomenon gets worse if you start the recipe with room temperature, softened butter.

If you want your cookies to maintain their shape and cook evenly, use cold butter, and cream it only until the lumps are gone, no more. If you want to be double sure that the fat is solid before baking, chill the dough. If you are creaming by hand, softened butter is fine, but be aware that you can go too far.

Thinking Ahead

One of my favorite things to do with cookie dough is to make it in advance. It keeps for several weeks in the freezer if wrapped well, and makes whipping up a batch of cookies effortless.

The best way to freeze cookie dough is in logs. From logs, cookies can be sliced off and baked within minutes. To make a cookie dough log, start with a piece of plastic wrap about 18 inches long. Place 2 to 3 cups of dough down the center length of the plastic wrap, and with your hands, form a log 1 to 2 inches in diameter. The fatter the log is, the bigger the cookie will be. Wrap the plastic around the dough and twist it tight at the ends. The pressure of twisting the plastic will push the dough into a sausage shape. Store the dough logs in the fridge for 3 to 4 days, or freeze them for 2 to 3 weeks.

When the time comes to bake your dough, bring a log out to a cutting board, unwrap, and slice off ½-inch coins. Spread them out evenly on a cookie sheet, with 1 to 2 inches between, depending on the dough. Dough that spreads will form nicely into a cookie shape. Dough that is meant to hold its shape, like sugar cookie dough, will maintain the sliced coin shape when baked.

> **Kitchen Tips**
>
> Roll logs of sugar cookie dough in colored sugar, chopped nuts, or jimmies before slicing the log to give the cookies a decorative frame.

Nuts to You

Nuts are a familiar ingredient in baking. Because they can be expensive, I try to buy them in bulk whenever possible. They are loaded with oil, and so I store them in the refrigerator to keep them from turning rancid.

If nuts are going inside of dough, toast them first to release the most flavor. Spread them in one even layer on a baking sheet. Bake at 350°F until the color begins to change and you can smell them. They can be chopped before or after baking. Be sure to cool them completely before adding them into the dough. The heat of warm toasty nuts will melt the butter in a dough and cause the cookie to spread.

If nuts are going on the outside of cookies as a topper or an outer coating, do not toast them in advance. They will be toasted when the cookie bakes. If you pretoast them in this instance, they will get double toasted, too dark, and probably burnt.

Coconut is another common cookie additive that is improved by toasting. But beware. Shredded coconut is thin, and toasts very fast. Spread a thin layer onto a baking sheet and toast at 350°F, stirring every 5 to 6 minutes to ensure even browning.

Preparing Pans

Cookie sheets, or baking sheets, come in many forms, and are made from many materials, including nonstick varieties. But regardless of what the pan is made of, I always suggest lining it with paper.

Paper is a good idea because it keeps food from sticking without having to use butter or pan spray. These oils cook onto your pans, and build up over repeated use, even when pans are cleaned thoroughly. This shortens the useful life of the pan, and looks pretty bad. Paper also makes baking more fun by speeding cleanup. Just throw the paper away! No heavy-duty scrubbing is required, which prolongs the life of your pans.

Professional chefs use parchment paper. It comes in rolls for the home cook, and is specially treated so that it doesn't burn and food doesn't stick to it. Many large food-warehouse stores carry professional-grade parchment in large sheets, which is worth the investment if you bake a lot. Wax paper is a viable alternative.

If you are baking bars, a pan lined with paper makes them hard to cut and serve out of the pan. In this case, a light coating of butter or pan spray is fine.

Chocolate Chip Cookies

The variations of this cookie are limited only by your imagination. The recipe will hold at least one additional cup of garnish, such as chopped nuts or candies. I like to make s'mores cookies with 1 cup each of chocolate chips, crushed graham crackers, and mini-marshmallows.

2¾ cup all-purpose flour

1 tsp. baking soda

½ tsp. salt

6 oz. (1½ sticks) butter

1 cup sugar

1 cup brown sugar

1 TB. vanilla extract

2 eggs

2 cups chocolate chips

Makes about 2 dozen cookies
Prep time: 15 minutes
Cook time: 30 minutes for entire batch
Chilling time: 30 minutes

1. Preheat oven to 350°F. Line two baking sheets with parchment paper. Sift together flour, baking soda, and salt and set aside. In a large bowl, using a sturdy spoon or an electric mixer, cream butter and sugars together until lump-free. Add vanilla and eggs, one by one. Slowly add sifted ingredients. Mix well to fully incorporate, and fold in chips. Chill dough for 30 minutes.

2. Drop cookie dough onto lined baking sheets 2 inches apart. Bake for 10 to 12 minutes, until golden brown around the edges. Cool 5 minutes before removing from baking sheet.

Blondies: Bake cookie dough in a 9×13 baking dish at 350°F for 20 to 30 minutes, until the center is firm and golden. To serve, cut into squares.

Chocolate-Chocolate Chip: Replace ¼ cup flour with ¼ cup cocoa powder. Take care not to overbake, as judging the color is difficult with chocolate dough.

White Chocolate-Macadamia Nut: Replace the chocolate chips with white chocolate chips or chunks, and add 1 cup of chopped macadamia nuts.

Oatmeal Fudge Drops

This is the perfect cookie for a hot summer day, because you never have to turn on the oven! But look out. These things are addictive.

Makes about 2 dozen cookies
Prep time: 10 minutes
Chilling time: 30 minutes

2 cups sugar

2 oz. (½ stick) butter

2 oz. bittersweet chocolate, chopped

½ cup milk

⅔ cup peanut butter

3 cups quick-cooking oatmeal

1. In a large saucepan, combine sugar, butter, chocolate, and milk. Set over medium heat and melt gently, stirring occasionally, being careful not to scorch or boil. Remove from heat when smooth and stir in peanut butter and oatmeal.

2. Mix thoroughly, then drop by tablespoonful onto wax paper. Chill for 30 minutes before serving. Store in an airtight container in the refrigerator or freezer.

Fudge Brownies

This is my favorite brownie recipe. They are very dense and a little gooey. Be sure to serve with a big glass of milk.

10 oz. (2½ sticks) butter

2 cups bittersweet chocolate chips (or 12 oz. chopped chocolate)

1½ cup all-purpose flour

½ tsp. salt

6 eggs

2½ cups sugar

¾ cup chopped nuts (optional)

> *Makes about 2 dozen 11/2-inch brownies*
>
> **Prep time:** 20 minutes
> **Cook time:** 30 minutes

1. Preheat oven to 350°F. Lightly butter a 9×13 brownie pan. Melt butter and chocolate in a double boiler or a bowl set over simmering water. Set aside.

2. Sift together the flour and salt and set aside. In a medium bowl using a whisk or an electric mixer, whip the eggs and sugar until thick and pale yellow. Add the chocolate, then fold in sifted ingredients. Fold in nuts, if using. Transfer to brownie pan and bake for 30 minutes, until the top looks shiny and set. Cool for 20 minutes before cutting.

Marble Brownies: In a medium bowl beat until smooth one (8-oz.) package of cream cheese, ⅓ cup sugar, 1 TB. vanilla extract, and one egg. Swirl this mixture on top of the brownie batter before baking.

Dress It Up: Ganache Glazed Brownies

Ganache is truly a miracle food. Spread it hot, as in this recipe, for a shiny chocolate glaze. Chill it, and roll it for rich chocolate truffles. Whip it stiff into a smooth creamy frosting. And my favorite of all, add it to warm milk for the best hot chocolate on earth!

Makes enough to cover two dozen 11/2-inch brownies

Prep time: 10 minutes
Cook time: 5 minutes
Chilling time: 60 minutes

---

1 recipe baked fudge brownies (see previous recipe)

2 cups bittersweet chocolate chips (or 12 oz. chopped chocolate)

2 TB. butter

1 cup heavy cream

1. Combine the chocolate and butter in a large bowl and set aside. In a small saucepan, bring the cream to a boil over high heat. Just before it boils over, pour it over the chocolate and butter.

2. Let the bowl sit undisturbed for 3 minutes, then whisk until smooth. Immediately spread over brownies and refrigerate until firm, about 1 hour. To cut the brownies neatly, use a warm knife, and wipe it clean with a damp towel after each cut.

Oatmeal-Raisin Cookies

Because these have oatmeal and raisins inside, my kids initially refused to eat them. That is, until they had one by accident. Now they're on the top 10 list.

1½ cup all-purpose flour	1 cup sugar
1 tsp. baking soda	1 cup brown sugar
2 cups rolled oats	1 TB. vanilla extract
½ tsp. salt	2 eggs
6 oz. (1½ sticks) butter	2 cups raisins

Makes about 2 dozen cookies

Prep time: 15 minutes
Cook time: 30 minutes for entire batch
Chilling time: 30 minutes

1. Preheat oven to 350°F. Line two baking sheets with parchment paper. Sift together flour, baking soda, oats, and salt and set aside. In a large bowl, using a sturdy spoon or an electric mixer, cream butter and sugars together until lump-free. Add vanilla and eggs, one by one. Slowly add sifted ingredients, mixing well to fully incorporate. Fold in raisins. Chill dough for 30 minutes.

2. Drop cookie dough onto lined baking sheets 2 inches apart. Bake for 10 to 12 minutes, until golden brown on the edges. Cool 5 minutes before removing from baking sheet.

Ranger Cookies: For these old-time favorites, replace the raisins with 1 cup chocolate chips, 1 cup peanuts, 1 cup shredded coconut, and 1 cup corn- or wheat-flake cereal.

Lemon Bars

Many lemon bar recipes use the traditional French tart dough pâté sucrée for the base. But I've found that this sugar cookie recipe, while very similar in structure to French pâté sucrée, tastes better and is easier to handle.

Makes about 2 dozen 11/2-inch bars
Prep time: 20 minutes
Cook time: 35 minutes
Chilling time: 60 minutes

1 recipe sugar cookie dough (see recipe later in this chapter)

6 whole eggs

5 egg yolks (reserve whites)

1¾ cup sugar

Zest of 4 lemons

1⅓ cup lemon juice

¼ tsp. salt

8 oz. (2 sticks) butter

½ cup powdered sugar

1. Preheat oven to 350°F. Lightly butter a 9×13 brownie pan. Press cookie dough into pan, lining the bottom with a ¼-inch thick layer of dough. Bake until golden brown, about 15 minutes. Cool.

2. In a large saucepan, combine whole eggs and yolks, sugar, lemon zest and juice, salt, and butter. Mix well and set over high heat. Stir continuously until mixture thickens to sour cream consistency. Pour immediately onto precooked cookie-dough lined pan. Reduce oven temperature to 325°F and bake until golden brown and just set, about 15 to 20 minutes. Cool completely, than refrigerate until firm, about 1 hour. Dust with powdered sugar before cutting into squares.

Lime-Tangerine Bars: Replace the lemon juice and zest with ⅔ cups each tangerine and lime juice and zest.

Raspberry Bars: Replace 1 cup lemon juice with raspberry purée.

Cranberry Bars: Replace 1 cup lemon juice with cranberry purée.

Date Bars

Dates are an ancient fruit, and this recipe takes advantage of their luscious flavor. If you have a good source for fresh dates, choose them over prechopped packages. It's worth the extra chopping effort.

1 egg	2 tsp. baking powder
1 cup sugar	1 cup all-purpose flour
½ tsp. salt	1½ cup dates, pitted and chopped
½ cup milk	1 cup pecans
1 TB. vanilla	2 cups powdered sugar, sifted

> *Makes about 2 dozen 1½-inch bars*
>
> **Prep time:** 20 minutes
> **Cook time:** 30 minutes

1. Preheat oven to 350°F. Lightly butter a 9×13 brownie pan. In a large bowl stir together egg and sugar. Add salt, milk, and vanilla and stir to combine. Sift together baking powder and flour, and mix well into egg mixture. Fold in dates and pecans.

2. Pour batter into prepared pan and bake until golden brown, 20 to 30 minutes. Cool completely, cut into bars, and coat each bar in powdered sugar.

3. Store in an airtight container at room temperature for 1 week, or freeze for up to one month.

Peanut Butter Cookies

It doesn't matter what your peanut butter preference is—smooth or chunky, these are the top seller at every bake sale.

Makes about 2 dozen cookies
Prep time: 15 minutes
Cook time: 30 minutes
Chilling time: 30 minutes

1¼ cup all-purpose flour

½ tsp. baking powder

½ tsp. salt

4 oz. (1 stick) butter

½ cup peanut butter

1½ cup sugar, divided

½ cup brown sugar

1 TB. vanilla extract

1 egg

1. Preheat oven to 325°F. Line two baking sheets with parchment paper. Sift together flour, baking soda, and salt and set aside. In a large bowl, using a sturdy spoon or an electric mixer, cream butter, peanut butter, ½ cup granulated sugar, and brown sugar together until lump-free. Add vanilla and egg. Slowly add sifted ingredients. Mix well to fully incorporate. Chill dough for 30 minutes.

2. Fill a small bowl with the remaining granulated sugar. Roll cookie dough into walnut-sized balls, coat them with sugar, and set onto lined baking sheets 2 inches apart. Use a fork dipped in sugar to make a cross-hatch design on top of each cookie. Bake for 10 to 12 minutes, until golden brown around the edges. Cool 5 minutes before removing from baking sheet.

Peanut Butter Kisses: Roll dough into balls, set on the baking sheet, press an unwrapped chocolate kiss into the center of each cookie, and bake.

Snickerdoodles

Recipes for small cakes flavored with cinnamon go back to medieval times, but the name of this cookie is definitely modern. Snickerdoodle is a tiny adventure hero who drives a peanut car and saves the day with the help of his uncle Yankee and his cousin Polly Wolly.

2¼ cups all-purpose flour	2 cup sugar, divided
2 tsp. baking soda	1 TB. vanilla extract
2 tsp. cream of tartar	2 eggs
¼ tsp. salt	⅓ cup cinnamon
8 oz. (2 sticks) butter	

> *Makes about 2 dozen cookies*
>
> **Prep time:** 15 minutes
> **Cook time:** 30 minutes
> **Chilling time:** 30 minutes

1. Preheat oven to 350°F. Line two baking sheets with parchment paper. Sift together flour, baking soda, cream of tartar, and salt and set aside. In a large bowl, using a sturdy spoon or an electric mixer, cream butter and 1 cup sugar together until lump-free. Add vanilla and eggs, one by one. Slowly add sifted ingredients and mix well to fully incorporate. Chill dough for 30 minutes.

2. In a small bowl combine remaining cup of sugar and cinnamon. Roll cookie dough into walnut-sized balls, coat them with cinnamon sugar, and set onto lined baking sheets 2 inches apart. Bake for 10 to 12 minutes, until golden brown around the edges. Cool 5 minutes before removing from baking sheet.

Sugar Cookies

This dough holds its shape perfectly in the oven, making it just the thing for fanciful shapes and decorative icing. It also makes a great refrigerator cookie. Form it into logs, roll them in chopped nuts or colored sugar, chill, slice, and bake.

Makes about 2 dozen cookies

Prep time: 15 minutes
Cook time: 45 minutes
Chilling time: 30 minutes

2⅓ cup all-purpose flour	3⅔ cup sugar
¾ tsp. baking powder	1 TB. vanilla extract
¼ tsp. salt	1 egg
8 oz. (2 sticks) butter	1 TB. milk

1. Preheat oven to 350°F. Line two baking sheets with parchment paper. Sift together flour, baking powder, and salt and set aside. In a large bowl, using a sturdy spoon or an electric mixer, cream butter and sugar together until lump-free. Add vanilla, egg, and milk. Slowly add sifted ingredients and mix well to fully incorporate. Chill dough for 30 minutes.

2. Roll out chilled cookie dough on a floured surface to ¼-inch thick. Use a floured cutter and place cookie-dough shapes onto lined baking sheets 1 inch apart. Bake for 10 to 12 minutes, until golden brown around the edges. Cool 5 minutes before removing from baking sheet.

Gingersnaps

This is my very favorite cookie. Even though the name says *snap*, I like mine a little chewy. The longer you bake them, the snappier they get.

2⅓ cup all-purpose flour	¼ tsp. salt
1 TB. ground ginger	4 oz. (1 stick) butter
2 tsp. cinnamon	3 cups sugar, divided
2 tsp. nutmeg	½ cup molasses
¼ tsp. clove	1 tsp. vanilla
1½ tsp. baking powder	1 egg

Makes about 2 dozen cookies
Prep time: 45 minutes
Cook time: 30 minutes
Chilling time: 30 minutes

1. Preheat oven to 350°F. Line two baking sheets with parchment paper. Sift together flour, ginger, cinnamon, nutmeg, clove, baking powder, and salt and set aside. In a large bowl, using a sturdy spoon or an electric mixer, cream butter and 1 cup sugar together until lump-free. Add molasses, vanilla, and egg. Slowly add sifted ingredients and mix well to fully incorporate. Chill dough for 30 minutes.

2. Place the remaining 2 cups of sugar in a small bowl. Roll cookie dough into walnut-sized balls, coat them with sugar, and set onto lined baking sheets 2 inches apart. Bake for 8 to 10 minutes, until golden brown on the edges. Cool 5 minutes before removing from baking sheet.

Molasses Crisps: Add an extra ½ cup of flour to the dough, and once chilled, roll out on a floured surface to ¼-inch thick. Cut with a floured circle cutter, sprinkle with granulated sugar, and bake at 325°F for 8 to 10 minutes, until golden brown around the edges.

Candied Gingersnaps: Fold 1 cup of chopped candied ginger into the dough.

Dress It Up: Gingerbread Men

Who says you have to make men? Make women, kids, dogs, cats, whatever you like. One year I made gingerbread cars. Unfortunately, my husband ate all the wheels, thinking they were cookies. We refer to that as "The Year He Ate Christmas."

Makes about 2 dozen cookies, depending on size and shape

Prep time: 30 minutes

Cook time: 30 minutes

Chilling time: 30 minutes

Finishing time: 20–60 minutes

---

3 cups all-purpose flour

¼ tsp. salt

¾ tsp. baking soda

1 TB. ginger

1 TB. cinnamon

½ tsp. nutmeg

¼ tsp. clove

4 oz. (1 stick) butter

½ cup sugar

1 egg

⅔ cup molasses

For the icing

1 (1-lb.) box powdered sugar, sifted

½ tsp. cream of tartar

2 egg whites

1–2 TB. lemon juice

Food coloring

Red-hot candies, raisins, chocolate chips, gum drops, or whatever you like for decorating

1. Preheat oven to 350°F. Line two baking sheets with parchment paper. Sift together flour, salt, baking soda, ginger, cinnamon, nutmeg, and clove and set aside. In a large bowl, using a sturdy spoon or an electric mixer, cream butter and sugar together until lump-free. Add egg and molasses. Slowly add sifted ingredients. Mix well to fully incorporate and chill for 30 minutes.

2. Roll out chilled dough on a floured surface to ¼-inch thick. Use a floured cutter and place cookie-dough shapes onto lined baking sheets 1 inch apart. Decorate with candies now, or add them after baking, using icing as glue. Bake for 10 to 12 minutes, until golden brown around the edges. Cool 5 minutes before removing from baking sheet.

3. For icing, use a sturdy spoon or an electric mixer to combine the sugar, cream of tartar, and egg whites and beat until smooth. Add lemon juice slowly as needed to achieve thin but spreadable texture. When you lift up the spoon and drizzle the icing back into the bowl it should hold a ribbon on the surface for about 5 seconds. Add food coloring as desired. Icing can be used to coat the entire cookie, draw on features, or glue on candies. For gluing and drawing, make a thicker icing by adding slightly less lemon juice.

Mexican Wedding Cookies

These melt-in-your-mouth morsels are known in many cultures, by many other names, including Russian tea cakes, butterballs, snowballs, sandies, polvorones, mandulas, and kourabi. They appear as a special treat in so many countries because the ingredients—butter, sugar, and nuts—are usually saved for special occasions.

3¼ cup all-purpose flour

16 oz. (4 sticks) butter

⅔ cup powdered sugar

½ tsp. salt

2 cups pecans, toasted and chopped

1 tsp. vanilla extract

2 cups sifted powdered sugar

Makes about 4 dozen cookies
Prep time: 15 minutes
Cook time: 30 minutes
Chilling time: 30 minutes

1. Preheat oven to 350°F. Line two baking sheets with parchment paper. Sift flour and set aside. In a large bowl, using a sturdy spoon or an electric mixer, cream butter and powdered sugar together until lump-free. Add salt, nuts, and vanilla and mix thoroughly. Slowly add sifted flour and mix well to fully incorporate. Chill dough for 30 minutes.

2. Roll cookie dough into walnut-sized balls and set on lined baking sheets, 1 inch apart. Bake for 15 to 20 minutes, until golden brown around the edges. Cool 5 minutes before removing from baking sheet. When cookies are completely cool, coat thoroughly in sifted powdered sugar. Store in an airtight container at room temperature for 1 week, or freeze for up to 2 months.

Snowballs: Omit nuts and add ¼ teaspoon of almond extract.

Pfeffernusse: Traditional pfeffernusse are made without butter, and come out of the oven very hard. They are then allowed to age for 4 to 6 weeks, which softens the texture and mellows the flavor. For a quick version, omit the nuts in this recipe and add 1 teaspoon each cinnamon, nutmeg, cardamom, and black pepper; ½ teaspoon each of white pepper, allspice, and ginger; and ¼ teaspoon of clove.

Macaroons

These are delicious and very low in fat. You can further increase the healthy nature of this cookie by using unsweetened coconut and replacing the sugar with an equivalent amount of sugar substitute.

Makes about 3 dozen cookies
Prep time: 20 minutes
Cook time: 30 minutes

3 egg whites

½ tsp. salt

½ cup sugar

4 cups shredded coconut

1 TB. vanilla extract

1. Preheat oven to 350°F. Line two baking sheets with parchment paper. In a large bowl, using a whisk or an electric mixer, whip the egg whites with salt until medium peaks form. Slowly begin adding the sugar, 1 tablespoon at a time, until the whites are stiff and shiny. Fold in coconut and vanilla and mix well.

2. Drop by tablespoonful onto prepared baking sheets, 1 inch apart. Using wet fingers, shape into mounds or peaks. Bake until golden brown, 10 to 15 minutes.

3. Cool 5 minutes before removing from baking sheet. Store in an airtight container at room temperature for 1 week, or freeze up to 1 month.

Chocolate Macaroons: Fold in 1 cup of chocolate chips or chocolate chunks with the coconut.

Chapter 16

Down-Home Desserts

In This Chapter

- How to cook custards
- Tips for cooking with sugar
- Oven-baked and stovetop custards and puddings
- Fruity desserts
- Campfire treats and kids' favorites
- Home-style candies

When it's cold outside and the wind is howling, what could be better than a bowl of steaming bread pudding or rice pudding? When you're entertaining on a warm summer night, who doesn't love a good strawberry shortcake? What's camping without s'mores, or Halloween without caramel apples? These recipes will comfort you no matter what season it is.

Mastering Custards

Many of the desserts in this chapter are based on egg custards. The custards vary in flavor and texture, but they all include eggs and liquid. Baked slowly, these custards can set smooth and creamy, with a gelled consistency that's soft, not rubbery. When baked too quickly, the eggs will coagulate too fast and the finishing texture is more like scrambled eggs. The gentle cooking is important, too, for flavor. Overcooked custards taste overwhelmingly of eggs, which is a flavor more suited to breakfast than dessert.

Eggs contain protein. When protein is heated, it coagulates. The hotter it gets, the tighter it becomes. Using a steak as an example, the texture is much softer when cooked rare than when it is cooked well done. To achieve a soft and creamy texture, cook baked custards at low temperatures. Often recipes call for a protective water bath to slow the conduction of heat and prevent scorching. When cooking stovetop custards, stirring must remain constant to keep the eggs from settling on the bottom where they will heat and solidify quickly.

Once you feel comfortable with the custards, you have a world of fabulous dessert possibilities available to you. Oven-baked custards like bread pudding and flan are but a stepping stone to rich crème brûlée and pot de crème, and they are easily altered to fit the savory side of the table by omitting the sugar and adding a multitude of herbs and spices, vegetables, and cheeses (see the recipe for strata in Chapter 1). Stovetop custards like chocolate pudding are great on their own but become something quite exceptional when you pour them into a pie shell or pipe them into a cream puff (see the recipe for chocolate cream pie in Chapter 14).

Cooking with Sugar

Candy making can be easy and fun, especially if you have a microwave. Many cooks stay away from candy making because they are worried about crystallization, an event that can ruin a batch of sugar within minutes. Sugar starts out in crystalline form. Once liquefied, the two single sugar molecules, glucose and fructose, separate. During cooking they naturally try to rejoin with each other. If a stray crystal, or a spec of anything foreign, enters the pot, the molecules will gravitate towards it, grab hold, and start forming a gigantic crystal. (This same phenomenon was demonstrated when you made rock candy in science class.) To prevent those pesky molecules from taking over, recipes contain extra glucose (in the form of corn syrup) or acid. These ingredients discourage the reforming of crystals.

There are also some precautions you can take while the sugar is cooking. Never stir a pot of sugar unless a recipe tells you to (when there are other ingredients in the pot, like butter, for example). The agitation will bring any foreign particles into play.

If crystals begin to accumulate on the side of the pan as the sugar cooks, they can be dissolved and wiped away with a moist, clean pastry brush. Be careful not to simply wash the crystals down into the pot.

Kitchen Tips

The best defense against crystallization is to simply use a clean pan, clean sugar, and wipe the sides of the pot clean of any stray grains of sugar before the pot hits the heat. Set the pot over high heat and do not touch it until it is done. The more you wiggle, stir, shake, and jostle the syrup, the closer to the edge of crystallization you push it.

When cooking sugar on top of the stove, a candy thermometer makes the task super simple, provided that the thermometer is accurate. The old-fashioned method of testing sugar stages with ice water is easy, too, and in most cases more reliable. Have a bowl of ice at the ready as the sugar cooks. As the bubbles get larger and the mixture starts to thicken, spoon out a small amount into the ice water. Immediately feel its consistency. If the recipe calls for soft-ball sugar, you should easily be able to form the sugar into a ball. Hard-ball sugar will keep the ball shape once formed. Crack stage will harden immediately once it hits the water, and will crack easily.

Sugar boiled on its own will be clear until it reaches the hard-crack stage, when it begins turning amber as it hits caramel, and on to black as it starts to burn. If the recipe has other ingredients, like butter or milk, it will begin to darken sooner, and hard-crack will be a rich caramel color.

Bread Pudding

The best part about a bread pudding is, of course, the bread. The richer it is, the better the pudding will be. Challah, brioche, and Hawaiian bread are good choices for this recipe. Other exceptional options include day-old Danish, croissants, cinnamon buns, sweet rolls, and even donuts.

Serves 6–8
Prep time: 15 minutes (plus 1 hour to overnight for refrigeration)
Cook time: 60–90 minutes

4–6 cups cubed bread

4 eggs

1 cup brown sugar

1 TB. cinnamon

2 tsp. nutmeg

1 TB. vanilla extract

4 cups milk

2 cups heavy cream

1 cup sugar

1. Lightly butter a 9×13 rectangular pan and fill it with the cubed bread. In a large bowl, whisk together the eggs, brown sugar, cinnamon, nutmeg, and vanilla. Slowly add the milk and whisk to combine thoroughly. Pour over the bread cubes and refrigerate for at least 1 hour, up to overnight.

2. Preheat oven to 325°F. Before baking, cover the top of pudding with heavy cream and sprinkle the sugar evenly over the top. Bake until golden brown and firmly set, about 1½ hours. Serve warm with a dollop of whipped or ice cream.

Bread Pudding with Fruit: Toss 1 to 2 cups of dried or fresh fruit in with the bread cubes. Try a mixture of dried fruits like golden raisins, dates, and apricots, or use fresh seasonal berries, stone fruit, sautéed apples, or pears.

Chocolate Bread Pudding: Before adding the milk to the egg custard, warm it on the stove. Off the heat, add 2 cups of chocolate chips, whisk until melted, then proceed with the recipe. You can toss some chocolate chips in with the bread cubes too, as well as some nuts or banana slices.

Gingerbread Pudding: Use stale gingerbread cake and add to the custard ¼ cup brandy; 2 tablespoons ground ginger; 1 tablespoon each allspice, nutmeg, cinnamon, and cardamom; and 1 teaspoon clove. Toss in with the bread cubes 1 cup of chopped crystallized ginger and 1 cup of raisins.

Dress It Up: Summer Pudding

This recipe requires no cooking, and yet produces one of the most beautiful desserts in town. The recipe calls for a 10×2 cake pan, but it can be easily adapted for smaller, individual molds. I like making these summer puddings in cupcake pans.

1 pint raspberries, rinsed	½ cup sugar
1 pint blackberries, rinsed	Zest and juice of 1 lemon
1 pint blueberries, rinsed	Pinch salt
1 pint strawberries, rinsed, trimmed, and quartered	1 loaf sliced egg bread, challah, or French *pain de mie*, crusts removed

Serves 6
Prep time: 45 minutes (plus 12–24 hours for refrigeration)

1. In a large bowl combine the berries, sugar, lemon zest and juice, and salt, mixing together gently, and set aside at room temperature to macerate for 30 minutes.

2. Line a 10×2 cake pan with two 18-inch-long pieces of plastic wrap placed in the pan to form an *X*. Trim three to four pieces of bread into triangles and place them at the bottom of the pan in one layer, overlapping a little. Cut three to four pieces of bread into rectangles and line the edges of the pan, overlapping a little. Fill the bread-lined pan with the berry mixture, including all the juice. Trim remaining bread to fit across the top of the berries, overlapping a little. Wrap plastic up and across the pudding. Top with a plate and a little weight, such as a can of tomato sauce, and refrigerate 12 hours or overnight. To serve, unwrap the plastic and invert onto a serving plate. Cut into wedges and top with a dollop of whipped cream.

Chefspeak

French *pain de mie* is a rich, dense white bread. It is baked in a rectangular mold with a lid, so the loaves come out with perfectly square edges. The dense nature of the crumb (and more specifically, the lack of big holes) makes it a perfect choice for this recipe. Look for it in fine bakeries.

Rice Pudding

The rice you choose for this recipe is simply a matter of taste. Short-grain rice has more starch and will yield a thicker, stickier pudding, while the long-grain varieties stay separated for a completely different, but no less delicious, texture. Just be sure not to use instant or quick-cook rice. If you do you'll have a gluey mess on your hands.

Serves 6
Prep time: 10 minutes
Cook time: 30 minutes

3 cups water

2 TB. cinnamon

Zest of 1 lime

1 cup rice (not quick cooking)

2 cups cream

¾ cup sugar

½ tsp. salt

4 egg yolks

1 cup raisins

2 oz. (½ stick) butter

1. In a large saucepan, bring water, cinnamon, and zest to a boil. At the boil, add the rice and reduce heat to a simmer. Cover and cook until all water is absorbed. Add cream, sugar, and salt and simmer until thick, about 20 minutes, stirring occasionally to prevent scorching. Remove from heat.

2. In a small bowl, combine the egg yolks with ½ cup of hot rice, stir quickly, then add warmed yolks to the pot. Stir quickly to incorporate evenly, and cook another 5 minutes. Add raisins and butter and mix well.

3. Pour rice pudding into dishes and serve warm or at room temperature with a dollop of whipped cream.

Coconut Rice Pudding: Use jasmine rice, and replace half the water with an equal amount of canned coconut milk. Replace the raisins with chopped dates, and top with some toasted coconut.

Indian Pudding

This is a New England classic. Historically, cornmeal was known as Indian meal and was used by colonists in the absence of wheat flour. The creamy texture and rich, molasses flavor are the perfect remedy for cold winter nights.

1 cup half-and-half	½ tsp. cinnamon
1 cup cornmeal	½ tsp. clove
3 cups milk	1 tsp. salt
1 cup sugar	½ cup molasses
1½ tsp. ginger	1 cup cream
1½ tsp. nutmeg	

Serves 6
Prep time: 15 minutes
Cook time: 90 minutes

1. Preheat oven to 300°F. Generously butter a 9x13 baking dish. In a small bowl, combine half-and-half and cornmeal and set aside.

2. In a large saucepan bring the milk to a boil. Reduce heat and stir in cornmeal mixture. Simmer, stirring, until thickened, about 5 minutes. Remove from heat.

3. Add sugar, ginger, nutmeg, cinnamon, clove, salt, molasses, and cream. Mix well and transfer to prepared baking dish.

4. Bake until firm and browned, about 1½ hours. Serve warm, topped with additional cream.

Chocolate Pudding

If you've only made pudding from a box, you'll be pleasantly surprised by the flavor of this recipe. Once you master it, you have the basis for an infinite number of sweet creations, including fillings for pies, tarts, cakes, and pastries.

Serves 6
Prep time: 10 minutes
Cook time: 10 minutes, plus 30–60 minutes for chilling

4 egg yolks

1 cup sugar

⅓ cup cornstarch

4 cups half-and-half

1 TB. vanilla extract

12 oz. bittersweet chocolate, chopped, or one (12-oz.) bag of chocolate chips

2 TB. butter

1. In a small bowl whisk together egg yolks, sugar, and cornstarch and set aside. In a large saucepan combine half-and-half and vanilla and bring to a boil over high heat. At the boil, ladle ½ cup of hot half-and-half into the yolks and whisk quickly to combine.

2. Pour the warmed yolks into the saucepan and, over high heat, whisk immediately and vigorously until the mixture begins to resemble thick sour cream, about 2 minutes.

3. Remove from heat, add chocolate and butter, and stir to combine. Pour immediately into serving dishes and chill until set, 30 to 60 minutes. Serve with a dollop of whipped cream.

Butterscotch Pudding: Replace the sugar with an equal amount of brown sugar, and replace the chocolate with ¼ cup of good-quality scotch whiskey. For kids, substitute one (12-oz.) bag butterscotch chips for the whiskey.

Vanilla Pudding: Increase the vanilla to 2 tablespoons, and add one vanilla been. Split the vanilla bean lengthwise and scrape out all its tiny seeds. Add the seeds to the half-and-half, and save the pod in a jar of sugar. The pod will infuse the sugar with its lovely essence.

Flan

Flan is the Spanish version of French crème caramel. The technique was brought to the New World by the Spanish, where it found great popularity. Central American, South American, and Caribbean recipes for flan often contain sweetened condensed or evaporated milk, as well as fruit or vegetable purées.

2 cups sugar	**6 eggs**
½ **cup water**	**1 TB. vanilla extract**
¾ **cup brown sugar**	**1½ cup milk**

Serves 6
Prep time: 30 minutes
Cook time: 60 minutes, plus 2–3 hours for chilling

1. Preheat oven to 325°F. In a small saucepan combine the sugar and the water. Mix well, and wipe any stray sugar off the sides of the pan. Place over high heat and cook, without moving or stirring, until the sugar is a dark, golden amber. Pour caramelized sugar immediately into custard cups, swirling it carefully up the sides. Set aside at room temperature to cool and harden.

2. In a large bowl combine brown sugar, eggs, vanilla, and milk. Mix well to incorporate and pour into custard cups. Set cups in a larger baking pan and fill it with water until it reaches halfway up the cups. Cover the entire pan with foil and bake until the custards are just set, 45 to 60 minutes. The flan should not rise or brown, and should have a subtle jiggle, like gelatin. Remove from the oven to cool, then chill for 2 to 3 hours in the refrigerator before serving. To unmold each cup, carefully run a knife around the rim and invert onto a plate. Serve with seasonal fresh fruit and crisp cookies.

Kitchen Tips

I like to make flan in 6-ounce ceramic or Pyrex glass ramekins. It is common to see large flan baked in an 8- or 10-inch round pan, but I feel they don't cook properly when they're that big.

Dress It Up: Pot De Crème

This is chocolate pudding's rich French cousin. Classic presentation calls for small porcelain pot de crème pots. They look like handleless tea cups with lids. Of course, regular custard cups or ramekins will suffice. After all, it's what's inside that counts.

Serves 6
Prep time: 15 minutes
Cook time: 60 minutes, plus 2 to 3 hours chilling

½ cup sugar

1 egg

4 egg yolks

1 TB. vanilla extract

2 cups milk

¾ cup cream

1½ cup chocolate chips, or 10 oz.chopped bittersweet chocolate

1. Preheat oven to 325°F. In a large bowl combine sugar, egg, yolks, and vanilla. Mix well and set aside. In a medium saucepan bring the milk and cream to a simmer. Remove from heat and stir in chocolate chips until melted.

2. Slowly pour milk into egg mixture, whisking to combine thoroughly, and pour into custard cups. Set cups in a larger baking pan and fill it with water until it reaches halfway up the cups. Cover the entire pan with foil and bake until the custards are just set, about 45 to 60 minutes. They should not rise or brown, and should have a subtle jiggle, like gelatin.

3. Remove from the oven to cool, then chill for 2 to 3 hours in the refrigerator before serving with a dollop of whipped cream.

Crème Brûlée: Replace the milk with an additional 1½ cups cream, and replace the egg with an additional two egg yolks. After the baked custard has chilled, top it with a thin layer of sugar. Using a propane or butane torch, caramelize the sugar. Let the sugar cool at room temperature for 5 minutes before serving.

Strawberry Shortcakes

This classic dessert has many incarnations, but it began as a way to use up last night's biscuits.

⅔ cup buttermilk

2 TB. vanilla extract, divided

2¼ cup all-purpose flour

½ cup sugar, divided

1 TB. baking powder

½ tsp. salt

4 oz. butter (1 stick), chilled and diced

1 egg yolk

2 TB. milk

2 cups heavy whipping cream

2 pints strawberries, rinsed, trimmed, and halved

Powdered sugar

Serves 6		
Prep time: 30 minutes		
Cook time: 20 minutes		

1. Preheat oven to 375°F. Line a cookie sheet with parchment paper. Combine buttermilk and 1 tablespoon vanilla and set aside. In a large bowl sift together flour, ¼ cup sugar, baking powder, and salt. Cut-in chilled butter to pea-size pieces with your fingertips or a pastry blender. Make a well in the center of the flour-butter mixture, pour in buttermilk, and stir gently until just moistened. Turn the dough out onto a lightly floured work surface and fold seven or eight times, until it holds together. Roll to 1 inch thick and cut into 2- or 3-inch biscuits with circle cookie cutter. Place on the cookie sheet 2 inches apart. Whisk together yolk and milk and brush it generously on top of each biscuit. Bake until golden brown, about 15 minutes.

2. Whip cream until soft peaks form with ¼ cup sugar and 1 tablespoon vanilla. Cut biscuits in half and use to sandwich berries and cream. Sprinkle with sifted powdered sugar and serve.

Peach Cobbler

This recipe can be used with any stone fruit (nectarine, apricot, cherry), any berry, rhubarb, and even tropical fruits like mango and pineapple. Apples and pears should be cooked first.

Serves 6–8
Prep time: 30 minutes
Cook time: 45 minutes

For the filling:

6 cups peaches, sliced

1 cup brown sugar

1 TB. cornstarch

½ tsp. salt

Grated zest and juice of 1 lemon

1 tsp. cinnamon

1 tsp. nutmeg

For the biscuit:

2¼ cup all-purpose flour

¼ **cup sugar**

1 TB. baking soda

½ tsp. salt

4 oz. butter (1 stick), chilled and diced

⅔ cup buttermilk

To glaze the top:

1 egg yolk

2 TB. cream

¼ **cup sugar**

1. Preheat oven to 350°F. In a large bowl, toss together peaches, brown sugar, cornstarch, salt, lemon zest and juice, cinnamon, and nutmeg. Mix well to thoroughly coat peaches. Taste to check for sweetness. If there is not enough sugar, add 2 to 3 tablespoons more as needed. Pour peaches into a 9×13 baking dish.

2. In a large bowl, sift together the flour, sugar, baking soda, and salt. Add the chilled butter and cut in to pea-size pieces. Stir in buttermilk until dough just holds together. Drop by spoonful, distributing as evenly as possible across fruit.

3. In a small bowl, combine egg yolk and cream. Brush over the biscuit dough, sprinkle with sugar, and bake for 30 to 45 minutes, until golden brown and bubbly.

Pie Crust Cobbler: Replace the biscuit with ½ recipe of basic pie dough (see recipe in Chapter 14), rolled out into a 9×13 rectangle.

Fruit Crisp: Replace the biscuit with 1 recipe of streusel (see Chapter 2). This dessert is also known as a crumble or a buckle.

Brown Betty: Top the same fruit filling with a mixture of 2 cups bread crumbs or cubes and 1 cup of brown sugar. The crumbs can be seasoned with spices or ground nuts, and are often layered under the fruit as well. Oats can also be used instead of bread.

Gelatin Parfait

This recipe is for strawberry parfait, but it can be made with any flavor of gelatin and any fresh fruit. Try lime, peach, cherry, or mix it up. How about lime gelatin with mangos, kiwis, and canned pineapple?

1 (3-oz.) package strawberry gelatin	1 (8-oz.) package cream cheese, softened
⅔ cup boiling water	2 cups whipped topping
⅔ cup cold water	1 pint fresh strawberries, rinsed, trimmed, and sliced
1 TB. lime juice	

Serves 6
Prep time: 15 minutes
Cook time: 15 minutes, plus 60 to 90 minutes chilling

1. Combine gelatin and boiling water, stirring until gelatin is completely dissolved. Add cold water and lime juice and mix well. Place cream cheese in a large bowl and beat until smooth. Slowly add gelatin. Mix thoroughly, then refrigerate until nearly set, about 1 hour.

2. Fold whipped topping into partially set gelatin. Layer in parfait glasses with sliced strawberries and refrigerate until ready to serve.

Chiffon Pie: Whip three egg whites with a pinch of salt and ¼ cup of sugar until stiff peaks form. Fold this into the gelatin along with the whipped topping. Pour into a graham cracker pie crust and chill to set. Top with additional whipped cream.

S'Mores

Of course, it's possible that you have never had a s'more, the campfire staple of Girl and Boy Scouts. But mark my words, even staunch anti-Scouts will succumb to its pleasures. Consider yourself warned.

Serves 4
Prep time: 5 minutes
Cook time: 10 minutes

4 large marshmallows   **8 graham crackers**

4 squares of chocolate from a classic Hershey bar

1. Using a skewer, stick, or coat hanger, roast marshmallows to desired doneness over hot coals.

2. Stack the chocolate on top of one cracker, and put the hot marshmallow on the chocolate. Sandwich it with another cracker and enjoy!

Kitchen Tips

If you're short on campfires you can zap the marshmallows in the microwave. It only takes about 30 seconds. Take them out when they start to expand.

Caramel Apples

This is a favorite kids' treat, and adults love them, too. But if chomping into a giant gooey apple is not for you, try slicing the apple into thin wedges.

1 (1-lb.) box brown sugar

8 oz. (2 sticks) butter

1 (14-oz.) can sweetened condensed milk

1 cup corn syrup

1 TB. vanilla

½ tsp. salt

Assorted chopped nuts, chocolate chips, small candies, candy sprinkles, mini-marshmallows

6 apples

Popsicle sticks

Makes 6 apples
Prep time: 15 minutes
Cook time: 60–90 minutes

1. Generously butter a large piece of waxed paper. In a large saucepan, combine brown sugar, butter, condensed milk, corn syrup, vanilla, and salt. Place over high heat and cook, stirring occasionally, to 236°F on a candy thermometer (soft-ball stage). Remove from heat and let cool to 200°F.

2. Have ready several plates filled with chopped nuts, chocolate chips, small candies, candy sprinkles, and mini-marshmallows. Remove the apple stems and insert Popsicle sticks. Dip apples into caramel and allow excess to drip off over saucepan. Roll in desired topping and set on prepared waxed paper to cool until set, about 30 minutes.

Kitchen Tips

For this recipe, any apple will do. Pick the one you most enjoy eating out of hand. My favorite is the Fuji. It's not too tart, not too sweet.

Caramel Corn

This holiday favorite is great as is, or you can spice it up. Adding a teaspoon of crushed red pepper flakes or cayenne pepper makes a sweet-spicy treat that's perfect for cocktail parties.

Makes 1 quart
Prep time: 15 minutes
Cook time: 30 minutes

1½ cup nuts

3 cups popped popcorn

1½ cup sugar

½ cup corn syrup

⅓ cup cold water

3 TB. butter

1 tsp. salt

¼ tsp. baking soda

½ tsp. vanilla

1. Lightly butter a large sheet of waxed or parchment paper and set aside. Combine nuts and popped corn and keep warm in a 200°F oven.

2. In a large saucepan combine sugar, corn syrup, and water and bring to a boil. At the boil add butter, and cook to 300°F on a candy thermometer (hard-crack stage). Remove from heat and add salt, baking soda, and vanilla. Stir until foamy, then immediately fold in popcorn and nuts. Quickly transfer to prepared wax paper and spread out into small hunks. Cool completely before serving. Store in an airtight container at room temperature.

Fudge

A lot of good cooks shy away from fudge because it seems complicated. But this extremely simple recipe originated on a package of chocolate chips. The secret is the marshmallow cream.

3 cups chocolate chips

2 cups marshmallow cream

4 oz. (1 stick) butter

1 TB. vanilla

2 cups chopped nuts (optional)

1 (12-oz.) can evaporated milk

4½ cups sugar

Makes about 4 dozen slices
Prep time: 10 minutes
Cook time: 30 minutes, plus 2 hours for chilling

1. Butter a 12×18 jellyroll pan. In a large bowl combine chocolate, marshmallow cream, butter, vanilla, and nuts, if using, and set aside.

2. Combine the evaporated milk and sugar in a large saucepan and bring to a boil. Cook for 9 minutes, stirring constantly. Pour over chocolate mixture and beat by hand or electric mixer until thick. Pour into prepared pan, spread evenly and refrigerate until set, about 2 hours. Cut into small squares.

Peanut Brittle

Here's a recipe that has been made easier by the microwave. If you like, you can make it the traditional way. See the stove-top variation that follows.

Makes about 1 pound
Prep time: 10 minutes
Cook time: 30 minutes

1 cup sugar	1 TB. butter
½ cup corn syrup	1½ baking soda
1½ cup raw peanuts	1 tsp. vanilla

1. Lightly butter a baking sheet. In a large glass or ceramic bowl, combine sugar, corn syrup, and peanuts and microwave on high for 3 minutes. Add butter and heat another 3 minutes. Stir and heat a final 1 to 3 minutes, or until golden brown (hard-crack stage, 300°F).

2. Add baking soda and vanilla, and stir until foamy. Pour immediately onto prepared baking sheet and spread very thin. Cool completely before cracking into pieces. Store in an airtight container at room temperature.

Listen to Mom!

Please remember that boiled sugar is very, very hot!

Stove-Top Brittle: Cook the sugar, corn syrup, peanuts, and butter in a saucepan over high heat until it reaches hard-crack stage (300°F), stirring occasionally, then resume recipe as written.

Chapter 17

Anytime Snacks

In This Chapter

◆ Snacking through the years

◆ Cold-cut, cheese, and cracker concoctions

◆ Healthy treats that are fun to boot!

◆ Snacks to please a crowd

◆ Sweet-tooth snack attack

Snacking is not meant to be hard. It is designed to get you through the afternoon, sustain you during homework time, play time, and boring afternoon meeting time. Snacks fuel your hikes, tide you over until lunch, and ease your mind in the middle of the night.

The recipes in this chapter are true to this basic principle of snacking. They are easy, fun, and perfectly suited for cooks of any age. They are the things we experimented on in the kitchen as kids, or the things Mom left out for us when we had a friend over to play.

The Evolution of Snacking

Snacks, like people, grow and change over the years. When we are young, they remain simple: cookies, crackers, and things that Mom knew we liked, and would eat, and would keep us quiet.

For babies, Cheerios take longer to pick up than they do to eat, affording Mom enough time to put a load of dishes away or fold some laundry. As we get older, graham crackers are sweet, but still bland enough for our awakening palettes. (It's not until a few years later that they are accompanied by marshmallows and chocolate; see the recipe for s'mores in Chapter 16.)

Grammar school snacks often involved something that dips easily into a glass of milk. Everyone has their favorite dunkable, with Oreos ranking at the top of the list. Not only do they taste good, but their unique design provided an archeological activity. Oh, the joy of discovering a chocolate cookie facing backward!

The decision of what to eat during afternoon TV viewings was no small matter. If it was late spring or summer, frozen treats were necessary. Missile Pops, Push-Ups, and Otter Pops were top requests. If we were bored, sometimes we'd make our own frozen pops in a Dixie cup with Kool-Aid.

When I was a kid in the 1970s, my friends with hippie parents escaped from the granola by coming to my house. Oh, the hours lost in the backyard fort with a jar of peanut butter, a bag of chocolate chips, and a spoon!

As our teen years approached, we became more independent, and we preferred to prepare our own snacks. Cereal was a big hit, and it is a recipe all of us could handle. Peanut butter sandwiches were slightly more technical, and thus made us feel even more grown-up.

Tidbits

If you haven't shared your childhood snack memories with your kids, now is the time. Who knows, they may start some traditions of their own. No kids? Everyone feels young at heart. I'm sure you can find someone who needs a pick-me-up.

The microwave didn't appear in every household until I was in high school, at which time the afternoon baked potato was all the rage, steamy and hot in under 10 minutes! Frozen burritos were also big, but not quite as big as a study date at the pizza parlor. It was at that point that we cut the apron strings and ventured out into the culinary world on our own, leaving behind the cookies and milk.

It is here, in the land of snacking, that we recall some of our most comforting food memories. These are the foods of home, family, and friends.

Bologna Roll-Ups

These creations are also affectionately known as roller-coasters. You can dress this idea up for company by using interesting cured meats and foreign cheeses with funny names. But don't try to pass something like that off to your kids after school. Baloney!

8 slices American cheese   **8 slices bologna**

Serves 4
Prep time: 5 minutes

1. Layer one slice cheese on top of one slice bologna and roll up into a log.

2. Secure with a toothpick and serve.

Cream Cheese Roll-Ups: Spread softened cream cheese on the bologna, then roll it up. It tastes great on Italian salami, too.

Pretzel Roll-Ups: Add a pretzel stick in the center of your roll up for a crunchy surprise.

Roll-Up Canapés: Slice the roll-ups into thin wheels and present them on crackers.

Ants on a Log

This a terrifically healthful snack, with or without the "ants."

4 stalks celery, washed, trimmed and cut into 3-inch lengths   **½ cup peanut butter**
¼ cup raisins

Serves 4
Prep time: 10 minutes

1. Spread each celery stick with 1 tablespoon of peanut butter.

2. Sprinkle with five or six raisins.

Ladybugs on a Log: Replace raisins with dried cranberries.

Crickets on a Snowy Log: Replace peanut butter with cream cheese, and sprinkle with peanuts, walnuts, or almonds instead of raisins.

Cracker Canapés

This snack looks like you fussed, but its really just preassembled cheese and crackers. Use whatever cheese and crackers you like. It's the final topping that makes it fancy.

Serves 4
Prep time: 10 minutes

12 crackers

12 slices of cheese, cut into 1-inch squares

¼ cup cream cheese, softened

Assorted olives, pickles, and peppers

⅓ cup flat Italian parsley leaves

Paprika

1. On each cracker, layer a slice of cheese; a dollop of cream cheese; a small slice of olive, pickle, or pepper; and a small leaf of parsley.

2. Top with a dusting of paprika.

Peanut Butter Canapés: Spread a teaspoon of peanut butter on each cracker and top with a thin slice of banana, apple, or raisins. Finish with a sprinkle of cinnamon or a drizzle of honey.

Salty Seafood Canapés: Top each cracker with a teaspoon of cream cheese and a smoked oyster, anchovy, or sardine. Sprinkle with chopped dill.

Strawberries, Sour Cream, and Brown Sugar

This sounds weird, but it is incredibly luscious. I was first served this by a babysitter in 1970-something. I think she was trying to get on my good side. It remains one of my all-time favorite late-night treats.

Serves 4
Prep time: 10 minutes

1 pint big, ripe strawberries, washed and dried, with stems intact

1 pint sour cream

2 cups brown sugar

1. Arrange strawberries on a plate. Place sour cream and brown sugar in two bowls.

2. Dip a strawberry first in sour cream, then in sugar, and then pop into your mouth.

Toaster-Oven Pizza

The smell of this after-school classic can be detected wafting through the halls of every college dorm in America.

Serves 4
Prep time: 10 minutes
Cook time: 10 minutes

4 English muffins, split

1 (15-oz.) can pizza, spaghetti, or tomato sauce

2 cups mozzarella cheese, grated

Assorted pizza toppings, including pepperoni, cooked sausage, mushrooms, peppers, onions, olives, anchovies, or pineapple and ham.

1. Spread each muffin with 1 to 2 tablespoons of sauce. Top with a generous handful of cheese and desired toppings.

2. Place in the toaster oven at 350°F, high, or broil, and cook until cheese is melted, about 3 to 5 minutes.

Pita Pizza: Try the same thing on a round of pita bread. To serve, cut it into wedges.

French Bread Pizza: Build the pizza on thick slices of French, Italian, or sourdough bread.

Pita Chips

This is a surprisingly satisfying and healthy snack—crisp like a chip or a cracker, but baked, not fried. Get the kids to help with this one.

Serves 4
Prep time: 10 minutes
Cook time: 10 minutes

½ cup olive oil

¼ cup Parmesan cheese

1 TB. dried oregano

2 cloves garlic, minced

½ tsp. pepper

4 pita rounds

1. Preheat oven to 400°F. Combine olive oil, cheese, oregano, garlic, and pepper in a small bowl and set aside.

2. Slice each pita round into eight wedges. Separate each wedge into two triangles and spread in one layer on a baking sheet. Use a pastry brush to coat each triangle lightly with the flavored oil. Bake until golden brown and crisp, about 3 minutes. Store in an airtight container at room temperature.

Cheesy Pita Chips: Rather than brushing with oil, sprinkle the pita triangles with a mixture of finely grated cheese. Try Parmesan, cheddar, or Gruyere.

Sweet Pita Chips: Sprinkle the pita triangles with cinnamon sugar. For a sugar–free version, mix cinnamon with a sugar substitute.

Buffalo Wings

This American classic is said to have been concocted late one night in a bar in Buffalo, New York, for the hungry owners. Apparently the only thing on hand was chicken wings, hot sauce, celery, and blue cheese dressing. Those Buffalonians certainly are resourceful!

1 cup canola oil	1 tsp. salt
3–4-lb. chicken wings	1 tsp. pepper
3 oz. (¾ stick) butter	1 tsp. garlic powder
2–4 TB. hot pepper sauce	1 TB. dried oregano
3 TB. red or white wine vinegar	Celery sticks and blue cheese dressing for serving

Serves 4–6

Prep time: 15 minutes
Cook time: 45 minutes

1. Heat oil in a heavy skillet over high heat until it reaches 375°F. Fry the wings in batches until golden brown, about 5 minutes. Do not crowd. Drain on paper towels.

2. Melt butter in a large saucepan. Add pepper sauce, vinegar, and spices and mix well. Remove from heat and add wings, tossing to coat. Serve with celery sticks and blue cheese dressing.

Nachos

Are you so used to movie theater/ballpark/race-track nachos that you've forgotten what real nachos taste like? For starters, they're made with actual cheese from a cow, not a can.

Serves 4
Prep time: 15 minutes
Cook time: 30 minutes

1 (10–12-oz.) bag of corn tortilla chips

1 (16-oz.) can refried beans

2 cups grated cheddar cheese

1 ripe tomato, diced

2 scallions, chopped

1 cup sour cream

1 cup guacamole

1 (2¼-oz.) can sliced black olives

1 (7-oz.) can jalapeños

1. Preheat oven to 375°F. Spread chips out evenly on a 12×18 baking sheet or a large ovenproof platter. Evenly distribute the beans on top of the chips in dollops, and top with grated cheese. Sprinkle tomato and scallions over the cheese.

2. Bake for 20 to 30 minutes until melted. Before serving, top with sour cream, guacamole, olives, and jalapeños.

Tidbits

Nachos are said to have been invented by restaurateur Ignacio "Nacho" Anaya in a Mexican town, Piedras Negras, just across the border from a Texas air base. The dish was a favorite of military wives, who helped popularize the dish throughout Texas.

TV Mix

Much of our popular food culture stems from clever corporate recipe developers. This cereal party mix is no exception. Initially developed in the 1950s as a way to sell more cereal, it became so popular that the company now sells it premixed, in flavors such as ranch, honey nut, and pizza.

4 TB. butter (½ stick), melted

3 TB. Worcestershire sauce

2 tsp. salt

1 tsp. pepper

½ tsp. garlic powder

½ tsp. onion powder

2 TB. hot pepper sauce (optional)

3 cups each corn, rice, and wheat Chex cereal

1 cup mixed nuts

1 cup pretzel sticks

Makes about 11 cups
Prep time: 10 minutes
Cook time: 60 minutes

1. Preheat oven to 250°F. In a large bowl stir the butter, Worcestershire, salt, pepper, garlic powder, onion powder, and pepper sauce, if using. Stir in the cereal, nuts, and pretzels until evenly coated.

2. Spread mix onto baking sheets and bake for 1 hour, stirring every 10 to 15 minutes, until well toasted. Store in an airtight container at room temperature.

Sweet Cereal Mix: In a microwave or double boiler melt 2 oz. (½ stick) butter and 1 cup chocolate chips. Add ½ cup peanut butter and 1 TB. vanilla extract and stir until smooth. Add cereal and stir to coat completely. Spread out to dry, then toss with 1½ cups sifted powdered sugar.

GORP

This snack, also known as trail mix, is a great source of quick energy and protein. The name stands for Good Ol' Raisins and Peanuts, but the fun moms always added chocolate.

Makes about 6 cups
Prep time: 15 minutes

2 cups roasted, salted peanuts   **2 cups M&Ms**

2 cups raisins

1. Combine all ingredients in a large bowl and mix well.

2. Store in an airtight container at room temperature.

Tropical GORP: Combine dried banana chips, dried pineapple, chopped dates, macadamia or cashew nuts, and large pieces of shaved coconut.

Autumn GORP: Add your favorite dried fruits and nuts. I like cranberries, apricots, dried apples, pecans, and walnuts.

Rice Krispies Treats

This recipe has appeared on the box of Rice Krispies cereal since the 1940s. Recently I have seen this treat sold at bakeries and candy counters on a Popsicle stick and dipped in chocolate. At Disneyland they come in the shape of Mickey.

Makes about 2 dozen 1½-inch bars
Prep time: 5 minutes
Cook time: 30 minutes

4 TB. (½ stick) butter   **1 tsp. vanilla extract**

1 (10-oz.) package marshmallows   **6 cups puffed rice cereal**

1. Lightly butter a 9×13 pan. In a large saucepan, melt the butter over medium heat. Add marshmallows and vanilla, stirring until completely melted. Remove from heat, add cereal, and mix thoroughly.

2. Pour into prepared pan and spread evenly. Cool completely, about 20 minutes, before cutting. Store airtight at room temperature.

Glossary

adobo A Philippine method of meat preparation which includes chilies, pepper, vinegar, soy sauce, garlic, and bay leaves. The sauce is typically used to braise chicken and pork. Mexican adobo is a red chile sauce, often used in the canning of chipotle chilies.

ahi A type of tuna fish, also known as yellow fin and big eye. The raw meat is bright red in color.

ajo blanco Spanish white cold soup, made with garlic, bread, almonds, and grapes.

al dente An Italian term that means "to the tooth," and refers to the degree to which certain foods, usually pasta and vegetables, are cooked. These foods are cooked until done but still have a slight texture when bitten. They are not raw or crunchy, nor are they soft.

amaretti Crunchy Italian macaroon cookies flavored with bitter almonds.

amaretto An Italian liqueur with the distinctive flavor of bitter almonds.

andouille French spiced and smoked sausage originally from the regions of Brittany and Normandy. When the French migrated to Nova Scotia, and then to Louisiana, their traditions followed. The Cajun version of andouille is quite a bit hotter than its French counterpart.

angel food pan   A round cake pan with a hollow interior tube that allows heat to penetrate the batter from the middle. The resulting cake has a hole in the center, like a giant donut.

annatto   Derived from the seed of the achiote tree, this red spice is used as a coloring for butter, cheese, candies, oils, stocks, and sauces throughout Central American, Mexican, and Philippine cuisines.

arugula   A small salad green with a bitter, peppery flavor. Also known as *rocket*.

bacalao   The Spanish name for dried salted cod.

baste   To coat food as it cooks with fat or liquid to preserve moisture. A bulb baster is a suction-based tool.

béchamel   French white cream sauce made by adding milk to a roux. Béchamel is traditionally flavored with nutmeg and an onion pierced with a clove and bay leaf, known as onion piqué.

blanch   To boil briefly, then submerge in ice water to halt cooking. The process is used to loosen the skin and intensify the color of vegetables and fruits. Also referred to as *parboil*.

Boston butt   The rear front shoulder of a hog. The name comes from the New England colonial tradition of packing meat in barrels or butts for shipment.

bouquet garni   An aromatic sachet of herbs and spices used in all kinds of classic French stocks, stews, and soups. The classic preparation uses a wilted leek green to wrap a bay leaf, parsley stem, thyme sprig, three peppercorns, and a clove. Today, the ingredients are often wrapped in cheesecloth. The bundle is tied with a long piece of kitchen twine and secured to the pot handle for easy removal.

brisket   A flat cut of beef from the breast, under the first five ribs.

broiler/fryer   A 2- to 3-month-old chicken that weighs from 3½ to 4 pounds.

bromaline   An enzyme found in pineapples that breaks down protein. This works as a meat tenderizer, a digestive aid, and a skin irritant. It also prevents gelatin from setting. These properties are eliminated when the enzyme is heated.

buckle   Similar to a coffee cake, with fruit added to the batter and streusel added to the top.

buckwheat   The seed from a plant in the rhubarb family which is ground into flour, or cooked the same way as rice under the name Kasha.

butterfly   To split food down the center, cutting almost, but not quite, all the way through. The food is opened up to reveal two identical sides, like a butterfly's wings.

Cajun seasoning   A blend of herbs and spices which typically includes garlic, onions, chilies, pepper, and mustard.

cake flour   A soft flour containing less protein and more starch than all-purpose flour, perfect for cakes and other delicate baked goods that don't need a strong elastic dough structure.

capers   Small buds from an evergreen shrub, pickled in salty, vinegar-based brine.

challah   A rich, braided loaf of bread traditionally served on the Jewish table for Sabbath, holidays, and ceremonies.

cherrystone   A medium-size clam, from 2 to 2½ inches in diameter.

chili sauce   A condiment similar to ketchup, made with chilies, chile powder, tomatoes, and vinegar.

clarify   The term means to clear, and refers to removing cloudy sediment from a stock, soup, sauce, or liquefied fat.

clotted cream   Thick cream from unpasteurized milk. Also known as Devonshire cream.

cod   A mild, low-fat, white fish used in a variety of preparations worldwide. Also marketed under the name cod are haddock, pollock, and whiting.

concassé   The term technically refers to food that is coarsely chopped, but is most often applied to tomatoes that have been skinned, seeded, and diced.

confit   Anything cooked in its own juice, including fruit, vegetables, or meat. Confit de canard is a classic French dish of preserved duck, salted and cooked slowly in its own fat, then covered in the fat for prolonged storage.

cornichon   The French name for gherkin, a small pickling cucumber.

crab boil   A blend of herbs and spices, typically containing mustard, chilies, allspice, and bay leaf.

creaming   A term used to describe the blending of two ingredients into a creamy, smooth, pastelike texture.

crumble   A dessert also known as a crisp, consisting of fruit with a streusel topping.

crustacean   A classification of shellfish with hard exoskeletons, including crabs, lobsters, and shrimp.

curing   A method of preserving food with salt (corned), acid (pickled), or smoke.

deglaze   A method of removing cooked food, and flavor, from the bottom of a sauté or roasting pan, by adding liquid, heating, and scraping.

Devonshire cream   See *clotted cream.*

double boiler   Two pots fitted one on top of the other, designed to allow steam from the bottom to rise up and warm the ingredients of the top. It is used when direct heat is too severe.

dried currants   Tiny raisins made from the miniature *zante* grape. Do not confuse them with red, white, or black currants, which are small berries used for preserves, pastries, and the liqueur cassis.

dry rub   A method of flavoring meat, in which a blend of spices is rubbed into raw meat and allowed to penetrate for several hours before the meat is cooked.

durham   A strain of wheat, very high in protein, used to make semolina flour.

fennel   The edible bulb, leaves, and seeds from an aromatic vegetable with a subtle licorice flavor. Known as *finocchio* in Italian, it is a common ingredient in many Mediterranean cuisines.

finocchio   See *fennel.*

flat fish   Fish that swim horizontally along the ocean floor. They have flat, platelike bodies, with both eyes on the top side. Flat fish species include sole and halibut.

Florentine   Food preparations in the style of Florence, Italy, usually including spinach, which is an ingredient supposedly popularized by the Florentine-born queen of France, Catherine de Medici. It is also a thin Viennese wafer made with nuts.

foam   A culinary term for anything with air whipped into it, usually eggs, egg yolks, or egg whites.

food mill   A tool used to grind and press cooked food through small holes in preparation for purée.

free range   Animals that are allowed to roam freely for a portion of the day in order to improve the quality and flavor of their meat.

gherkin   A small cucumber used specifically in pickling.

grana   Hard, grainy cheese, such as Parmesan or Romano, used for grating.

gratinée, au gratin   The melting and browning of the top of a dish.

gremolada, gremolata   An Italian garnish made of chopped garlic, lemon zest, parsley, and anchovy.

Guinness Stout   A dark Irish porter-style beer.

ham hock   The bottom half of a hog's hind leg, usually cured, smoked, and cut into 2- to 3-inch pieces. Used to flavor and enrich long-cooking soups and stews.

hard-crack stage   Sugar cooked to between 300°F and 310°F, used in candy and pastry making. When cooled, the sugar will harden and snaps or cracks easily.

haricot vert   Small, thin French green beans.

herbes de Provençe   A blend of herbs commonly used in Mediterranean cuisine, including lavender, thyme, sage, marjoram, basil, rosemary, fennel, and savory.

hors d'oeuvre   A dish served outside the main meal as an appetizer.

horseradish   A spicy root used as a condiment, grated fresh and mixed with cream or preserved in vinegar.

instant-read   A thermometer designed to determine the internal temperatures of food.

kalamata   Greek black olives marinated in wine and olive oil.

kalua pork   A method of slow roasting pork in an underground oven. The distinctive flavor of smoked ti leaves makes this dish a luau staple.

Kasha   See *buckwheat.*

kosher   Food that conforms to strict Jewish law, prepared under the supervision of a rabbi, and given the kosher seal.

krumkake   Thin Norwegian wafer cookies, flavored with lemon or cardamom, and baked in a decorative waffle iron.

latkes   Potato pancakes, traditionally served at Hanukkah to commemorate the Miracle of the Oil.

legumes   Dried beans from seed pods that split open along the side when ripe. Legume varieties include soybeans, peas, garbanzo beans, and peanuts.

lemon curd   A tart, lemon custard used as a spread or a filling.

littleneck   Small clams, under 2 inches in diameter.

macerate   To soak food, usually fruit, in liquid to infuse flavor.

mandoline   A handheld grater designed to slice foods into precise, uniform wafers, sticks, or waffles. Also known as a v-slicer.

masa harina   Flour made from dried hominy corn, used for corn tortillas and tamales.

microplane   A fine grater used for citrus zest and grana cheeses. The tool was originally a carpenter's rasp used for sanding wood.

millet   A tiny, bland grain packed with protein, which can be boiled like rice or ground into a flour.

mirepoix   A blend of aromatic vegetables used in stocks, soups, and stew. Typically the mix consists of carrot, onion, and celery sautéed in butter.

mollusk   A classification of shellfish with one or two shells, like clams, oysters, and abalone.

Mornay   A French cheese sauce, made by adding Swiss cheese to sauce béchamel.

msickquatash   A New England Native American word for boiled whole grains or kernels, the forerunner of succotash.

mutton   Lamb over 2 years old, with a strong flavor and tough flesh.

natural   Foods raised, grown, and manufactured without artificial ingredients, or preservatives.

Niçoise   In the style of Nice, a Mediterranean coastal city in southern France. Dishes *à la Niçoise* typically contain ingredients indigenous to the region, including garlic, tomatoes, fresh herbs, and seafood.

organic   Foods raised, grown, and manufactured without artificial ingredients, preservatives, hormones, antibiotics, pesticides, fertilizers, radiation, or food additives.

osso bucco   An Italian dish of veal shank braised in wine, herbs, and aromatic vegetables, garnished with gremolata.

oyster liquor   The juice found inside an oyster shell.

paella   Spanish rice dish, made in a pan of the same name, flavored with saffron, and filled with a variety of meat, shellfish, vegetables, and aromatics.

pain perdu   The French name for French toast, which means, literally, "lost bread."

panko   Thick, coarse Japanese bread crumbs.

parboil   See *blanch*.

parchment paper   Heavy paper that withstands heat, water, and grease, used to line pans and wrap foods.

pâté sucrée   A sweet, crisp pastry dough used for tart shells.

picnic roast   A roast cut from the upper foreleg and shoulder of a hog.

pimentos   Sweet red peppers, available fresh in limited areas in late summer, readily available peeled and preserved in a brine. Pimento peppers are the basis for paprika, and are stuffed into green Spanish olives.

pizzelle   Thin Italian wafer cookies flavored with anise and baked in a decorative waffle iron.

pomme   The French word for apple.

pomme de terre   The French term for potato, meaning literally "apple of the earth."

pork butt   See *Boston butt*.

pot likker   The broth in which vegetables and meat are cooked. The term originated in the Southern United States and commonly refers to the broth of collard greens.

potato ricer   A plungerlike tool used to press cooked food through fine holes in preparation for purée.

poulet   The French word for chicken.

pulses   Dried legumes.

radiatore   Small ruffled pasta shapes, whose name is Italian for little radiators.

ramekin   A small glass or ceramic dish used for individual chilled or baked foods and side servings.

reduce   A culinary term meaning to cook the water out of a dish, reducing its volume, intensifying its flavor, and thickening its consistency.

roaster   A high-fat chicken, weighing between 3 and 5 pounds, and between 6 and 8 months old. The increased fat helps baste the bird in the oven.

Romano   An Italian grana cheese from Rome. Pecorino Romano is made from sheep's milk, while others can be made from goat or cow's milk.

Roquefort   A French blue cheese made specifically from sheep's milk, exposed to penicillium roqueforte mold spores, and aged in limestone caves in southwestern France.

round fish   Fish that swim above the ocean floor and are circular in cross section.

roux   A thickening agent made with equal parts melted fat (usually butter) and flour.

Satay   Indonesian marinated, skewered, and grilled meat, usually served with peanut sauce.

sauce Bolognese   Traditional Italian red sauce from the Bologna region of northern Italy, made with slow-cooked meats and vegetables. In Italy this style of sauce is known as a ragu.

sauté   To cook food quickly, over high heat, constantly stirring for even browning. The term means "to jump," and sauté pans are designed with a curved lip, making constant motion as easy as a flick of the wrist.

scrod   Young cod and haddock weighing under 3 pounds.

seasoning   1. To flavor a dish. 2. To smooth the roughness of iron pans, thereby preventing food from sticking. It is done by oiling and heating the pan for an extended period of time. Once seasoned, pans need only be gently cleaned. Reseasoning may be necessary if pan is scratched or scrubbed, but typically the seasoning lasts for several years.

seize   A term that refers to the thickening and hardening of melted chocolate that occurs when a small amount of moisture is added.

shallot   A member of the onion family. The shallot grows in large cloves like garlic, has multiple layers like the onion, and reddish-brown papery skin. The flavor is more subtle than both.

shank   Meat from the upper portion of an animal's front or hind leg.

shellfish   Aquatic animals with a shell. They are categorized as either mollusks (animals with one or two hinged shells), or crustaceans (animals with an exoskeleton). Cephalopods are mollusks with tentacles and no shell, such as the octopus and the squid.

sherry   A fortified wine from the Andalusian region of southern Spain. There are several varieties, ranging from dry manzanillas to sweet olorosos.

soft-ball stage   Sugar cooked to between 234°F and 240°F, used in candy and pastry making. When cooled, the sugar can be formed into a soft ball.

soft-crack stage   Sugar cooked to between 270°F and 290°F, used in candy and pastry making. When cooled, the sugar is hard, but still bends.

split to the bone   See *butterfly*.

stockpot   A large pot with a round base, straight sides, and two handles, capable of holding anywhere from 6 to 20 quarts of liquid.

stone fruit   A tree fruit that contains a pit or stone, such as peaches, apricots, cherries, and plums.

sugar pie   A small, round, sweet variety of pumpkin bred specifically for use in baking.

sweet anise   Another name for fennel, though the actual herb anise is unrelated to fennel.

swiss chard   A leafy green vegetable with red or white stalks, related to beets, with a texture and flavor similar to spinach.

Tabasco   A small red pepper from the Mexican state of Tabasco, grown in Louisiana specifically for use in the pepper sauce of the same name.

tagine, tajine   Not only the name of the recipe, but also the cooking vessel. Stews of meat, vegetable, olives, preserved lemons, and spices are slow-cooked in these terra-cotta pots with distinctive conical lids. The pot doubles as a serving dish, and is presented to the table, always accompanied by a dish of couscous.

tandoor   An Indian brick and clay oven used to cook meats over a smoky fire at very high temperature.

tapas   Small dishes served as appetizers or snacks, served with sherry in bars and restaurants throughout Spain.

teriyaki   Meat barbecued Japanese style, marinated in sake, soy sauce, ginger, sesame, and sugar.

tomato concassé   See *concassé*.

turmeric   A spice derived from the root of a plant in the ginger family, used for its bitter flavor and bright yellow color.

water bath   A method in which a pan of food is cooked resting in another, larger pan of water. The method slows the conduction of heat, cooking slowly and gently. The method is known in French as *bain marie*.

white pepper   The same berry as the black peppercorn, allowed to ripen, and dry, resulting in a slightly hotter flavor.

yellow fin   See *ahi*.

zester   A small tool designed to strip the aromatic, colorful, oil-rich skin from citrus fruit.

Common Ingredient Substitutions and Equivalents

If Recipe Calls for This	You Can Substitute This
Baking powder, 1 tsp.	¼ tsp. baking soda + ⅝ tsp. cream of tartar, or ¼ tsp. baking soda + ½ cup buttermilk
Broth or stock, 1 cup	1 bouillon cube + 1 cup hot water
Buttermilk, 1 cup	1 cup yogurt, or 1 cup milk + 1 TB. lemon juice, or 1 cup milk + 1 TB. vinegar, or 1 cup milk + 1 tsp. cream of tartar
Cake flour, 1 cup	1 cup all-purpose flour + 1 TB. cornstarch
Cornstarch, 1 TB.	2 TB. all-purpose flour
Corn syrup, 1 cup	1¼ cups sugar + ¼ cup water
Cream, 1 cup	¾ cup whole milk + ⅓ cup butter
Egg, 1 whole	2 yolks, or 2 whites, or 3½ TB. egg substitute

continues

continued

If Recipe Calls for This	You Can Substitute This
Egg white, 1	1 TB. powdered egg white, or 2 TB. frozen egg whites
Egg yolk, 1	2 TB. powdered yolk, or 3½ tsp. frozen yolk
Herbs, 1 TB. fresh	1 tsp. dry
Honey, 1 cup	1¼ cup white sugar, and increase recipe liquid by ¼ cup
Milk, 1 cup	½ cup evaporated milk + ½ cup water, or ¼ cup powdered milk + ⅔ cup water
Mustard, 1 TB.	1 tsp. powdered mustard

This Amount	Equals This
Apples, 1 lb.	3 cups sliced
Bananas, 1 lb.	2 cups sliced, 1½ cup mashed
Beef, ground, 1 lb.	2 cups
Green beans, 1 lb.	3½ cups
Beans, canned, 15 oz.	1½ cups
Beans, dried, 1 lb.	2½ cups
Butter, 1 lb.	2 cups
Carrots, 1 lb.	3 cups chopped
Cheddar cheese, 1 lb.	4 cups grated
Chocolate chips, 6 oz.	1 cup
Corn, frozen, 1 lb.	3⅓ cups
Cornmeal, 1 lb.	3 cups
Cornstarch, 1 lb.	3 cups
Cream, liquid, 1 cup	2 cups whipped
Eggs, 1 cup	5 medium
Egg whites, 1 cup	8 medium
Egg yolks, 1 cup	12 medium

This Amount	Equals This
Flour, all-purpose, 1 lb.	4 cups
Flour, bread, unsifted, 1 lb.	3 cups
Flour, cake, unsifted, 1 lb.	4½ cups
Gelatin, unflavored, ¼ oz.	1 TB. or 3½ sheets
Graham crackers, 16 squares	1 cup crumbs
Lemons, 6–7	1 cup juice
Limes, 1–2	1 TB. juice
Marshmallows, 1 lb.	60 large
Mushrooms, 1 lb.	6 cups sliced
Nuts, chopped, 1 lb.	3½ cups
Oats, 1 lb.	5 cups
Pasta, 1 lb.	3 cups raw, 4 cups cooked
Peas, frozen, 10 oz.	2 cups
Pumpkin, fresh, 1 lb.	1 cup purée
Pumpkin, canned, 17 oz.	2 cups purée
Raisins, 1 lb.	3 cups
Rice, white, 1 lb.	2½ cups raw, 7½ cups cooked
Rice, brown, 1 lb.	2⅓ cups raw, 7 cups cooked
Rhubarb, fresh, 1 lb.	2 cups chopped
Sugar, brown, 1 lb.	2⅓ cups, packed
Sugar, granulated, 1 lb.	2¼ cups
Sugar, powdered, 1 lb.	3¾ cups, unsifted
Spinach, fresh, 1 lb.	10 cups raw, chopped, 1 cup cooked
Spinach, frozen, 10.oz.	1¼ cups
Tomatoes, fresh, 1 lb.	2 cups chopped
Yeast, dry, 1 (¼-oz.) package	2½ tsp.

Conversion Tables

Measurement Equivalents

1½ tsp.	= ½ TB.	= ¼ fl. oz.	
3 tsp.	= 1 TB.	= ½ fl. oz.	
1 TB.	= 3 tsp.	= ½ fl. oz.	
2 TB.	= ⅛ cup	= 1 fl. oz.	
4 TB.	= ¼ cup	= 2 fl. oz.	
8 TB.	= ½ cup	= 4 fl. oz.	
12 TB.	= ¾ cup	= 6 fl. oz.	
16 TB.	= 1 cup	= 8 fl. oz.	
1 cup	= 16 TB.	= 8 fl. oz.	
2 cups	= 1 pt.	= 16 fl. oz.	
4 cups	= 2 pt.	= 32 fl. oz.	= 1 qt.
16 cups	= 4 qt.	= 128 fl. oz.	= 1 gal.

Temperature

To convert Fahrenheit to Celsius, subtract 32, divide by 9, multiply by 5.

To convert Celsius to Fahrenheit, divide by 5, multiply by 9, add 32.

Fahrenheit	Celsius
32°F	0°C (Freezing)
50°F	10°C
100°F	37.8°C
120°F	48.9°C
150°F	65.6°C
200°F	93.3°C
212°F	100°C (boiling)
240°F	115°C (soft ball)
250°F	121°C (hard ball)
270°F	132°C (soft crack)
300°F	149°C (hard crack)
320°F	160°C (caramel)
350°F	177°C
400°F	205°C
450°F	233°C
500°F	260°C

Weight

To convert ounces to grams, multiply by 28.35.

To convert grams into ounces, multiply by 0.03527.

To convert kilograms into pounds, multiply by 2.2046.

When multiplying large weight, round to nearest whole number.

United States	Metric (Approximate)
½ oz.	15g
⅔ oz.	20g
¾ oz.	22g
1 oz.	30g
2 oz.	55g
4 oz. (¼ lb.)	115g
5 oz.	140g
8 oz. (½ lb.)	225g
12 oz.	340g
16 oz. (1 lb.)	455g
2 lb.	910g
3 lb.	1kg, 365g
4 lb.	1kg, 820g
5 lb.	2kg, 275g

Volume

To convert milliliters into ounces, multiply by 0.0338.

To convert milliliters into pints, multiply by 0.0021125.

To convert liters into ounces, multiply by 33.8.

To convert liters into pints, multiply by 2.1125.

To convert liters into quarts, multiply by 1.05625.

To convert quarts into liters, multiply by 0.946.

When multiplying large volume, round to nearest whole number.

United States	Metric (Approximate)
½ tsp.	2.5ml
1 tsp.	5ml
1 TB.	15ml

continues

continued

United States	Metric (Approximate)
1 cup	237ml
1 pint	475ml
1 quart	950ml

Length

To convert inches into centimeters, multiply by 25.4.

To convert centimeters into inches, multiply by 0.3937.

To convert meters into inches, multiply by 39.3701.

United States	Metric (Approximate)
1 in.	2.5cm
6 in.	15cm
8 in.	20cm
9 in.	22.5cm
12 in. (1 ft.)	30cm
13 in.	32.5cm
2 ft.	60cm
3 ft. (1 yd.)	90cm

Index

Also by Leslie Bilderback,
Certified Master Chef and Baker

ISBN: 978-1-59257-562-6

Coming Soon!

The Complete Idiot's Guide® to Spices & Herbs
ISBN: 978-1-59257-674-6

The Complete Idiot's Guide® to Good Food from the Good Book
ISBN: 978-1-59257-728-6

idiotsguides.com